Charles J Tibbits

**Folklore and legends : England and Scotland**

Charles J Tibbits

**Folklore and legends : England and Scotland**

ISBN/EAN: 9783743346109

Manufactured in Europe, USA, Canada, Australia, Japa

Cover: Foto ©ninafisch / pixelio.de

Manufactured and distributed by brebook publishing software (www.brebook.com)

Charles J Tibbits

**Folklore and legends : England and Scotland**

# FOLK-LORE

AND

# LEGENDS

ENGLAND AND SCOTLAND

GIBBINGS AND COMPANY, LIMITED
18 BURY ST., LONDON, W.C.
1894

# INTRODUCTORY NOTE.

The old English Folklore Tales are fast dying out. The simplicity of character necessary for the retaining of old memories and beliefs is being lost, more rapidly in England, perhaps, than in any other part of the world. Our folk are giving up the old myths for new ones. Before remorseless "progress," and the struggle for existence, the poetry of life is being quickly blotted out. In editing this volume I have endeavoured to select some of the best specimens of our Folklore. With regard to the nursery tales, I have taken pains to give them as they are in the earliest editions I could find. I must say, however, that, while I have taken every care to alter only as much as was absolutely necessary in these tales, some excision and slight alteration has at times been required.

C. J. T.

# CONTENTS.

|  | PAGE |
|---|---|
| A Dissertation on Fairies, | 1 |
| Nelly the Knocker, | 39 |
| The Three Fools, | 42 |
| Some Merry Tales of the Wise Men of Gotham, | 46 |
| The Tulip Fairies, | 54 |
| The History of Jack and the Giants, | 57 |
| The Fairies' Cup, | 84 |
| The White Lady, | 86 |
| A Pleasant and Delightful History of Thomas Hickathrift, | 89 |
| The Spectre Coach, | 117 |
| The Baker's Daughter, | 123 |
| The Fairy Children, | 126 |
| The History of Jack and the Beanstalk, | 129 |
| Johnny Reed's Cat, | 150 |
| Lame Molly, | 156 |
| The Brown man of the Moors, | 159 |

| | PAGE |
|---|---|
| How the Cobbler cheated the Devil, | 161 |
| The Tavistock Witch, | 165 |
| The Worm of Lambton, | 168 |
| The Old Woman and the Crooked Sixpence, | 174 |
| The Yorkshire Boggart, | 177 |
| The Duergar, | 181 |
| The Barn Elves, | 185 |
| Legends of King Arthur, | 187 |
| Silky, | 192 |

# A DISSERTATION ON FAIRIES.

## BY JOSEPH RITSON, ESQ.

THE earliest mention of Fairies is made by Homer, if, that is, his English translator has, in this instance, done him justice :—

> "Where round the bed, whence Achelöus springs,
> The wat'ry Fairies dance in mazy rings."
> (*Iliad*, B. xxiv. 617.)

These Nymphs he supposes to frequent or reside in woods, hills, the sea, fountains, grottos, etc., whence they are peculiarly called Naiads, Dryads and Nereids :

> "What sounds are those that gather from the shores,
> The voice of nymphs that haunt the sylvan bowers,
> The fair-hair'd dryads of the shady wood,
> Or azure daughters of the silver flood?"
> (*Odyss.* B. vi. 122.)

The original word, indeed, is *nymphs*, which, it must be confessed, furnishes an accurate idea of the *fays* (*fées* or *fates*) of the ancient French and Italian romances; wherein they are represented as females of inexpressible beauty, elegance, and every kind of personal accomplishment, united with magic or supernatural power; such, for instance, as the Calypso of Homer, or the Alcina of Ariosto. Agreeably to this idea it is that Shakespeare makes Antony say in allusion to Cleopatra—

"To this great fairy I'll commend thy acts,"

meaning this grand assemblage of power and beauty. Such, also, is the character of the ancient nymphs, spoken of by the Roman poets, as Virgil, for instance:

" Fortunatus et ille, deos qui novit agrestes,
Panaque, Sylvanumque senem, Nymphasque sorores."
(*Geor.* ii. 493.)

They, likewise, occur in other passages as well as in Horace—

" —— gelidum nemus
Nympharumque leves cum Satyris chori."
(*Carmina*, I., O. 1, v. 30.)

and, still more frequently, in Ovid.

Not far from Rome, as we are told by Chorier, was a place formerly called "Ad Nymphas," and, at this day, "Santa Ninfa," which without doubt, he adds, in the language of our ancestors, would have been called "The Place of Fays" (*Recherches des Antiquitez, de Vienne*, Lyon, 1659).

The word *faée*, or *fée*, among the French, is derived, according to Du Cange, from the barbarous Latin *fadus* or *fada*, in Italian *fata*. Gervase of Tilbury, in his *Otia Imperialia* (D. 3, c. 88), speaks of "some of this kind of *larvæ*, which they named *fadæ*, we have heard to be lovers," and in his relation of a nocturnal contest between two knights (c. 94) he exclaims, "What shall I say? I know not if it were a true *horse*, or if it were a fairy (*fadus*), as men assert." From the *Roman de Partenay*, or *de Lezignan*, MS. Du Cange cites—

> "Le chasteau fut fait d'une fée
> Si comme il est partout retrait."

Hence, he says, *faërie* for spectres:

> "Plusieurs parlant de Guenart,
> Du Lou, de l'Asne, et de Renart,
> De faëries, et de songes,
> De fantosmes, et de mensonges."

The same Gervase explains the Latin *fata* (*fée*, French) a divining woman, an enchantress, or a witch (D. 3, c. 88).

Master Wace, in his *Histoire des Ducs de Normendie* (confounded by many with the *Roman de Rou*), describing the fountain of Berenton, in Bretagne, says—

> "En la forest et environ,
> Mais jo ne sais par quel raison
> La seut l'en les fées veeir,
> Se li Breton nos dient veir, etc."
>
> (In the forest and around,
> I wot not by what reason found,
> There may a man the fairies spy,
> If Britons do not tell a lie.)

but it may be difficult to conceive an accurate idea, from the mere name, of the popular French *fays* or *fairies* of the twelfth century.

In Vienne, in Dauphiny, is *Le puit des fées*, or Fairy-well. These *fays*, it must be confessed, have a strong resemblance to the nymphs of the ancients, who inhabited caves and fountains. Upon a little rock which overlooks the Rhone are three round holes which nature alone has formed, although it seem, at first sight, that art has laboured after her. They say that they were formerly frequented by Fays; that they were full of water when it rained; and that they there frequently took the pleasure of the bath; than which they had not one more charming (Chorier, *Recherches*, etc.).

Pomponius Mela, an eminent geographer, and, in point of time, far anterior to Pliny, relates, that beyond a mountain in Æthiopia, called by the Greeks the "High Mountain," burning, he says, with perpetual fire, is a hill spread over a long tract by extended shores, whence they rather go to see wide plains than to behold [the habitations] of Pans and Satyrs. Hence, he adds, this opinion received faith, that, whereas, in these parts is nothing of culture, no seats of inhabitants, no footsteps—a waste solitude in the day, and a mere waste silence—frequent fires shine by night; and camps, as it were, are seen widely spread; cymbals and tympans sound; and sounding pipes are heard more than human

(B. 3, c. 9). These invisible essences, however, are both anonymous and nondescript.

The *penates* of the Romans, according to honest Reginald Scot, were "the domesticall gods, or rather divels, that were said to make men live quietlie within doores. But some think that *Lares* are such as trouble private houses. *Larvæ* are said to be spirits that walk onelie by night. *Vinculi terrei* are such as was Robin Good-fellowe, that would supplie the office of servants, speciallie of maides, as to make a fier in the morning, sweepe the house, grind mustard and malt, drawe water, etc. These also rumble in houses, drawe latches, go up and down stairs," etc. (*Discoverie of Witchcraft*, London, 1584, p. 521). A more modern writer says "The Latins have called the fairies *lares* and *larvæ*, frequenting, as they say, houses, delighting in neatness, pinching the slut, and rewarding the good housewife with money in her shoe" (*Pleasaunt Treatise of Witches*, 1673, p. 53). This, however, is nothing but the character of an English fairy applied to the name of a Roman *lar* or *larva*. It might have been wished, too, that Scot, a man unquestionably of great learning, had referred, by name and work and book and chapter, to those ancient authors from whom he derived his information upon the Roman *penates*, etc.

What idea our Saxon ancestors had of the fairy which they called *ælf*, a word explained by Lye as equivalent to *lamia, larva, incubus, ephialtes*, we are utterly at a loss to conceive.

The nymphs, the satyrs, and the fauns, are frequently noticed by the old traditional historians of the north; particularly *Saxo-grammaticus*, who has a curious story of three nymphs of the forest, and Hother, King of Sweden and Denmark, being apparently the originals of the weird, or wizard, sisters of Macbeth (B. 3, p. 39). Others are preserved by Olaus Magnus, who says they had so deeply impressed into the earth, that the place they have been used to, having been (apparently) eaten up in a circular form with flagrant heat, never brings forth fresh grass from the dry turf. This nocturnal sport of monsters, he adds, the natives call The Dance of the Elves (B. 3, c. 10).

> "In John Milesius any man may reade
> Of divels in Sarmatia honored,
> Call'd *Kottri*, or *Kibaldi*; such as wee
> Pugs and Hob-goblins call. Their dwellings bee
> In corners of old houses least frequented,
> Or beneath stacks of wood: and these convented,
> Make fearfull noise in buttries and in dairies;
> Robin Goodfellowes some, some call them fairies.
> In solitarie roomes these uprores keepe,
> And beat at dores to wake men from their sleepe;
> Seeming to force locks, be they ne're so strong,
> And keeping Christmasse gambols all night long.
> Pots, glasses, trenchers, dishes, pannes, and kettles,
> They will make dance about the shelves and settles,
> As if about the kitchen tost and cast,
> Yet in the morning nothing found misplac't."
> 
> (Heywood's *Hierarchie of Angells*, 1635, fo. p. 574.)

Milton, a prodigious reader of romance, has, likewise, given an apt idea of the ancient fays—

> "Fairer than famed of old, or fabled since
> Of fairy damsels met in forest wide,
> By knights of Logres, and of Liones,
> Lancelot or Pelleas, or Pellenore."

These ladies, in fact, are by no means unfrequent in those fabulous, it must be confessed, but, at the same time, ingenious and entertaining histories; as, for instance, *Melusine*, or *Merlusine*, the heroine of a very ancient romance in French verse, and who was occasionally turned into a serpent; *Morgan-la-faée*, the reputed half-sister of King Arthur; and *the Lady of the Lake*, so frequently noticed in Sir Thomas Malory's old history of that monarch.

Le Grand is of opinion that what is called Fairy comes to us from the Orientals, and that it is their *génies* which have produced our *fairies*; a species of nymphs, of an order superior to those women magicians, to whom they nevertheless gave the same name. In Asia, he says, where the women imprisoned in the harems, prove still, beyond the general servitude, a particular slavery, the romancers have imagined the *Peris*, who, flying in the air, come to soften their captivity, and render them happy (*Fabliaux*, 12mo. i. 112). Whether this be so or not, it is certain that we call the *auroræ boreales*, or active clouds, in the night, *perry-dancers*.

After all, Sir William Ouseley finds it impossible

to give an accurate idea of what the Persian poets designed by a Perie, this aërial being not resembling our fairies. The strongest resemblance he can find is in the description of Milton in *Comus*. The sublime idea which Milton entertained of a fairy vision corresponds rather with that which the Persian poets have conceived of the Peries.

> "Their port was more than human as they stood;
> I took it for a faëry vision
> Of some gay creatures of the element,
> That in the colours of the rainbow live
> And play i' th' plighted clouds."
>
> (D'Israeli's *Romances*, p. 13.)

It is by no means credible, however, that Milton had any knowledge of the Oriental Peries, though his enthusiastic or poetical imagination might have easily peopled the air with spirits.

There are two sorts of *fays*, according to M. Le Grand. The one a species of nymphs or divinities; the other more properly called sorceresses, or women instructed in magic. From time immemorial, in the abbey of Poissy, founded by St. Lewis, they said every year a mass to preserve the nuns from the power of the *fays*. When the process of the Damsel of Orleans was made, the doctors demanded, for the first question, "If she had any knowledge of those who went to the Sabbath with the *fays*? or if she had not assisted at the assemblies held at the fountain of the *fays*, near Domprein, around which dance malignant spirits?" The Journal of Paris, under Charles VI. and Charles VII. pretends that she confessed that, at the age of twenty-seven years, she frequently went, in spite of her father and mother, to a fair fountain in the county of Lorraine, which she named the "Good Fountain to the Fays Our Lord" (*Ib.* p. 75).

Gervase of Tilbury, in his chapter "of Fauns and Satyrs," says,—"there are likewise others, whom the vulgar call *Follets*, who inhabit the houses of the simple rustics, and can be driven away neither by holy water, nor exorcisms; and because they are not seen, they afflict those, who are entering, with stones, billets, and domestic furniture, whose words for certain are heard in the human manner, and their forms do not appear" (*Otia imperialia*, D. i. c. 18). He is speaking of England.

This Follet seems to resemble Puck, or Robin Goodfellow, whose pranks were recorded in an old song and who was sometimes useful, and sometimes mischievous. Whether or not he was the fairy-spirit of whom Milton

> "Tells how the drudging goblin swet,
> To ern his cream-bowle duly set,
> When, in one night, ere glimpse of morn,
> His shadowy flail hath thresh'd the corn,
> That ten day-labourers could not end,
> Then lies him down, the lubbar fend;
> And stretch'd out all the chimney's length,
> Basks at the fire his hairy strength;
> And crop-full out of dores he flings,
> Ere the first cock his matin rings." (*L'Allegro*).

is a matter of some difficulty. Perhaps the giant son of the witch, that had the devil's mark about her (of whom "there is a pretty tale"), that was called *Lob-lye-by-the-fire*, was a very different personage from Robin Good-fellow, whom, however, he in some respects appears to resemble. A near female relation of the compiler, who was born and brought up in a small village in the bishopric of Durham, related to him many years ago, several circumstances which confirmed the exactitude of Milton's description; she particularly told of his threshing the corn, churning the butter, drinking the milk, etc., and, when all was done, " lying before the fire like a great rough hurgin bear."

In another chapter Gervase says—"As among men, nature produces certain wonderful things, so spirits, in airy bodies, who assume by divine permission the mocks they make. For, behold! England has certain dæmons (dæmons, I call them, though I know not, but I should say secret forms of unknown generation), whom the French call *Neptunes*, the English *Portunes*. With these it is natural that they take advantage of the simplicity of fortunate peasants; and when, by reason of their domestic labours, they perform their nocturnal vigils, of a sudden, the doors being shut, they warm themselves at the fire, and eat little frogs, cast out of their bosoms and put upon the burning coals; with an antiquated countenance; a wrinkled face; diminutive in stature, not having [in length] half a thumb. They are clothed with rags patched together; and if anything should be to be carried on in the house, or any kind of laborious work to be done, they join themselves to the work, and expedite it with more than human facility. It is natural to these, that they may be obsequious, and may not be hurtful. But one little mode, as it were, they have of hurting. For when, among the ambiguous shades of night, the English occasionally ride alone, the *Portune*, sometimes, unseen, couples himself to the rider; and, when he has accompanied him, going on, a very long time, at length, the bridle being seized, he leads him up to the hand in the mud, in which while, infixed, he wallows, the *Portune*, departing, sets up a laugh; and so, in this kind of way, derides human simplicity" (*Otia imperialia*, D. 3, c. 61).

This spirit seems to have some resemblance to the *Picktree-brag*, a mischievous barguest that used to haunt that part of the country, in the shape of different animals, particularly of a little galloway; in which shape a farmer, still or lately living thereabout, reported that it had come to him one night as he was going home; that he got upon it, and rode very quietly till it came to a great pond, to which it ran and threw him in, and went laughing away.

He further says there is, in England, a certain species of demons, which in their language they call *Grant*, like a one-year old foal, with straight legs, and sparkling eyes. This kind of demon very often appears in the streets, in the very heat of the day, or about sunset; and as often as it makes its appearance, portends that there is about to be a fire in that city or town. When, therefore, in the following day or night the danger is urgent, in the streets, running to and fro, it provokes the dogs to bark, and, while it pretends flight invites them, following, to pursue, in the vain hope of overtaking it. This kind of illusion provokes caution to the watchmen who have the custody of fire, and so the officious race of demons, while they terrify the beholders, are wont to secure the ignorant by their arrival (Gervase, D. 3, c. 62).

Gower, in his tale of Narcissus, professedly from Ovid, says—

> "—— As he cast his loke
> Into the well,——
> He sawe the like of his visage,
> And wende there were an ymage
> Of such a nymphe, as tho was faye."
>
> (*Confessio amantis*, fo. 20, b.)

In his *Legend of Constance* is this passage:—

> "Thy wife which is of fairie
> Of suche a childe delivered is,
> Fro kinde, whiche stante all amis."
>
> (*Ibid.* fo. 32, b.)

In another part of his book is a story "Howe

the Kynge of Armenis daughter mette on a tyme a companie of the *fairy.*" These "ladies," ride aside "on fayre [white] ambulende horses," clad, very magnificently, but all alike, in white and blue, and wore "corownes on their heades;" but they are not called *fays* in the poem, nor does the word *fay* or *fairie* once occur therein.

The fairies or elves of the British isles are peculiar to this part of the world, and are not, so far as literary information or oral tradition enables us to judge, to be found in any other country. For this fact the authority of father Chaucer will be decisive, till we acquire evidence of equal antiquity in favour of other nations:—

> "In olde dayes of the King Artour,
> Of which the Bretons speken gret honour,
> All was this lond fulfilled of faerie;
> The elf-quene, with hire joly compagnie,
> Danced ful oft in many a grene mede.
> This was the old opinion as I rede;
> I speke of many hundred yeres ago;
> But now can no man see non elves mo,
> For now the grete charitee and prayers
> Of limitoures and other holy freres,
> That serchen every land, and every streme,
> As thickke as motes in the sunnebeme,
> Blissing halles, chambres, kichenes, and boures,
> Citees and burghes, castles highe and toures,
> Thropes and bernes, shepenes and dairies,
> This maketh that ther ben no faeries."
>
> (*Wif of Bathes Tale.*)

The fairy may be defined as a species of being partly material, partly spiritual, with a power to change its appearance, and be, to mankind, visible or invisible, according to its pleasure. In the old song, printed by Peck, Robin Good-fellow, a well-known fairy, professes that he had played his pranks from the time of Merlin, who was the contemporary of Arthur.

Chaucer uses the word *faërie* as well for the *individual* as for the *country* or *system*, or what we should now call *fairy-land*, or *faryism*. He knew nothing, it would seem, of *Oberon*, *Titania*, or *Mab*, but speaks of—

> "Pluto, that is the King of Faerie,
> And many a ladie in his compagnie,
> Folwing his wif, the quene Proserpina, etc."
>      (*The Marchantes Tale*, i. 10101.)

From this passage of Chaucer Mr. Tyrwhitt "cannot help thinking that his *Pluto* and *Proserpina* were the true progenitors of *Oberon* and *Titania*."

In the progress of *The Wif of Bathes Tale*, it happed the knight,

> "———in his way . . . . . to ride
> In all his care, under a forest side,
> Whereas he saw upon a dance go
> Of ladies foure-and-twenty, and yet mo.
> Toward this ilke dance, he drow ful yerne,
> In hope that he som wisdom shulde lerne,
> But, certainly, er he came fully there,
> Yvanished was this dance, he wiste not wher."

These *ladies* appear to have been *fairies*, though nothing is insinuated of their size. Milton seems to have been upon the prowl here for his "forest-side."

In *A Midsummer-Night's Dream*, a fairy addresses Bottom the weaver—

"Hail, *mortal*, hail!"

which sufficiently shows she was not so herself.

Puck, or Robin Good-fellow, in the same play, calls Oberon,

"—— King of *shadows*,"

and in the old song just mentioned,

"The King of *ghosts* and *shadows*,"

and this mighty monarch asserts of himself, and his subjects,

"But we are *spirits* of another sort."

The fairies, as we already see, were male and female. Their government was monarchical, and Oberon, the King of Fairyland, must have been a sovereign of very extensive territory. The name of his queen was Titania. Both are mentioned by Shakespeare, being personages of no little importance in the above play, where they, in an ill-humour, thus encounter:

Obe. Ill met by moon-light, proud Titania.
Tita. What, jealous Oberon? Fairy, skip hence;
        I have forsworn his bed and company."

That the name [Oberon] was not the invention of our great dramatist is sufficiently proved. The allegorical Spenser gives it to King Henry the Eighth. Robert Greene was the author of a play entitled " The Scottishe history of James the Fourthe .... intermixed with a pleasant comedie presented by *Oberon, king of the fairies.*" He is, likewise, a character in the old French romances of *Huon de Bourdeaux*, and *Ogier le Danois*; and there even seems to be one upon his own exploits, *Roman d' Auberon*. What authority, however, Shakespeare had for the name Titania, it does not appear, nor is she so called by any other writer. He himself, at the same time, as well as many others, gives to the queen of fairies the name of Mab, though no one, except Drayton, mentions her as the wife of Oberon:

" O then, I see, queen Mab hath been with you,
She is the fairy's midwife, and she comes
In shape no bigger than an agate-stone
On the fore-finger of an alderman,
Drawn with a team of little atomics
Athwart men's noses as they lie asleep;
Her waggon-spokes made of long spinner's legs;
The cover, of the wings of grasshoppers;
The traces, of the smallest spider's web;
The collars, of the moonshine's wat'ry beams:
Her whip, of cricket's bone; the lash, of film:
Her waggoner, a small grey-coated gnat,
Not half so big as a round little worm
Pricked from the lazy finger of a maid:
Her chariot is an empty hazel-nut,

Made by the joiner squirrel, or old grub,
Time out of mind the fairies' coachmakers.
And in this state she gallops night by night
Through lovers' brains, and then they dream of love!
. . . This is that very Mab,
That plats the manes of horses in the night;
And bakes the elf-locks in foul sluttish hairs,
Which, once untangled, much misfortune bodes."
                                        (*Romeo and Juliet.*)

Ben Jonson, in his "Entertainment of the Queen and Prince at Althrope," in 1603, describes to come "tripping up the lawn a bevy of fairies attending on Mab their queen, who, falling into an artificial ring that was there cut in the path, began to dance around."—(*Works*, v. 201.)

In the same masque the queen is thus characterised by a satyr :—

"This is Mab, the mistress fairy,
 That doth nightly rob the dairy,
 And can hurt or help the churning,
 (As she please) without discerning.
 She that pinches country-wenches
 If they rub not clean their benches,
 And with sharper nails remembers
 When they rake not up their embers;
 But, if so they chance to feast her,
 In a shoe she drops a tester.
 This is she that empties cradles,
 Takes out children, puts in ladles;
 Trains forth midwives in their slumber,
 With a sieve the holes to number;

> And thus leads them from her boroughs,
> Home through ponds and water-furrows.
> She can start our franklin's daughters,
> In their sleep, with shrieks and laughters,
> And on sweet St. Agnes' night
> Feed them with a promised sight,
> Some of husbands, some of lovers,
> Which an empty dream discovers."

Fairies, they tell you, have frequently been heard and seen—nay, that there are some living who were stolen away by them, and confined seven years. According to the description they give who pretend to have seen them, they are in the shape of men, exceeding little. They are always clad in green, and frequent the woods and fields; when they make cakes (which is a work they have been often heard at) they are very noisy; and when they have done, they are full of mirth and pastime. But generally they dance in moonlight when mortals are asleep and not capable of seeing them, as may be observed on the following morn—their dancing-places being very distinguishable. For as they dance hand in hand, and so make a circle in their dance, so next day there will be seen rings and circles on the grass.—(Bourne's *Antiquitates Vulgares,* Newcastle, 1725, 8vo, p. 82.)

These circles are thus described by Browne, the author of *Britannia's Pastorals* :—

> " . . . A pleasant meade,
> Where fairies often did their measures treade,
> Which in the meadow made such circles greene,
> As if with garlands it had crowned beene.

> Within one of these rounds was to be seene
> A hillock rise, where oft the fairie queene
> At twy-light sate, and did command her elves
> To pinch those maids that had not swept their shelves;
> And further, if by maidens' over-sight
> Within doores water were not brought at night,
> Or if they spred no table, set no bread,
> They should have nips from toe unto the head;
> And for the maid that had perform'd each thing,
> She in the water-pail bad leave a ring."

The same poet, in his "Shepeards Pipe," having inserted Hoccleve's tale of *Jonathas*, and conceiving a strange unnatural affection for that stupid fellow, describes him as a great favourite of the fairies, alleging, that—

> "Many times he hath been seene
> With the fairies on the greene,
> And to them his pipe did sound,
> While they danced in a round,
> Mickle solace would they make him,
> And at midnight often wake him,
> And convey him from his roome
> To a field of yellow broome;
> Or into the medowes, where
> Mints perfume the gentle aire,
> And where Flora spends her treasure,
> There they would begin their measure.
> If it chanc'd night's sable shrowds
> Muffled Cynthia up in clowds,
> Safely home they then would see him,
> And from brakes and quagmires free him."

The fairies were exceedingly diminutive, but, it must be confessed, we shall not readily find their real dimensions. They were small enough, however, if we may believe one of queen Titania's maids of honour, to conceal themselves in acorn shells. Speaking of a difference between the king and queen, she says :—

"But they do square; that all the elves for fear
Creep into acorn cups, and hide them there."

They uniformly and constantly wore green vests, unless when they had some reason for changing their dress. Of this circumstance we meet with many proofs. Thus in *The Merry Wives of Windsor*—

"Like urchins, ouphes, and fairies green."

In fact we meet with them of all colours; as in the same play—

"Fairies black, grey, green, and white."

That white, on some occasions, was the dress of a female, we learn from Reginald Scot. He gives a charm "to go invisible by [means of] these three sisters of fairies," *Milia, Achilia, Sibylia*: "I charge you that you doo appeare before me visible, in forme and shape of faire women, in white vestures, and to bring with you to me the ring of invisibilitie, by the which I may go invisible at mine owne will and pleasure, and that in all hours and minutes."

It was fatal, if we may believe Shakespeare, to speak to a fairy. Falstaff, in *The Merry Wives of Windsor*, is made to say, "They are fairies. He that speaks to them shall die."

They were accustomed to enrich their favourites, as we learn from the clown in *A Winter's Tale*—

"It was told me I should be rich by the fairies."

They delighted in neatness, could not endure sluts, and even hated fibsters, tell-tales, and divulgers of secrets, whom they would slily and severely bepinch when they little expected it. They were as generous and benevolent, on the contrary, to young women of a different description, procuring them the sweetest sleep, the pleasantest dreams, and, on their departure in the morning, always slipping a tester in their shoe.

They are supposed by some to have been malignant, but this, it may be, was mere calumny, as being utterly inconsistent with their general character, which was singularly innocent and amiable.

Imogen, in Shakespeare's *Cymbeline*, prays, on going to sleep—

"From fairies, and the tempters of the night,
Guard me, beseech you."

It must have been the *Incubus* she was so afraid of.

Hamlet, too, notices this imputed malignity of the fairies:—

> " . . . Then no planets strike,
> No fairy takes, nor witch has power to charm."

Thus, also, in *The Comedy of Errors* :—

> " A fiend, a fairy, pitiless and rough."

They were amazingly expeditious in their journeys. Puck, or Robin Good-fellow, answers Oberon, who was about to send him on a secret expedition—

> " I'll put a girdle round about the earth
> In forty minutes."

Again the same goblin addresses him thus :—

> " Fairy king, attend and mark,
> I do hear the morning lark.
>   *Obe.* Then, my queen, in silence sad,
> Trip we after the night's shade—
> We the globe can compass soon,
> Swifter than the wand'ring moon."

In another place Puck says—

> " My fairy lord this must be done in haste ;
> For night's swift dragons cut the clouds full fast,
> And yonder shines Aurora's harbinger,
> At whose approach ghosts, wandering here and there,
> Troop home to churchyards," etc.

To which Oberon replies—

> " But we are spirits of another sort :
> I with the morning's love have oft made sport ;
> And, like a forester, the groves may tread,
> Even till the eastern gate, all fiery-red,
> Opening on Neptune with fair blessed beams,
> Turns into yellow gold his salt-green streams."

Compare, likewise, what Robin himself says on this subject in the old song of his exploits.

They never ate—

> "But that it eats our victuals, I should think,
> Here were a fairy,"

says Belarius at the first sight of Imogen, as Fidele.

They were humanely attentive to the youthful dead. Thus Guiderius at the funeral of the above lady—

> "With female fairies will his tomb be haunted."

Or, as in the pathetic dirge of Collins on the same occasion :—

> "No wither'd witch shall here be seen,
> No goblins lead their nightly crew;
> The female fays shall haunt the green,
> And dress the grave with pearly dew."

This amiable quality is, likewise, thus beautifully alluded to by the same poet :—

> "By fairy hands their knell is rung,
> By forms unseen their dirge is sung."

Their employment is thus charmingly represented by Shakespeare, in the address of Prospero :—

> "Ye elves of hills, brooks, standing lakes, and groves;
> And ye, that on the sands, with printless foot
> Do chase the ebbing Neptune, and do fly him
> When he comes back; you demi-puppets, that

> By moon-shine do the green-sour ringlets make,
> Whereof the ewe not bites; and you, whose pastime
> Is to make midnight mushrooms; that rejoice
> To hear the solemn curfew."

In *The Midsummer Night's Dream*, the queen, Titania, being desirous to take a nap, says to her female attendants—

> "Come, now a roundel, and a fairy song;
> Then, for the third part of a minute hence;
> Some to kill cankers in the musk-rosebuds;
> Some, war with rear-mice for their leathern wings,
> To make my small elves coats; and some keep back
> The clamorous owl that nightly hoots, and wonders
> At our quaint spirits.  Sing me now asleep;
> Then to your offices, and let me rest."

Milton gives a most beautiful and accurate description of the little green-coats of his native soil, than which nothing can be more happily or justly expressed. He had certainly seen them, in this situation, with "the poet's eye":—

> ". . . Fairie elves,
> Whose midnight revels, by a forest side
> Or fountain, some belated peasant sees,
> Or dreams he sees, while overhead the moon,
> Sits arbitress, and nearer to the earth
> Wheels her pale course, they, on thir mirth and dance
> Intent, with jocond music charm his ear;
> At once with joy and fear his heart rebounds."

The impression they made upon his imagination

in early life appears from his "Vacation Exercise," at the age of nineteen:—

> "Good luck befriend thee, son; for, at thy birth
> The faiery ladies daunc't upon the hearth;
> The drowsie nurse hath sworn she did them spie
> Come tripping to the room where thou didst lie,
> And, sweetly singing round about thy bed,
> Strew all their blessings on thy sleeping head."

L'Abbé Bourdelon, in his *Ridiculous Extravagances of M. Ouflé*, describes "The fairies of which," he says, "grandmothers and nurses tell so many tales to children. These fairies," adds he, "I mean, who are affirmed to be blind at home, and very clear-sighted abroad; who dance in the moonshine when they have nothing else to do; who steal shepherds and children, to carry them up to their caves," etc. —(English translation, p. 190.)

The fairies have already called themselves *spirits*, *ghosts*, or *shadows*, and consequently they never died, a position, at the same time, of which there is every kind of proof that a fact can require. The reviser of Johnson and Steevens's edition of *Shakespeare*, in 1785, makes a ridiculous reference to the allegories of Spenser, and a palpably false one to Tickell's *Kensington Gardens*, which he affirms "will show that the opinion of fairies dying prevailed in the last century," whereas, in fact, it is found, on the slightest glance into the poem, to maintain the direct reverse:—

> "Meanwhile sad Kenna, loath to quit the grove,
> Hung o'er the body of her breathless love,
> Try'd every art (vain arts!) to change his doom,
> And vow'd (vain vows!) to join him in the tomb.
> What would she do? The Fates alike deny
> The dead to live, or fairy forms to die."

The fact is so positively proved, that no editor or commentator of Shakespeare, present or future, will ever have the folly or impudence to assert "that in Shakespeare's time the notion of fairies dying was generally known."

Ariosto informs us (in Harington's translation, Bk. x. s. 47) that

> ". . . (Either auncient folke believ'd a lie,
> Or this is true) a fayrie cannot die."

And again (Bk. xliii. s. 92),

> "I am a fayrie, and, to make you know,
> To be a fayrie what it doth import:
> We cannot dye, how old so ear we grow.
> Of paines and harmes of ev'rie other sort
> We tast, onelie no death we nature ow."

Beaumont and Fletcher, in *The Faithful Shepherdess*, describe—

> "A virtuous well, about whose flow'ry banks
> The nimble-footed fairies dance their rounds,
> By the pale moonshine, dipping oftentimes
> Their stolen children, so to make 'em free
> From dying flesh, and dull mortality."

Puck, *alias* Robin Good-fellow, is the most active and extraordinary fellow of a fairy that we anywhere meet with, and it is believed we find him nowhere but in our own country, and, peradventure also, only in the South. Spenser, it would seem, is the first that alludes to his name of Puck :—

> " Ne let the *Pouke,* nor other evill spright,
> Ne let Hob-goblins, names whose sense we see not,
> Fray us with things that be not."

"In our childhood," says Reginald Scot, "our mothers' maids have so terrified us with an oughe divell having hornes on his head, fier in his mouth, and a taile, eies like a bason, fanges like a dog, clawes like a beare, a skin like a niger, and a voice roaring like a lion, whereby we start and are afraid when we heare one crie Bough! and they have so fraied us with bull-beggers, spirits, witches, urchens, elves, hags, fairies, satyrs, pans, sylens, Kit with the cansticke, tritons, centaurs, dwarfes, giants, imps, calcars, conjurors, nymphes, changling, Incubus, Robin Goodfellow, the spoorne, the mare, the man in the oke, the hell wain, the fier drake, the puckle, Tom Thombe, Hob gobblin, Tom Tumbler, boneles, and such other bugs, that we are afraid of our owne shadowes."—(*Discoverie of Witchcraft,* London, 1584, 4to, p. 153.) "And know you this by the waie," he says, "that heretofore Robin Goodfellow and Hob goblin were as terrible, and also as credible, to the people as hags and witches be now. . . . And in truth, they that mainteine walking spirits have no reason to denie Robin Goodfellow, upon whom there hath gone as manie and as credible tales as upon witches, saving that it hath not pleased the translators of the Bible to call spirits by the name of Robin Goodfellow."—(P. 131.)

"Your grandams' maides," says he, "were woont to set a boll of milke before Incubus and his cousine Robin Goodfellow for grinding of malt or mustard, and sweeping the house at midnight; and you have also heard that he would chafe exceedingly if the maid or good-wife of the house, having compassion of his naked state, laid anie clothes for him, besides his messe of white bread and milke, which was his standing fee. For in that case he saith, What have we here?

"Hemton, hamton,
Here will I never more tread nor stampen."
(*Discoverie of Witchcraft*, p. 85.)

Robin is thus characterised in *The Midsummer Night's Dream* by a female fairy:—

"Either I mistake your shape and making quite,
Or else you are that shrewd and knavish sprite
Call'd Robin Goodfellow: are you not he
That fright the maidens of the villagery;
Skim milk; and sometimes labour in the quern,
And bootless make the breathless housewife churn;
And sometime make the drink to bear no barm;
Mislead night-wanderers, laughing at their harm?
Those that Hobgoblin call you, and sweet Puck,
You do their work, and they shall have good luck."

To these questions Robin thus replies:—

> "Thou speak'st aright;
> I am that merry wanderer of the night.
> I jest to Oberon, and make him smile,
> When I a fat and bean-fed horse beguile,
> Neighing in likeness of a filly foal:
> And sometimes lurk I in a gossip's bowl,
> In very likeness of a roasted crab;
> And, when she drinks, against her lips I bob,
> And on her wither'd dewlap pour the ale.
> The wisest aunt, telling the saddest tale,
> Sometime for three-foot stool mistaketh me;
> Then slip I from her bum, down topples she,
> And 'tailor,' cries, and falls into a cough;
> And then the whole quire hold their hips, and laugh;
> And waxen in their mirth, and neeze, and swear,
> A merrier hour was never wasted there."

His usual exclamation in this play is Ho, ho, ho!

> "Ho, ho, ho! Coward, why com'st thou not?"

So in *Grim, the Collier of Croydon*:—

> "Ho, ho, ho! my masters! No good fellowship!
> Is Robin Goodfellow a bugbear grown,
> That he is not worthy to be bid sit down?"

In the song printed by Peck, he concludes every stanza with Ho, ho, ho!

"If that the bowle of curds and creame were not duly set out for Robin Goodfellow, the frier, and Sisse the dairymaid, why, then, either the pottage was so burnt to next day in the pot, or the cheeses would not curdle, or the butter would not come, or the ale in the fat never would have good head. But if a Peter-penny, or an housle-egge were behind, or a patch of tythe unpaid, then 'ware of bull-beggars, spirits," etc.

This frolicsome spirit thus describes himself in Jonson's masque of *Love Restored*: "Robin Goodfellow, he that sweeps the hearth and the house clean, riddles for the country maids, and does all their other drudgery, while they are at hot-cockles; one that has conversed with your court spirits ere now." Having recounted several ineffectual attempts he had made to gain admittance, he adds: "In this despair, when all invention and translation too failed me, I e'en went back and stuck to this shape you see me in of mine own, with my broom and my canles, and came on confidently." The mention of his broom reminds us of a passage in another play, *Midsummer Night's Dream*, where he tells the audience—

"I am sent with broom before,
To sweep the dust behind the door."

He is likewise one of the *dramatis personæ* in the old play of *Wily Beguiled*, in which he says—

"Tush! fear not the dodge. I'll rather put on my flashing red nose, and my flaming face, and come wrap'd in a calf-skin, and cry *Bo, bo!* I'll pay the scholar, I warrant thee."—(Harsnet's *Declaration*, London, 1604, 4to.) His character, however, in this piece, is so diabolical, and so different from anything one could expect in Robin Good-fellow, that it is unworthy of further quotation.

He appears, likewise, in another, entitled *Grim, the Collier of Croydon*, in which he enters "in a suit of leather close to his body; his face and hands coloured russet colour, with a flail."

He is here, too, in most respects, the same strange and diabolical personage that he is represented in *Wily Beguiled*, only there is a single passage which reminds us of his old habits :—

"When as I list in this transform'd disguise
I'll fright the country people as I pass;
And sometimes turn me to some other form,
And so delude them with fantastic shows,
But woe betide the silly dairymaids,
For I shall fleet their cream-bowls night by night."

In another scene he enters while some of the other characters are at a bowl of cream, upon which he says—

"I love a mess of cream as well as they;
I think it were best I stept in and made one :
Ho, ho, ho! my masters! No good fellowship!
Is Robin Goodfellow a bugbear grown
That he is not worthy to be bid sit down?"

There is, indeed, something characteristic in this passage, but all the rest is totally foreign.

Doctor Percy, Bishop of Dromore, has reprinted in his *Reliques of Ancient English Poetry* a very curious and excellent old ballad originally published by Peck, who attributes it, but with no similitude, to Ben Jonson, in which Robin Good-fellow relates his exploits with singular humour. To one of these copies, he says, "were prefixed two wooden cuts, which seem to represent the dresses in which this whimsical character was formerly exhibited upon the stage." In this conjecture, however, the learned and ingenious editor was most egregiously mistaken, these cuts being manifestly printed from the identical blocks made use of by Bulwer in his "Artificial Changeling," printed in 1615, the first being intended for one of the black and white gallants of Scale-bay adorned with the moon, stars, etc., the other a hairy savage.

Burton, speaking of fairies, says that " a bigger kind there is of them, called with Hobgoblins, and Robin Goodfellowes, that would in those superstitious times, grinde corne for a messe of milke, cut wood, or do any kind of drudgery worke." Afterward, of the dæmons that mislead men in the night, he says, "We commonly call them Pucks."—(*Anatomy of Melancholie*.)

Cartwright, in *The Ordinary*, introduces *Moth*, repeating this curious charm :—

> " Saint Frances and Saint Benedight
> Blesse this house from wicked wight,
> From the nightmare, and the goblin
> That is hight Goodfellow Robin ;

> Keep it from all evil spirits,
> Fairies, weezels, rats, and ferrets;
> From curfew time
> To the next prime."
> (Act III. Sc. 1.)

This Puck, or Robin Good-fellow, seems, likewise, to be the illusory candle-holder, so fatal to travellers, and who is more usually called *Jack-a-lantern*, or *Will-with-a-wisp*; and, as it would seem from a passage elsewhere cited from Scot, *Kit with the canstick*. Thus a fairy, in a passage of Shakespeare already quoted, asks Robin—

> ". . . Are you not he
> That frights the maidens of the villagery,
> Misleads night-wanderers laughing at their harm?"

Milton alludes to this deceptive gleam in the following lines—

> ". . . A wandering fire,
> Compact of unctuous vapour, which the night
> Condenses, and the cold environs round,
> Kindled through agitation to a flame,
> Which oft, they say, some evil spirit attends,
> Hovering and blazing with delusive light,
> Misleads th' amazed night-wanderer from his way
> To bogs and mires, and oft through pond and pool."
> (*Paradise Lost*, Bk. 9).

He elsewhere calls him "the frier's lantern."—(*L'Allegro*).

This facetious spirit only misleads the benighted traveller (generally an honest farmer, in his way from the market, in a state of intoxication) for the joke's sake, as one very seldom, if ever, hears any of his deluded followers (who take it to be the torch of Hero in some hospitable mansion, affording "provision for man and horse") perishing in these ponds or pools, through which they dance or plunge after him so merrily.

"There go as manie tales," says Reginald Scot, "upon Hudgin, in some parts of Germanie, as there did in England of Robin Good-fellow. . . . Frier Rush was for all the world such another fellow as this Hudgin, and brought up even in the same schoole— to wit, in a kitchen, inasmuch as the selfe-same tale is written of the one as of the other, concerning the skullian, who is said to have beene slaine, etc., for the reading whereof I referre you to frier Rush his storie, or else to John Wierus, *De Præstigiis Dæmonum*."

In the old play of *Gammer Gurton's Needle*, printed in 1575, Hodge, describing a "great black devil" which had been raised by Diccon, the bedlam, and being asked by Gammer—

"But, Hodge, had he no horns to push?"

replies—

"As long as your two arms. Saw ye never Fryer Rushe,
Painted on a cloth, with a side-long cowe's tayle,
And crooked cloven feet, and many a hoked nayle?
For al the world (if I schuld judg) chould reckon him his
    brother ;
Loke even what face frier Rush had, the devil had such
    another."

The fairies frequented many parts of the bishopric of Durham. There is a hillock, or tumulus, near Bishopton, and a large hill near Billingham, both which used, in former time, to be "haunted by fairies." Even Ferry-hill, a well-known stage between Darlington and Durham, is evidently a corruption of Fairy-hill. When seen, by accident or favour, they are described as of the smallest size, and uniformly habited in green. They could, however, occasionally assume a different size and appearance; as a woman, who had been admitted into their society, challenged one of the guests, whom she espied in the market, selling fairy-butter. This freedom was deeply resented, and cost her the eye she first saw him with. Mr. Brand mentions his having met with a man, who said he had seen one who had seen the fairies. Truth, he adds, is to be come at in most cases. None, he believes, ever came nearer to it in this than he has done. However that may be, the present editor cannot pretend to have been more fortunate. His informant related that an acquaintance in Westmoreland, having a great desire, and praying earnestly, to see a fairy, was told by a friend, if not a fairy in disguise, that on the side of such a hill, at such a time of day, he should have a sight of one, and accordingly, at the time and place appointed, "the hobgoblin," in his own words, "stood before him in the likeness of a green-coat lad," but in the same instant, the spectator's eye glancing, vanished into the hill. This, he said, the man told him.

"The streets of Newcastle," says Mr. Brand, "were formerly (so vulgar tradition has it) haunted by a nightly *guest*, which appeared in the shape of a mastiff dog, etc., and terrified such as were afraid of shadows. I have heard," he adds, "when a boy, many stories concerning it."

The no less famous *barguest* of Durham, and the Picktree-*brag*, have been already alluded to. The former, beside its many other pranks, would sometimes, at the dead of night, in passing through the different streets, set up the most horrid and continuous shrieks to scare the poor girls who might happen to be out of bed. The compiler of the present sheets remembers, when very young, to have heard a respectable old woman, then a midwife at Stockton, relate that when, in her youthful days, she was a servant at Durham, being up late one Saturday night cleaning the irons in the kitchen, she heard these *skrikes*, first at a great and then at a less distance, till at length the loudest and most horrible that can be conceived, just at the kitchen window, sent her upstairs, she did not know how, where she fell into the arms of a fellow-servant, who could scarcely prevent her fainting away.

"Pioneers or diggers for metal," according to Lavater, "do affirme that in many mines there appeare straunge shapes and spirites, who are apparelled like unto other laborers in the pit. These wander up and down in caves and underminings, and seeme to bestuire themselves in all kinde of labour, as to digge after the veine, to carrie togither oare, to put it in baskets, and to turne the winding-whele to draw it up, when, in very deede, they do nothing lesse. They very seldome hurte the labourers (as they say) except they provoke them by laughing and rayling at them, for then they threw gravel stones at them, or hurt them by some other means. These are especially haunting in pittes where mettall moste aboundeth."—(*Of ghostes*, etc., London, 1572, 4to, p. 73.)

This is our great Milton's

"Swart faëry of the mine."

"Simple foolish men imagine, I know not howe, that there be certayne elves or fairies of the earth, and tell many straunge and marvellous tales of them, which they have heard of their grandmothers and mothers, howe they have appeared unto those of the house, have done service, have rocked the cradell, and (which is a signe of good luck) do continually tarry in the house."—(*Of ghostes*, etc., p. 49.)

Mallet, though without citing any authority, says, "after all, the notion is not everywhere exploded that there are in the bowels-of the earth, fairies, or a kind of dwarfish and tiny beings of human shape, and remarkable for their riches, their activity, and malevolence. In many countries of the north, the people are still firmly persuaded of their existence. In Ireland, at this day, the good folk show the very rocks and hills in which they maintain that there are swarms of these small subterraneous men, of the most tiny size, but the most delicate figures."—(*Northern Antiquities*, etc., ii. 47.)

There is not a more generally received opinion throughout the principality of Wales than that of the existence of fairies. Amongst the commonalty it is, indeed, universal, and by no means unfrequently credited by the second ranks.

Fairies are said, at a distant period, "to have frequented Bussers-hill in St. Mary's island, but their nightly pranks, aërial gambols, and cockleshell abodes, are now quite unknown."—(Heath's *Account of the Islands of Scilly*, p. 129.)

"Evil spirits, called fairies, are frequently seen in several of the isles [of Orkney], dancing and making merry, and sometimes seen in armour."—(Brand's *Description of Orkney*, Edin., 1703, p. 61.)

## NELLY, THE KNOCKER.

A FARM-STEADING situated near the borders of Northumberland, a few miles from Haltwhistle, was once occupied by a family of the name of W—— K——n. In front of the dwelling-house, and at about sixty yards' distance, lay a stone of vast size, as ancient, for so tradition amplifies the date, as the flood. On this stone, at the dead hour of the night, might be discerned a female figure, wrapped in a grey cloak, with one of those low-crowned black bonnets, so familiar to our grandmothers, upon her head. She was incessantly knock, knock, knocking, in a fruitless endeavour to split the impenetrable rock. Duly as night came round, she occupied her lonely station, in the same low crouching attitude, and pursued the dreary obligations of her destiny, till the grey streaks of the dawn gave admonition to depart. From this, the only perceptible action in which she engaged, she obtained the name of Nelly, the Knocker. So perfectly had the inmates of the farmhouse in the lapse of time, which will reconcile sights and events the most disagreeable and alarming, become accustomed to

Nelly's undeviating nightly din, that the work went forward unimpeded and undisturbed by any apprehension accruing from her shadowy presence. Did the servant-man make his punctual resort to the neighbouring cottages, he took the liberty of scrutinising Nelly's antiquated garb that varied not with the vicissitudes of seasons, or he pried sympathetically into the progress of her monotonous occupation, and though her pale, ghastly, contracted features gave a momentary pang of terror, it was rapidly effaced in the vortex of good fellowship into which he was speedily drawn. Did the loon venture an appointment with his mistress at the rustic style of the stack-garth, Nelly's unwearied hammer, instead of proving a barrier, only served, by imparting a grateful sense of mutual danger, to render more intense the raptures of the hour of meeting. So apathetic were the feelings cherished towards her, and so little jealousy existed of her power to injure, that the relater of these circumstances states that on several occasions she has passed Nelly at her laborious toil, without evincing the slightest perturbation, beyond a hurried step, as she stole a glance at the inexplicable and mysterious form.

An event, in the course of years, disclosed the secrets that marvellous stone shrouded, and drove poor Nelly for ever from the scene so inscrutably linked with her fate.

Two of the sons of the farmer were rapidly approaching maturity, when one of them, more reflecting and shrewd than his compeers, suggested the idea of relieving Nelly from her toilsome avocation, and of taking possession of the alluring legacy to which she was evidently and urgently summoning. He proposed, conjointly with his father and brother, to blast the stone, as the most expeditious mode of gaining access to her arcana, and, this in the open daylight, in order that any tutelary protection she might be disposed to extend to her favourite haunt might, as she was a thing of darkness and the night, be effectually countervailed. Nor were their hopes frustrated, for, upon clearing away the earth and fragments that resulted from the explosion, there was revealed to their elated and admiring gaze, a precious booty of closely packed urns copiously enriched with gold. Anxious that no intimation of their good fortune should transpire, they had taken the precaution to despatch the female servant on a needless errand, and ere her return the whole treasure was efficiently and completely secured. So completely did they succeed in keeping their own counsel, and so successfully did their reputation keep pace with the cautious production of their undivulged treasures, that for many years afterwards they were never suspected of gaining any advantage from poor Nelly's "knocking"; their improved appearance, and the somewhat imposing figure they made in their little district, being solely attributed to their superior judgment, and to the good management of their lucky farm.

# THE THREE FOOLS.

THERE was once a good-looking girl, the daughter of well-off country folk, who was loved by an honest young fellow named John. He courted her for a long time, and at last got her and her parents to consent to his marrying her, which was to come off in a few weeks' time.

One day as the girl's father was working in his garden he sat down to rest himself by the well, and, looking in, and seeing how deep it was, he fell a-thinking.

"If Jane had a child," said he to himself, "who knows but that one day it might play about here and fall in and be killed?"

The thought of such a thing filled him with sorrow, and he sat crying into the well for some time until his wife came to him.

"What is the matter?" asked she. "What are you crying for?"

Then the man told her his thoughts—

"If Jane marries and has a child," said he, "who knows but it might play about here and some day fall into the well and be killed?"

"Alack!" cried the woman, "I never thought of that before. It is, indeed, possible."

So she sat down and wept with her husband.

As neither of them came to the house the daughter shortly came to look for them, and when she found them sitting crying into the well—

"What is the matter?" asked she. "Why do you weep?"

So her father told her of the thought that had struck him.

"Yes," said she, "it might happen."

So she too sat down with her father and mother, and wept into the well.

They had sat there a good while when John comes to them.

"What has made you so sad?" asked he.

So the father told him what had occurred, and said that he should be afraid to let him have his daughter seeing her child might fall into the well.

"You are three fools," said the young man, when he had heard him to an end, and leaving them, he thought over whether he should try to get Jane for his wife or not. At length he decided that he would marry her if he could find three people more foolish than her and her father and mother. He put on his boots and went out.

"I will walk till I wear these boots out," said he, "and if I find three more foolish people before I am barefoot, I will marry her."

So he went on, and walked very far till he came to a barn, at the door of which stood a man with a shovel in his hands. He seemed to be working very hard, shovelling the air in at the door.

"What are you doing?" asked John.

"I am shovelling in the sunbeams," replied the man, "to ripen the corn."

"Why don't you have the corn out in the sun for it to ripen it?" asked John.

"Good," said the man. "Why, I never thought of that! Good luck to you, for you have saved me many a weary day's work."

"That's fool number one," said John, and went on.

He travelled a long way, until one day he came to a cottage, against the wall of it was placed a ladder, and a man was trying to pull a cow up it by means of a rope, one end of which was round the cow's neck.

"What are you about?" asked John.

"Why," replied the man, "I want the cow up on the roof to eat off that fine tuft of grass you see growing there."

"Why don't you cut the grass and give it to the cow?" asked John.

"Why, now, I never thought of that!" answered the man. "So I will, of course, and many thanks, for many a good cow have I killed in trying to get it up there."

"That's fool number two," said John to himself.

He walked on a long way, thinking there were more fools in the world than he had thought, and wondering what would be the next one he should meet. He had to wait a long time, however, and to walk very far, and his boots were almost worn out before he found another.

One day, however, he came to a field, in the middle of which he saw a pair of trousers standing up, being held up by sticks. A man was running about them and jumping over and over them.

"Hullo!" cried John. "What are you about?"

"Why," said the man, "what need is there to ask? Don't you see I want to get the trousers on?" so saying he took two or three more runs and jumps, but always jumped either to this side or that of the trousers.

"Why don't you take the trousers and draw them on?" asked John.

"Good," said the man. "Why, I never thought of it! Many thanks. I only wish you had come before, for I have lost a great deal of time in trying to jump into them."

"That," said John, "is fool number three."

So, as his boots were not yet quite worn out, he returned to his home and went again to ask Jane of her father and mother. At last they gave her to him, and they lived very happily together, for John had a rail put round the well and the child did *not* fall into it.

# SOME MERRY TALES OF THE WISE MEN OF GOTHAM.

[From a chap-book printed at Hull in the beginning of the present century.]

### TALE FIRST.

THERE were two men of Gotham, and one of them was going to the market at Nottingham to buy sheep, and the other was coming from the market, and both met together on Nottingham bridge.

"Well met," said the one to the other.

"Whither are you a-going?" said he that came from Nottingham.

"Marry," said he that was going thither, "I am going to the market to buy sheep."

"Buy sheep," said the other; "and which way will you bring them home?"

"Marry," said the other, "I will bring them over this bridge."

"By Robin Hood," said he that came from Nottingham, "but thou shalt not."

"By maid Marjoram," said he that was going thither, "but I will."

"Thou shalt not," said the one.

"I will," said the other.

"Tut here," said the one, and "Tut there," said the other. Then they beat their staves against the ground one against the other, as if there had been a hundred sheep betwixt them.

"Hold them there," said one.

"Beware of the leaping over the bridge of my sheep," said the other.

"I care not."

"They shall all come this way," said the one.

"But they shall not," said the other.

As they were in contention, another wise man that belonged to Gotham came from the market with a sack of meal upon his horse, and seeing and hearing his neighbours at strife about sheep, and none betwixt them, said he—

"Ah, fools! will you never learn wit? Then help me," said he that had the meal, "and lay this sack upon my shoulder."

They did so, and he went to one side of the bridge, and unloosed the mouth of the sack, and shook out the meal into the river. Then said he—

"How much meal is there in the sack, neighbours?"

"Marry," answered they, "none."

"Now, by my faith," replied this wise man, "even so much wit is there in your two heads, to strive concerning that thing which you have not."

Now, which was the wisest of all these three persons I leave you to judge.

## Tale Second.

On a time the men of Gotham fain would have pinned in the cuckoo, whereby she should sing all the year; and in the midst of the town they had a hedge made round in compass, and they got the cuckoo, and put her into it, and said—

"Sing here, and you shall lack neither meat nor drink all the year."

The cuckoo, when she perceived herself encompassed within the hedge, flew away.

"A vengeance on her," said the wise men, "we made not our hedge high enough."

## Tale Third.

There was a man of Gotham who went to the market of Nottingham to sell cheese, and, as he was going down the hill to Nottingham bridge, one of his cheese fell out of his wallet, and ran down the hill.

"What!" said the fellow, "can you run to the market alone? I will now send one after the other."

Then laying down the wallet, and taking out the cheese, he tumbled them down the hill, one after the other, and some ran into one bush and some into another, so at last he said—

"I do charge you to meet me in the market-place."

And when the man came into the market to meet the cheese, he stayed until the market was almost done, then went and inquired of his neighbours and other men if they did see his cheese come to market.

"Why, who should bring them?" said one of his neighbours.

"Marry, themselves!" said the fellow. "They knew the way well enough," said he. "A vengeance on them, for I was afraid, to see my cheese run so fast, that they would run beyond the market. I am persuaded that they are by this time almost at York."

So he immediately takes a horse, and rides after them to York, but was very much disappointed.

But to this day no man has ever heard of the cheese.

## Tale Fourth.

WHEN that Good Friday was come the men of Gotham did cast their heads together what to do with their white herrings, red herrings, their sprats, and salt fish. Then one counselled with the other, and agreed that all such fish should be cast into the pond or pool, which was in the middle of the town, that the number of them might increase against the next year. Therefore every one that had got any fish left did cast them into the pond. Then one said—

"I have as yet gotten left so many red herrings."

"Well," said the other, "and I have left so many whitings."

Another immediately cried out—

"I have as yet gotten so many sprats left."

"And," said the last, "I have got so many salt fishes. Let them all go together into the great pond without any distinction, and we may be sure to fare like lords the next year."

At the beginning of the next Lent they immediately went about drawing the pond, imagining they should have the fish, but were much surprised to find nothing but a great eel.

"Ah!" said they, "a mischief on this eel, for he hath eaten up our fish."

"What must we do with him?" said one to the other.

"Kill him!" said one to the other.

"Chop him into pieces," said another.

"Nay, not so," said the other, "but let us drown him."

"Be it accordingly so," replied they all.

So they immediately went to another pond, and did cast the eel into the water.

"Lie there," said these wise men, "and shift for thyself, since you can expect no help from us."

So they left the eel to be drowned.

## Tale Fifth.

On a certain time there were twelve men of Gotham that went a-fishing; and some did wade in the water, and some did stand upon dry land. And when they went homeward, one said to the other—

"We have ventured wonderful hard this day in wading, I pray God that none of us may have come from home to be drowned."

"Nay, marry," said one to the other, "let us see that, for there did twelve of us come out."

Then they told themselves, and every man told eleven, and the twelfth man did never tell himself.

"Alas!" said the one to the other, "there is some one of us drowned."

They went back to the brook where they had been fishing, and did make a great lamentation. A courtier did come riding by, and did ask what it was they sought for, and why they were so sorrowful.

"Oh!" said they, "this day we went to fish in the brook, and here did come out twelve of us, and one of us is drowned."

"Why," said the courtier, "tell how many there be of you," and the one said eleven, and he did not tell himself.

"Well," said the courtier, "what will you give me, and I will find out twelve men?"

"Sir," said they, "all the money we have got."

"Give me the money," said the courtier; and began with the first, and gave a recommendibus over the shoulders, which made him groan, saying, "Here is one;" and so he served them all, that they groaned at the matter. When he came to the last, he paid him well, saying—

"Here is the twelfth man."

"God's blessing on thy heart for finding out our dear brother."

## Tale Sixth.

A MAN'S wife of Gotham had a child, and the father bid the gossips, which were children of eight or ten years of age. The eldest child's name, who was to be godfather, was called Gilbert, the second child's name was Humphrey, and the godmother's name was Christabel. The friends of all of them did admonish them, saying, that divers of times they must say after the priest. When they were all come to the church-door, the priest said—

"Be you all agreed of the name?"

"Be you all," said Gilbert, "agreed of the name?"

The priest then said—

"Wherefore do you come hither?"

Gilbert said, "Wherefore do you come hither?" Humphrey said, "Wherefore do you come hither?"

And Christabel said, "Wherefore do you come hither?"

The priest being amazed, he could not tell what to say, but whistled and said "Whew!"

Gilbert whistled and said "Whew!" Humphrey whistled and said "Whew!" and so did Christabel. The priest being angry, said—

"Go home, fools, go home!"

Then said Gilbert and Humphrey and Christabel the same.

The priest then himself provided for god-fathers and god-mothers.

Here a man may see that children can do nothing without good instruction, and that they are not wise who regard them.

# THE TULIP FAIRIES.

NEAR a pixy field in the neighbourhood of Dartmoor, there lived, on a time, an old woman who possessed a cottage and a very pretty garden, wherein she cultivated a most beautiful bed of tulips. The pixies, it is traditionally averred, so delighted in this spot that they would carry their elfin babes thither, and sing them to rest. Often, at the dead hour of the night, a sweet lullaby was heard, and strains of the most melodious music would float in the air, that seemed to owe their origin to no other musicians than the beautiful tulips themselves, and whilst these delicate flowers waved their heads to the evening breeze, it sometimes seemed as if they were marking time to their own singing. As soon as the elfin babes were lulled asleep by such melodies, the pixies would return to the neighbouring field, and there commence dancing, making those rings on the green which showed, even to mortal eyes, what sort of gambols had occupied them during the night season.

At the first dawn of light the watchful pixies once more sought the tulips, and, though still invisible they could be heard kissing and caressing their babies. The tulips, thus favoured by a race of genii, retained their beauty much longer than any other flowers in the garden, whilst, though contrary to their nature, as the pixies breathed over them, they became as fragrant as roses, and so delighted at all was the old woman who kept the garden that she never suffered a single tulip to be plucked from its stem.

At length, however, she died, and the heir who succeeded her destroyed the enchanted flowers, and converted the spot into a parsley-bed, a circumstance which so disappointed and offended the pixies, that they caused all the parsley to wither away, and, indeed, for many years nothing would grow in the beds of the whole garden. These sprites, however, though eager in resenting an injury, were, like most warm spirits, equally capable of returning a benefit, and if they destroyed the product of the good old woman's garden when it had fallen into unworthy hands, they tended the bed that wrapped her clay with affectionate solicitude. They were heard lamenting and singing sweet dirges around her grave; nor did they neglect to pay this mournful tribute to her memory every night before the moon was at the full, for then their high solemnity of dancing, singing, and rejoicing took place to hail the queen of the night on completing her circle in the heavens. No human hand ever tended the grave of the poor old woman who had nurtured the tulip bed for the delight of these elfin creatures; but no rank weed was ever seen to grow upon it. The sod was ever green, and the prettiest flowers would spring up without sowing or planting, and so they continued to do until it was supposed the mortal body was reduced to its original dust.

# THE HISTORY OF JACK AND THE GIANTS.

## I.

[From a Chap-book printed and sold in Aldermary Churchyard, London. Probable date, 1780.]

In the reign of King Arthur, near to the Land's End of England, in the County of Cornwall, lived a wealthy farmer, who had a son named Jack. He was brisk and of a ready wit, so that whatever he could not perform by force and strength he completed by wit and policy. Never was any person heard of that could worst him. Nay, the very learned many times he has baffled by his cunning and sharp inventions.

In those days the Mount of Cornwall was kept by a large and monstrous giant of eighteen feet high, and about three yards in circumference, of a fierce and grim countenance, the terror of the neighbouring towns and villages.

His habitation was in a cave in the midst of the Mount. Never would he suffer any living creature to keep near him. His feeding was on other men's cattle, which often became his prey, for whenever he wanted food, he would wade over to the mainland, where he would well furnish himself with whatever he could find, for the people at his approach would all forsake their habitations. Then would he seize upon their cows and oxen, of which he would think nothing to carry over upon his back half a dozen at one time: and as for their sheep and boys, he would tie them round his waist like a bunch of candles. This he practised for many years, so that a great part of the county of Cornwall was very much impoverished by him.

Jack having undertaken to destroy this voracious monster, he furnished himself with a horn, a shovel, and a pickaxe, and over to the mount he went in the beginning of a dark winter's evening, where he fell to work, and before morning had dug a pit twenty-two feet deep, and in width nearly the same, and covering it over with sticks and straw, and then strewing a little mould over it, it appeared like plain ground. Then, putting his horn to his mouth, he blew tan-tivy, tan-tivy, which noise awoke the giant, who came roaring towards Jack, crying out—

"You incorrigible villain, you shall pay dearly for disturbing me, for I will broil you for my breakfast."

These words were no sooner spoke, but he tumbled headlong into the pit, and the heavy fall made the foundation of the Mount to shake.

"O Mr. Giant, where are you now? Oh, faith, you are gotten into Lob's Pound, where I will surely plague you for your threatening words. What do you think now of broiling me for your breakfast? Will no other diet serve you but poor Jack?"

Having thus spoken and made merry with him a while, he struck him such a blow on the crown with his pole-axe that he tumbled down, and with a groan expired. This done, Jack threw the dirt in upon him and so buried him. Then, searching the cave, he found much treasure.

Now when the magistrates who employed Jack heard that the job was over, they sent for him, declaring that he should be henceforth called Jack the Giant Killer, and in honour thereof presented him with a sword and an embroidered belt, upon which these words were written in letters of gold—

> "Here's the valiant Cornish man,
> Who slew the giant, Cormoran."

The news of Jack's victory was soon spread over the western parts, so that another giant, called Old Blunderbore, hearing of it, vowed to be revenged on Jack, if it ever was his fortune to light on him. The giant kept an enchanted castle situated in the midst of a lonesome wood.

About four months after as Jack was walking by the borders of this wood, on his journey towards Wales, he grew weary, and therefore sat himself down by the side of a pleasant fountain, when a deep sleep suddenly seized him. At this time the giant, coming there for water, found him, and by the lines upon his belt immediately knew him to be Jack, who had killed his brother giant. So, without any words, he took him upon his shoulder to carry him to his enchanted castle. As he passed through a thicket, the jostling of the boughs awoke Jack, who, finding himself in the clutches of the giant was very much surprised, though it was but the beginning of his terrors, for, entering the walls of the castle, he found the floor strewn and the walls covered with the skulls and bones of dead men, when the giant told him his bones should enlarge the number of what he saw. He also told him that the next day he would eat him with pepper and vinegar, and he did not question but that he would find him a curious breakfast. This said, he locks up poor Jack in an upper room, leaving him there while he went out to fetch another giant who lived in the same wood, that he also might partake of the pleasure they should have in the destruction of honest Jack. While he was gone dreadful shrieks and cries affrighted Jack, especially a voice which continually cried—

> "Do what you can to get away,
> Or you'll become the giant's prey;
> He's gone to fetch his brother who
> Will likewise kill and torture you."

This dreadful noise so affrighted poor Jack, that he was ready to run distracted. Then, going to a window he opened the casement, and beheld afar off the two giants coming.

"So now," quoth Jack to himself, "my death or deliverance is at hand."

There were two strong cords in the room by him, at the end of which he made a noose, and as the giants were unlocking the iron gates, he threw the ropes over the giants' heads, and then threw the other end across a beam, when he pulled with all his might till he had throttled them. Then, fastening the ropes to a beam, he returned to the window, where he beheld the two giants black in the face, and so sliding down the ropes, he came upon the heads of the helpless giants, who could not defend themselves, and, drawing his own sword, he slew them both, and so delivered himself from their intended cruelty. Then, taking the bunch of keys, he entered the castle, where, upon strict search, he found three ladies tied up by the hair of their heads, and almost starved to death.

"Sweet ladies," said Jack, "I have destroyed the monster and his brutish brother, by which means I have obtained your liberties."

This said, he presented them with the keys of the castle, and proceeded on his journey to Wales.

Jack having got but little money, thought it prudent to make the best of his way by travelling hard, and at length, losing his road, he was benighted, and could not get a place of entertainment, till, coming to a valley between two hills, he found a large house in a lonesome place, and by reason of his present necessity he took courage to knock at the gate. To his amazement there came forth a monstrous giant, having two heads, yet he did not seem so fiery as the other two, for he was a Welsh giant, and all he did was by private and secret malice, under the false show of friendship. Jack, telling his condition, he bid him welcome, showing him into a room with a bed, where he might take his night's repose. Upon this Jack undressed himself, but as the giant was walking to another apartment Jack heard him mutter these words to himself—

"Tho' here you lodge with me this night,
You shall not see the morning light,
My club shall dash your brains out quite."

"Say you so?" says Jack. "Is this one of your Welsh tricks? I hope to be as cunning as you."

Then, getting out of bed, and feeling about the room in the dark, he found a thick billet of wood, and laid it in the bed in his stead, then he hid himself in a dark corner of the room. In the dead time of the night came the giant with his club, and he struck several blows on the bed where Jack had artfully laid the billet. Then the giant returned back to his own room, supposing he had broken all his bones. Early in the morning Jack came to thank him for his lodging.

"Oh," said the giant, "how have you rested? Did you see anything in the night?"

"No," said Jack, "but a rat gave me three or four slaps with his tail."

Soon after the giant went to breakfast on a great bowl of hasty pudding, giving Jack but a small quantity. Jack, being loath to let him know he could not eat with him, got a leather bag, and, putting it artfully under his coat, put the pudding into it. Then he told the giant he would show him a trick, and taking up a knife he ripped open the bag and out fell the pudding. The giant thought he had cut open his stomach and taken the pudding out.

"Odds splutters," says he, "hur can do that hurself," and, taking the knife up, he cut himself so badly that he fell down and died.

Thus Jack outwitted the Welsh giant and proceeded on his journey.

King Arthur's only son desired his father to furnish him with a certain sum of money, that he might go and seek his fortune in the principality of Wales, where a beautiful lady lived, whom he had heard was possessed with seven evil spirits.

The king, his father, counselled him against it, yet he could not be persuaded, so the favour was granted, which was one horse loaded with money, and another to ride on. Thus he went forth without any attendants, and after several days' travel he came to a large market-town in Wales, where he beheld a vast crowd of people gathered together. The king's son demanded the reason of it, and was told that they had arrested a corpse for many large sums of money, which the deceased owed before he died. The king's son replied—

"It is a pity that creditors should be so cruel. Go, bury the dead, and let the creditors come to my lodgings, and their debts shall be discharged."

Accordingly they came, and in such great numbers that before night he had almost left himself penniless. Now Jack the Giant Killer being there, and seeing the generosity of the king's son, desired to be his servant. It being agreed on, the next morning they set forward. As they were riding out of the town's end, an old woman cried out—

"He has owed me twopence seven years, pray, sir, pay me as well as the rest."

The king's son put his hand in his pocket and gave it her, it being the last money he had, then, turning to Jack, he said—

"Take no thought nor heed. Let me alone, and I warrant you we will never want."

Now Jack had a small spell in his pocket, the which served for a refreshment, after which they had but one penny left between them. They spent the forenoon in travel and familiar discourse, until the sun grew low, when the king's son said—

"Jack, since we have got no money where can we lodge to-night?"

Jack replied—

"Master, we will do well enough, for I have an uncle who lives within two miles of this place. He is a huge and monstrous giant, having three heads. He will beat five hundred men in armour, and make them fly before him."

"Alas!" said the king's son, "what shall we do there? He will eat us up at a mouthful—nay, we are scarce sufficient to fill one hollow tooth."

"It is no matter for that," says Jack. "I myself will go before and prepare the way for you. Tarry here, and wait my return."

He waited, and Jack rode full speed. Coming to the castle gate, he immediately began to knock with such force that all the neighbouring hills resounded. The giant, roaring with a voice like thunder, called—

"Who is there?"

"None, but your poor cousin Jack."

"And what news," said he, "with my cousin Jack?"

He replied—

"Dear uncle, heavy news."

"God wot! Prithee! what heavy news can come to me? I am a giant with three heads, and besides, thou knowest, I fight five hundred men in armour, and make them all fly like chaff before the wind."

"Oh," said Jack, "but here is a king's son coming

with a thousand men in armour to kill you, and to destroy all you have."

"O my cousin Jack, this is heavy news indeed, but I have a large vault underground where I will run and hide myself, and you shall lock, bolt, and bar me in, and keep the keys till the king's son is gone."

Jack, having now secured the giant, returned and fetched his master, and both made merry with the best dainties the house afforded. In the morning Jack furnished his master with fresh supplies of gold and silver, and having set him three miles on the road out of the giant's smell, he returned and let his uncle out of the hole, who asked Jack what he should give him for his care of him, seeing his castle was demolished.

"Why," said Jack, "I desire nothing but your old rusty sword, the coat in the closet, and the cap and the shoes at your bed's head."

"Ay," said the giant, "thou shalt have them, and be sure keep you them, for my sake. They are things of excellent use. The coat will keep you invisible, the cap will furnish you with knowledge, the sword cuts asunder whatever you strike, and the shoes are of extraordinary swiftness. They may be serviceable to you, so take them with all my heart."

Jack took them, and immediately followed his master. Having overtaken him, they soon arrived at the lady's dwelling, who, finding the king's son to be a suitor, prepared a banquet for him, which being ended, she wiped her mouth with a handkerchief, saying—"You must show me this to-morrow morning, or lose your head," and then she put it in her bosom.

The king's son went to bed right sorrowful, but Jack's cap of knowledge instructed him how to obtain the handkerchief. In the midst of the night the lady called upon her familiar to carry her to Lucifer. Jack whipped on his coat of darkness, with his shoes of swiftness, and was there before her, but could not be seen by reason of his coat, which rendered him perfectly invisible to Lucifer himself. When the lady came she gave him the handkerchief, from whom Jack took it, and brought it to his master, who, showing it the next morning to the lady, saved his life. This much surprised the lady, but he had yet a harder trial to undergo. The next night the lady salutes the king's son, telling him he must show her the next day the lips she kissed last or lose his head.

"So I will," replied he, "if you kiss none but mine."

"It is neither here nor there for that," says she. "If you do not, death is your portion."

At midnight she went again and chid Lucifer for letting the handkerchief go.

"But now," said she, "I shall be too hard for the king's son, for I will kiss thee, and he is to show me the lips I kissed last, and he can never show me thy lips."

Jack, standing up with his sword of sharpness, cut off the evil spirit's head, and brought it under his invisible coat to his master, who laid it at the end of his bolster, and in the morning, when the lady came up, he pulled it out and showed her the lips which she kissed last. Thus, she having been answered twice, the enchantment broke, and the evil spirit left her, to their mutual joy and satisfaction. Then she appeared her former self, both beauteous and virtuous. They were married the next morning, and soon after returned with joy to the court of King Arthur, where Jack, for his good services, was made one of the knights of the Round Table.

## II.

[From a Chap-book, printed and sold at Newcastle, by J. WHITE, 1711.]

JACK, having been successful in all his undertakings, and resolved not to be idle for the future, but to perform what service he could for the honour of his king and country, humbly requested of the king, his royal master, to fit him with a horse and money, to travel in search of strange and new adventures. "For," said he, "there are many giants yet living in the remote parts of the kingdom, and in the dominions of Wales, to the unspeakable damage of your majesty's liege subjects, wherefore, may it please your majesty to give me encouragement, and I doubt not but in a short time to cut them all off, root and branch, and so rid the realm of those cruel giants and devouring monsters in nature."

Now, when the king had heard these noble propositions, and had duly considered the mischievous practices of those bloodthirsty giants, he immediately granted what honest Jack requested. And on the first day of March, being thoroughly furnished with all necessaries for his progress, he took his leave, not only of King Arthur, but likewise of all the trusty and hardy knights belonging to the Round Table, who, after much salutation and friendly greeting, parted, the king and nobles to their courtly palaces, and Jack the Giant Killer to the eager pursuit of Fortune's favours, taking with him the cap of knowledge, sword of sharpness, shoes of swiftness, and likewise the invisible coat, the latter to perfect and complete the dangerous enterprises that lay before him.

He travelled over vast hills and wonderful mountains till, at the end of three days, he came to a large and spacious wood, through which he must needs pass, where, on a sudden, to his great amazement, he heard dreadful shrieks and cries. Casting his eyes around to observe what it might be, he beheld with wonder a giant rushing along with a

worthy knight and his fair lady, whom he held by
the hair of their heads in his hands, with as much
ease as if they had been but a pair of gloves, the
sight of which melted honest Jack into tears of pity
and compassion. Alighting off his horse, which he
left tied to an oak-tree, and then putting on his
invisible coat, under which he carried his sword of
sharpness, he came up to the giant, and, though he
made several passes at him, yet, nevertheless, he
could not reach the trunk of his body by reason of
his height, though he wounded his thighs in several
places. At length, giving him a swinging stroke,
he cut off both his legs, just below the knees, so
that the trunk of his body made not only the ground
to shake, but likewise the trees to tremble with the
force of its fall, at which, by mere fortune, the
knight and his lady escaped his rage. Then had
Jack time to talk with him, and, setting his foot
upon his neck, he said—

"Thou savage and barbarous wretch, I am come
to execute upon you the just reward of your villainy,"
and with that, running him through and through,
the monster sent forth a hideous groan, and yielded
up his life into the hands of the valiant conqueror,
Jack the Giant Killer, while the noble knight and
virtuous lady were both joyful spectators of his
sudden downfall and their deliverance.

This being done, the courteous knight and his
fair lady not only returned Jack hearty thanks for

their deliverance, but also invited him home, there to refresh himself after the dreadful encounter, as likewise to receive some ample reward, by way of gratuity, for his good service.

"No," quoth Jack; "I cannot be at ease till I find out the den which was this monster's habitation."

The knight, hearing this, waxed right sorrowful and replied—

"Noble stranger, it is too much to run a second risk, for note, this monster lived in a den under yon mountain with a brother of his, more fierce and fiery than himself. Therefore, if you should go thither and perish in that attempt it would be the heart-breaking of both me and my lady. Therefore let me persuade you to go with us, and desist from any further pursuit."

"Nay," quoth Jack, "if there be another—nay, were there twenty, I would shed the last drop of blood in my body before one of them should escape my fury. When I have finished this task I will come and pay my respects to you."

So, having taken the directions to their habitation, he mounted his horse, leaving them to return home, while he went in pursuit of the deceased giant's brother. He had not ridden past a mile and a half before he came in sight of the cave's mouth, near to the entrance of which he beheld the other giant sitting upon a huge block of timber with a knotted iron club lying by his side, waiting, as Jack supposed, for his brother's return. His goggle eyes appeared like terrible flames of fire. His countenance was grim and ugly, his cheeks being like a couple of large fat flitches of bacon. Moreover, the bristles of his beard seemed to resemble rods of iron wire. His locks hung down upon his broad shoulders, like curled snakes or hissing adders.

Jack alighted from his horse and put him into a thicket, then, with his coat of darkness, he came somewhat nearer to behold this figure, and said softly—

"Oh! are you there? It will be not long e'er I shall take you by the beard."

The giant all this time could not see him by reason of his invisible coat. So, coming up close to him, valiant Jack, fetching a blow at his head with his sword of sharpness, and missing something of his arm, cut off the giant's nose. The pain was terrible, and so he put up his hands to feel for his nose, and when he could not find it, he raved and roared louder than claps of thunder. Though he turned up his large eyes, he could not see from whence the blow came which had done him that great disaster, yet, nevertheless, he took up his iron-knotted club, and began to lay about him like one that was stark staring mad.

"Nay," quoth Jack, "if you are for that sport, then I will despatch you quickly, for I fear an accidental blow should fall on me."

Then, as the giant rose from his block, Jack makes no more to do but runs the sword up to the hilt in his body, where he left it sticking for a while, and stood himself laughing, with his hands akimbo, to see the giant caper and dance, crying out.

The giant continued raving for an hour or more, and at length fell down dead, whose dreadful fall had like to have crushed poor Jack had he not been nimble to avoid the same.

This being done, Jack cut off both the giants' heads and sent them to King Arthur by a wagoner whom he hired for the purpose, together with an account of his prosperous success in all his undertakings.

Jack, having thus despatched these monsters, resolved with himself to enter the cave in search of these giants' treasure. He passed along through many turnings and windings, which led him at length to a room paved with free-stone, at the upper end of which was a boiling cauldron. On the right hand stood a large table where, as he supposed, the giants used to dine. He came to an iron gate where was a window secured with bars of iron, through which he looked, and there beheld a vast many miserable captives, who, seeing Jack at a distance, cried out with a loud voice—

"Alas! young man, art thou come to be one amongst us in this miserable den?"

"Ay," quoth Jack, "I hope I shall not tarry

long here; but pray tell me what is the meaning of your captivity?"

"Why," said one young man, "I'll tell you. We are persons that have been taken by the giants that keep this cave, and here we are kept till such time as they have occasion for a particular feast, and then the fattest amongst us is slaughtered and prepared for their devouring jaws. It is not long since they took three for the same purpose."

"Say you so," quoth Jack; "well, I have given them both such a dinner that it will be long enough e'er they'll have occasion for any more."

The miserable captives were amazed at his words.

"You may believe me," quoth Jack, "for I have slain them with the point of my sword, and as for their monstrous heads, I sent them in a wagon to the court of King Arthur as trophies of my unparalleled victory."

For a testimony of the truth he had said, he unlocked the iron gate, setting the miserable captives at liberty, who all rejoiced like condemned malefactors at the sight of a reprieve. Then, leading them all together to the aforesaid room, he placed them round the table, and set before them two quarters of beef, as also bread and wine, so that he feasted them very plentifully. Supper being ended, they searched the giants' coffers, where, finding a vast store of gold and silver, Jack equally divided it among them. They all returned him hearty thanks for their treasure and miraculous deliverance. That night they went to their rest, and in the morning they arose and departed—the captives to their respective towns and places of abode, and Jack to the house of the knight whom he had formerly delivered from the hand of the giant.

It was about sun-rising when Jack mounted his horse to proceed on his journey, and by the help of his directions he came to the knight's house some time before noon, where he was received with all demonstrations of joy imaginable by the knight and his lady, who, in honourable respect to Jack, prepared a feast, which lasted for many days, inviting all the gentry in the adjacent parts, to whom the worthy knight was pleased to relate the manner of his former danger and the happy deliverance by the undaunted courage of Jack the Giant Killer. By way of gratitude he presented Jack with a ring of gold, on which was engraved, by curious art, the picture of the giant dragging a distressed knight and his fair lady by the hair of the head, with this motto—

> "We are in sad distress, you see,
> Under a giant's fierce command;
> But gained our lives and liberty
> By valiant Jack's victorious hand."

Now, among the vast assembly there present were five aged gentlemen who were fathers to some of those miserable captives which Jack had lately set at liberty, who, understanding that he was the person that performed those great wonders, immediately paid their venerable respects. After this their mirth increased, and the smiling bowls went freely round to the prosperous success of the victorious conqueror, but, in the midst of all this mirth, a dark cloud appeared which daunted all the hearts of the honourable assembly.

Thus it was. A messenger brought the dismal tidings of the approach of one Thunderdel, a huge giant with two heads, who, having heard of the death of his kinsmen, the above-named giants, was come from the northern dales in search of Jack to be revenged of him for their most miserable downfall. He was now within a mile of the knight's seat, the country people flying before him from their houses and habitations, like chaff before the wind. When they had related this, Jack, not a whit daunted, said—

"Let him come. I am prepared with a tool to pick his teeth. And you, gentlemen and ladies, walk but forth into the garden, and you shall be the joyful spectators of this monstrous giant's death and destruction."

To which they consented, every one wishing him good fortune in that great and dangerous enterprise.

The situation of this knight's house take as follows: It was placed in the midst of a small island, encompassed round with a vast moat, thirty feet deep and twenty feet wide, over which lay a drawbridge. Jack employed two men to cut this last on both sides, almost to the middle, and then, dressing himself in his coat of darkness, likewise putting on his shoes of swiftness, he marches forth against the giant, with his sword of sharpness ready drawn. When he came up to him, yet the giant could not see Jack, by reason of his invisible coat which he had on. Yet, nevertheless, he was sensible of some approaching danger, which made him cry out in these following words—

"Fe, fi, fo, fum!
I smell the blood of an Englishman;
Be he alive or be he dead
I'll grind his bones to make me bread."

"Sayest thou so?" quoth Jack, "then thou art a monstrous miller indeed. But what if I serve thee as I did the two giants of late? On my conscience, I should spoil your practice for the future."

At which time the giant spoke, in a voice as loud as thunder—

"Art thou that villain which destroyed my kinsmen? Then will I tear thee with my teeth, and, what is more, I will grind thy bones to powder."

"You will catch me first, sir," quoth Jack, and with that he threw off his coat of darkness that the giant might see him clearly, and then ran from him, as if through fear. The giant, with foaming mouth and glaring eyes, followed after, like a walking castle, making the foundation of the earth, as it were, to shake at every step. Jack led him a dance three or four times round the moat belonging to the knight's house, that the gentlemen and ladies might take a full view of this huge monster of nature, who followed Jack with all his might, but could not overtake him by reason of his shoes of swiftness, which carried him faster than the giant could follow. At last Jack, to finish the work, took over the bridge, the giant with full speed pursuing after him, with his iron club upon his shoulder, but, coming to the middle of the drawbridge, what with the weight of his body and the most dreadful steps that he took, it broke down, and he tumbled full into the water, where he rolled and wallowed like a whale. Jack, standing at the side of the moat, laughed at the giant and said—

"You told me you would grind my bones to powder. Here you have water enough. Pray, where is your mill?"

The giant fretted and foamed to hear him scoff at that rate, and though he plunged from place to place in the moat, yet he could not get out to be avenged on his adversary. Jack at length got a cast rope and cast it over the giant's two heads with a slip-knot, and, by the help of a train of horses, dragged him out again, with which the giant was near strangled, and before Jack would let him loose he cut off both his heads with his sword of sharpness, in the full view of all the worthy assembly of knights, gentlemen, and ladies, who gave a joyful shout when they saw the giant fairly despatched. Then, before he would either eat or drink, Jack sent the heads also, after the others, to the court of King Arthur, which being done, he, with the knights and ladies, returned to their mirth and pastime, which lasted for many days.

After some time spent in triumphant mirth and pastime, Jack grew weary of riotous living, wherefore, taking leave of the noble knights and ladies, he set forward in search of new adventures. Through many woods and groves he passed, meeting with nothing remarkable, till at length, coming near the foot of a high mountain, late at night, he knocked at the door of a lonesome house, at which time an ancient man, with a head as white as snow, arose and let him in.

"Father," said Jack, "have you any entertainment for a benighted traveller that has lost his way?"

"Yes," said the old man, "if you will accept of such accommodation as my poor cottage will afford, thou shalt be right welcome."

Jack returned him many thanks for his great civility, wherefore down they sat together, and the old man began to discourse him as follows—

"Son," said he, "I am sensible thou art the great

conqueror of giants, and it is in thy power to free this part of the country from an intolerable burden which we groan under. For, behold! my son, on the top of this high mountain there is an enchanted castle kept by a huge monstrous giant named Galligantus, who, by the help of an old conjuror, betrays many knights and ladies into this strong castle, where, by magic art, they are transformed into sundry shapes and forms. But, above all, I lament the fate of a duke's daughter, whom they snatched from her father's garden by magic art, carrying her through the air in a mourning chariot drawn, as it were, by two fiery dragons, and, being secured within the walls of the castle, she was immediately transformed into the real shape of a white hind, where she miserably moans her misfortune. Though many worthy knights have endeavoured to break the enchantment and work her deliverance, yet none of them could accomplish this great work, by reason of two dreadful griffins who were fixed by magic art at the entrance of the castle gate, which destroy any as soon as they see them. You, my son, being furnished with an invisible coat, may pass by them undiscovered, and on the brazen gates of the castle you will find engraved in large characters by what means the enchantment may be broken."

The old man having ended his discourse, Jack gave him his hand, with a faithful promise that in the morning he would venture his life to break the enchantment and free the lady, together with the rest that were miserable partners in her calamity.

Having refreshed themselves with a small morsel of meat, they laid them down to rest, and in the morning Jack arose and put on his invisible coat, cap of knowledge, and shoes of swiftness, and so prepares himself for the dangerous enterprises.

Now, when he had ascended to the top of the mountain, he soon discovered the two fiery griffins. He passed on between them without fear, for they could not see him by reason of his invisible coat. Now, when he was got beyond them, he cast his eyes around him, where he found upon the gates a golden trumpet, hung in a chain of fine silver, under which these lines were engraved—

> "Whosoever shall this trumpet blow
> Shall soon the giant overthrow,
> And break the black enchantment straight,
> So all shall be in happy state."

Jack had no sooner read this inscription but he blew the trumpet, at which time the vast foundation of the castle tumbled, and the giant, together with the conjuror, was in horrid confusion, biting their thumbs and tearing their hair, knowing their wicked reign was at an end. At that time Jack, standing at the giant's elbow, as he was stooping to take up his club, at one blow, with his sword of sharpness, cut off his head. The conjuror, seeing this, immediately mounted into the air and was carried away in a whirlwind. Thus was the whole enchantment broken, and every knight and lady, that had been for a long time transformed into birds and beasts, returned to their proper shapes and likeness again. As for the castle, though it seemed at first to be of vast strength and bigness, it vanished in a cloud of smoke, whereupon an universal joy appeared among the released knights and ladies. This being done, the head of Galligantus was likewise, according to the accustomed manner, conveyed to the court of King Arthur, as a present made to his majesty. The very next day, after having refreshed the knights and ladies at the old man's habitation (who lived at the foot of the mountain), Jack set forward for the court of King Arthur, with those knights and ladies he had so honourably delivered.

Coming to his majesty, and having related all the passages of his fierce encounters, his fame rang though the whole court, and, as a reward for his good services, the king prevailed with the aforesaid duke to bestow his daughter in marriage to honest Jack, protesting that there was no man so worthy of her as he, to all which the duke very honourably consented. So married they were, and not only the court, but likewise the kingdom were filled with joy and triumph at the wedding. After which the king, as a reward for all his good services done for the nation, bestowed upon him a noble habitation with a plentiful estate thereto belonging, where he and his lady lived the residue of their days in great joy and happiness.

## THE FAIRIES' CUP.

"In the province of the Deiri (Yorkshire), not far from my birthplace," says William of Newbury, "a wonderful thing occurred, which I have known from my boyhood. There is a town a few miles distant from the Eastern Sea, near which are those celebrated waters commonly called Gipse. . . . A peasant of this town went once to see a friend who lived in the next town, and it was late at night when he was coming back, not very sober, when, lo! from the adjoining barrow, which I have often seen, and which is not much over a quarter of a mile from the town, he heard the voices of people singing, and, as it were, joyfully feasting. He wondered who they could be that were breaking in that place, by their merriment, the silence of the dead night, and he wished to examine into the matter more closely. Seeing a door open in the side of the barrow he went up to it and looked in, and there he beheld a large and luminous house, full of people, women as well as men, who were reclining as at a solemn banquet. One of the attendants, seeing him standing at the door, offered him a cup.

He took it, but would not drink, and pouring out the contents, kept the vessel. A great tumult arose at the banquet on account of his taking away the cup, and all the guests pursued him, but he escaped by the fleetness of the beast he rode, and got into the town with his booty.

"Finally this vessel of unknown material, of unusual colour, and of extraordinary form, was presented to Henry the Elder, King of the English, as a valuable gift; was then given to the Queen's brother, David, King of the Scots, and was kept for several years in the treasury of Scotland. A few years ago, as I have heard from good authority, it was given by William, King of the Scots, to Henry the Second, who wished to see it."

# THE WHITE LADY

THERE was once on a time an old woman who lived near Heathfield, in Devonshire. She made a slight mistake, I do not know how, and got up at midnight, thinking it to be morning. This good woman mounted her horse, and set off, panniers, cloak, and all, on her way to market. Anon she heard a cry of hounds, and soon perceived a hare making rapidly towards her. The hare, however, took a turn and a leap and got on the top of the hedge, as if it would say to the old woman "Come, catch me." She liked such hunting as this very well, put forth her hand, secured the game, popped it into one of the panniers, covered it over, and rode forward. She had not gone far, when great was her alarm at perceiving on the dismal and solitary waste of Heathfield, advancing at full pace, a headless horse, bearing a black and grim rider, with horns sprouting from under a little jockey-cap, and having a cloven foot thrust into one stirrup. He was surrounded by a pack of hounds which had tails that whisked about and shone like fire, while the air itself had a strong sulphurous scent. These were signs not to be mistaken, and the poor old woman knew in a moment that huntsman and hounds were taking a ride from the regions below. It soon, however, appeared that however clever the rider might be, he was no conjuror, for he very civilly asked the old woman if she could set him right, and point out which way the hare was flown. The old woman probably thought it was no harm to pay the father of lies in his own coin, so she boldly gave him a negative, and he rode on, not suspecting the cheat. When he was out of sight the old woman perceived the hare in the pannier began to move, and at length, to her great amazement, it changed into a beautiful young lady, all in white, who thus addressed her preserver—

"Good dame, I admire your courage, and I thank you for the kindness with which you have saved me from a state of suffering that must not be told to human ears. Do not start when I tell you that I am not an inhabitant of the earth. For a great crime committed during the time I dwelt upon it, I was doomed, as a punishment in the other world, to be constantly pursued either above or below ground by evil spirits, until I could get behind their tails whilst they passed on in search of me. This difficult object, by your means, I have now happily effected, and, as a reward for your kindness, I promise that all your hens shall lay two eggs instead of one, and that your cows shall yield the most plentiful store of milk all the year round, that you shall talk twice as much as you ever did before, and your husband stand no chance in any matter between you to be settled by the tongue. But beware of the devil, and don't grumble about tithes, for my enemy and yours may do you an ill-turn when he finds out you were clever enough to cheat even him, since, like all great impostors, he does not like to be cheated himself. He can assume all shapes, except those of the lamb and dove."

The lady in white then vanished. The old woman found the best possible luck that morning in her traffic. And to this day the story goes in the town, that from the Saviour of the world having hallowed the form of the lamb, and the Holy Ghost that of the dove, they can never be assumed by the mortal enemy of the human race under any circumstances.

# A PLEASANT AND DELIGHTFUL HISTORY OF THOMAS HICKATHRIFT.

## I.

[From a Chap-book, printed at Whitehaven by Ann Dunn, Market Place. Probable date 1780.]

In the reign before William the Conqueror, I have read in an ancient history that there dwelt a man in the parish of the Isle of Ely, in the county of Cambridge, whose name was Thomas Hickathrift— a poor man and a day-labourer, yet he was a very stout man, and able to perform two days' work instead of one. He having one son and no more children in the world, he called him by his own name, Thomas Hickathrift. This old man put his son to good learning, but he would take none, for he was, as we call them in this age, none of the wisest sort, but something less, and had no docility at all in him.

His father being soon called out of the world, his mother was tender of him, and maintained him by her hand labour as well as she could, he being slothful and not willing to work to get a penny for his living, but all his delight was to be in the chimney-corner, and he would eat as much at one time as would serve four or five men. He was in height, when he was but ten years of age, about eight feet; and in thickness, five feet; and his hand was like unto a shoulder of mutton; and in all his parts, from top to toe, he was like unto a monster, and yet his great strength was not known.

The first time that his strength was known was by his mother's going to a rich farmer's house (she being but a poor woman) to desire a bottle of straw for herself and her son Thomas. The farmer, being a very honest, charitable man, bid her take what she would. She going home to her son Tom, said—

"I pray, go to such a place and fetch me a bottle of straw; I have asked him leave."

He swore he would not go.

"Nay, prithee, Tom, go," said his mother.

He swore again he would not go unless she would borrow him a cart-rope. She, being willing to please him, because she would have some straw, went and borrowed him a cart-rope to his desire.

He, taking it, went his way. Coming to the farmer's house, the master was in the barn, and two men a-thrashing. Said Tom—

"I am come for a bottle of straw."

"Tom," said the master, "take as much as thou canst carry."

He laid down the cart-rope and began to make his bottle. Said they—

"Tom, thy rope is too short," and jeered poor Tom, but he fitted the man well for it, for he made his bottle, and when he had finished it, there was supposed to be a load of straw in it of two thousand pounds weight. Said they—

"What a great fool art thou. Thou canst not carry the tenth of it."

Tom took the bottle, and flung it over his shoulder, and made no more of it than we would do of a hundredweight, to the great admiration of master and man.

Tom Hickathrift's strength being then known in the town they would no longer let him lie baking by the fire in the chimney-corner. Every one would be hiring him for work. They seeing him to have so much strength told him that it was a shame for him to live such a lazy course of life, and to be idle day after day, as he did.

Tom seeing them bate him in such a manner as they did, went first to one work and then to another, but at length came to a man who would hire him to go to the wood, for he had a tree to bring home, and he would content him. Tom went with him, and took with him four men besides; but when they came to the wood they set the cart to the tree, and began to draw it up with pulleys. Tom seeing them not able to stir it, said—

"Stand away, ye fools!" then takes it up and sets it on one end and lays it in the cart.

"Now," says he, "see what a man can do!"

"Marry, it is true," said they.

When they had done, as they came through the wood, they met the woodman. Tom asked him for a stick to make his mother a fire with.

"Ay," says the woodman. "Take one that thou canst carry."

Tom espied a tree bigger than that one that was in the cart, and lays it on his shoulder, and goes home with it as fast as the cart and the six horses could draw it. This was the second time that Tom's strength was known.

When Tom began to know that he had more strength than twenty men, he then began to be merry and very tractable, and would run or jump; took great delight to be amongst company, and to go to fairs and meetings, to see sports and pastimes.

Going to a feast, the young men were all met, some to cudgels, some to wrestling, some throwing the hammer, and the like. Tom stood a little to see the sport, and at last goes to them that were throwing the hammer. Standing a little to see their manlike sport, at last he takes the hammer in his hand, to feel the weight of it, and bid them stand out of the way, for he would throw it as far as he could.

"Ay," said the smith, and jeered poor Tom. "You'll throw it a great way, I'll warrant you."

Tom took the hammer in his hand and flung it. And there was a river about five or six furlongs off, and he flung it into that. When he had done, he bid the smith fetch the hammer, and laughed the smith to scorn.

When Tom had done this exploit he would go to wrestling, though he had no more skill of it than an ass but what he did by strength, yet he flung all that came to oppose him, for if he once laid hold of them they were gone. Some he would throw over his head, some he would lay down slyly and how he pleased. He would not like to strike at their heels, but flung them two or three yards from him, ready to break their necks asunder. So that none at last durst go into the ring to wrestle with him, for they took him to be some devil that was come among them. So Tom's fame spread more and more in the country.

Tom's fame being spread abroad both far and near, there was not a man durst give him an angry word, for he was something fool-hardy, and did not care what he did unto them, so that all they that knew him would not in the least displease him. At length there was a brewer at Lynn that wanted a good lusty man to carry his beer to the Marsh and to Wisbeach, hearing of Tom, went to hire him, but Tom seemed coy, and would not be his man until his mother and friends persuaded him, and his master entreated him. He likewise promised him that he should have a new suit of clothes and everything answerable from top to toe, besides he should eat of the best. Tom at last yielded to be his man, and his master told him how far he must go, for you must understand there was a monstrous giant kept some part of the Marsh, and none durst go that way, for if they did he would keep them or kill them, or else he would make bond slaves of them.

But to come to Tom and his master. He did more work in one day than all his men could do in three, so that his master, seeing him very tractable, and to look well after his business, made him his head man to go into the Marsh to carry beer by himself, for he needed no man with him. Tom went every day in the week to Wisbeach, which was a very good journey, and it was twenty miles the roadway.

Tom—going so long that wearisome journey; and finding that way the giant kept was nearer by half, and Tom having now got much more strength than before by being so well kept and drinking so much strong ale as he did—one day as he was going to Wisbeach, and not saying anything to his master or to any of his fellow-servants, he was resolved to make the nearest way to the wood or lose his life, to win the horse or lose the saddle, to kill or be killed, if he met with the giant. And with this resolution he goes the nearest way with his cart and horses to go to Wisbeach; but the giant, perceiving him, and seeing him to be bold, thought to prevent him, and came, intending to take his cart for a prize, but he cared not a bit for him.

The giant met Tom like a lion, as though he would have swallowed him up at a mouthful.

"Sirrah," said he, "who gave you authority to come this way? Do you not know I make all stand in fear of my sight, and you, like an impudent rogue, must come and fling my gates open at your pleasure? How dare you presume to do this? Are you so careless of your life? I will make thee an example for all rogues under the sun. Dost thou not care what thou dost? Do you see how many heads hang upon yonder tree that have offended my law? Thy head shall hang higher than all the rest for an example!"

Tom made him answer—

"A fig for your news, for you shall not find me like one of them."

"No?" said the giant. "Why? Thou art but a fool if thou comest to fight with such a one as I am, and bring no weapon to defend thyself withal."

Said Tom—

"I have a weapon here will make you understand you are a traitorly rogue."

"Ay, sirrah," said the giant; and took that word in high disdain that Tom should call him a traitorly might become the mansion of a great feudal lord or prince.

Thirty carcasses of deer were lying on the massive kitchen board, under the hands of numerous cooks, who toiled to cut them up and dress them, while the gigantic greyhounds which had taken the spoil lay lapping the blood, and enjoying the sight of the slain game. They came next to the royal hall, where the king received his loving consort; knights and ladies, dancing by threes, occupied the floor of the hall; and Thomas, the fatigue of his journey from the Eildon Hills forgotten, went forward and joined in the revelry. After a period, however, which seemed to him a very short one, the queen spoke with him apart, and bade him prepare to return to his own country.

"Now," said the queen, "how long think you that you have been here?"

"Certes, fair lady," answered Thomas, "not above these seven days."

"You are deceived," answered the queen; "you have been seven years in this castle, and it is full time you were gone. Know, Thomas, that the archfiend will come to this castle to-morrow to demand his tribute, and so handsome a man as you will attract his eye. For all the world would I not suffer you to be betrayed to such a fate; therefore up, and let us be going."

This terrible news reconciled Thomas to his departure from Elfinland; and the queen was not long in placing him upon Huntly Bank, where the birds were singing. She took leave of him, and to ensure his reputation bestowed on him the tongue which *could not lie*. Thomas in vain objected to this inconvenient and involuntary adhesion to veracity, which would make him, as he thought, unfit for church or for market, for king's court or for lady's bower. But all his remonstrances were disregarded by the lady; and Thomas the Rhymer, whenever the discourse turned on the future, gained the credit of a prophet whether he would or not, for he could say nothing but what was sure to come to pass.

Thomas remained several years in his own tower near Ercildoun, and enjoyed the fame of his predictions, several of which are current among the country people to this day. At length, as the prophet was entertaining the Earl of March in his dwelling, a cry of astonishment arose in the village, on the appearance of a hart and hind, which left the forest, and, contrary to their shy nature, came quietly onward, traversing the village towards the dwelling of Thomas. The prophet instantly rose from the board, and acknowledging the prodigy as the summons of his fate, he accompanied the hart and hind into the forest, and though occasionally seen by individuals to whom he has chosen to show himself, he has never again mixed familiarly with mankind.

*Scotch.*

he put his cart together again, loaded it, and drove it to Wisbeach and delivered his beer, and, coming home to his master, he told it to him. His master was so overjoyed at the news that he would not believe him till he had seen; and, getting up the next day, he and his master went to see if he spoke the truth or not, together with most of the town of Lynn. When they came to the place and found the giant dead, he then showed the place where the head was, and what silver and gold there was in the cave. All of them leaped for joy, for this monster was a great enemy to all the country.

This news was spread all up and down the country, how Tom Hickathrift had killed the giant, and well was he that could run or go to see the giant and his cave. Then all the folks made bonfires for joy, and Tom was a better respected man than before.

Tom took possession of the giant's cave by consent of the whole country, and every one said he deserved twice as much more. Tom pulled down the cave and built him a fine house where the cave stood, and in the ground that the giant kept by force and strength, some of which he gave to the poor for their common, the rest he made pastures of, and divided the most part into tillage to maintain him and his mother, Jane Hickathrift.

Tom's fame was spread both far and near throughout the country, and it was no longer Tom but Mr. Hickathrift, so that he was now the chiefest man among them, for the people feared Tom's anger as much as they did the giant before. Tom kept men and maid servants, and lived most bravely. He made a park to keep deer in. Near to his house he built a church and gave it the name of St. James's Church, because he killed the giant on that day, which is so called to this hour. He did many good deeds, and became a public benefactor to all persons that lived near him.

Tom having got so much money about him, and being not used to it, could hardly tell how to dispose of it, but yet he did use the means to do it, for he kept a pack of hounds and men to hunt with him, and who but Tom then? So he took such delight in sports that he would go far and near to any meetings, as cudgel-play, bear baiting, football, and the like.

Now as Tom was riding one day, he alighted off his horse to see that sport, for they were playing for a wager. Tom was a stranger, and none did know him there. But Tom spoiled their sport, for he, meeting the football, took it such a kick, that they never found their ball more. They could see it fly, but whither none could tell. They all wondered at it, and began to quarrel with Tom, but some of them got nothing by it, for Tom gets a great spar which belonged to a house that was blown down, and all that stood in his way he knocked down, so that all the county was up in arms to take Tom, but all in vain, for he manfully made way wherever he came.

When he was gone from them, and returning homewards, he chanced to be somewhat late in the evening on the road. There met him four stout, lusty rogues that had been robbing passengers that way, and none could escape them, for they robbed all they met, both rich and poor. They thought when they met with Tom he would be a good prize for them, and, perceiving he was alone made cock-sure of his money, but they were mistaken, for he got a prize by them. Whereupon, meeting him, they bid him stand and deliver.

"What," said Tom, "shall I deliver?"

"Your money, sirrah," said they.

"But," said Tom, "you will give me better words for it, and you must be better armed."

"Come, come," said they, "we do not come here to parley, but we come for money, and money we will have before we stir from this place."

"Ay!" said Tom. "Is it so? Then get it and take it."

So then one of them made at him, but he presently unarmed him and took away his sword, which was made of good trusty steel, and smote so hard at the others that they began to put spurs to their horses and be-gone. But he soon stayed their journey, for one of them having a portmanteau behind him, Tom, supposing there was money in it, fought with a great deal of more courage than before, till at last he killed two of the four, and the other two he wounded very sore so that they cried out for quarter. With much ado he gave them their lives, but took all their money, which was about two hundred pounds, to bear his expenses home. Now when Tom came home he told them how he had served the football-players and the four highwaymen, which caused a laughter from his old mother. Then, refreshing himself, he went to see how all things were, and what his men had done since he went from home.

Then going into his forest, he walked up and down, and at last met with a lusty tinker that had a good staff on his shoulder, and a great dog to carry his leather bag and tools of work. Tom asked the tinker from whence he came, and whither he was going, for that was no highway. The tinker, being a sturdy fellow, bid him go look, and what was that to him, for fools would be meddling.

"No," says Tom, "but I'll make you know, before you and I part, it is me."

"Ay!" said the tinker, "I have been this three long years, and have had no combat with any man, and none durst make me an answer. I think they be all cowards in this country, except it be a man who is called Thomas Hickathrift who killed a giant. Him I would fain see to have one combat with him."

"Ay!" said Tom, "but, methinks, I might be

master in your mouth. I am the man: what have you to say to me?"

"Why," said the tinker, "verily, I am glad we have met so happily together, that we may have one single combat."

"Sure," said Tom, "you do but jest?"

"Marry," said the tinker, "I am in earnest."

"A match," said Tom. "Will you give me leave to get a twig?"

"Ay," says the tinker. "Hang him that will fight a man unarmed. I scorn that."

Tom steps to the gate, and takes one of the rails for his staff. So they fell to work. The tinker at Tom and Tom at the tinker, like unto two giants, they laid one at the other. The tinker had on a leathern coat, and at every blow Tom gave the tinker his coat cracked again, yet the tinker did not give way to Tom an inch, but Tom gave the tinker a blow on the side of the head which felled the tinker to the ground.

"Now, tinker, where are you?" said Tom.

But the tinker, being a man of metal, leaped up again, and gave Tom a blow which made him reel again, and followed his blows, and then took Tom on the other side, which made Tom's neck crack again. Tom flung down the weapon, and yielded the tinker to be the best man, and took him home to his house, where I shall leave Tom and the tinker to be recovered of their many wounds and bruises, which relation is more enlarged as you may read in the second part of Thomas Hickathrift.

## II.

[From a Chap-book. The book bears no date or note as to where or by whom it was printed. It was probably printed at London about the year 1780.]

IN and about the Isle of Ely many disaffected persons, to the number of ten thousand and upwards, drew themselves up in a body, presuming to contend for their pretended ancient rights and liberties, insomuch that the gentry and civil magistrates of the country were in great danger, at which time the sheriff, by night, privately got into the house of Thomas Hickathrift as a secure place of refuge in so imminent a time of danger, where before Thomas Hickathrift he laid open the villainous intent of this headstrong, giddy-brained multitude.

"Mr. Sheriff," quoth Tom, "what service my brother" (meaning the tinker) "and I can perform shall not be wanting."

This said, in the morning by daybreak, with trusty clubs, they both went forth, desiring the Sheriff to be their guide in conducting them to the place of the rebels' rendezvous. When they came there, Tom and the tinker marched up to the head of the multitude, and demanded of them the reason why they disturbed the government, to which they answered with a loud cry—

"Our will's our law, and by that alone we will be governed."

"Nay," quoth Tom, "if it be so, these trusty clubs are our weapons, and by them you shall be chastised," which words were no sooner out of his mouth than the tinker and he put themselves both together in the midst of the throng, and with their clubs beat the multitude down, trampling them under their feet. Every blow which they struck laid twenty or thirty before them, nay—remarkable it was, the tinker struck a tall man, just upon the nape of the neck, with that force that his head flew off and was carried violently fourteen feet from him, where it knocked down one of their chief ringleaders,—Tom, on the other hand, still pressing forward, till by an unfortunate blow he broke his club. Yet he was not in the least dismayed, for he presently seized upon a lusty, stout, raw-boned miller, and made use of him for a weapon, till at length they cleared the field, so that there was not found one that dare lift up a hand against them, having run to holes and corners to hide themselves. Shortly after some of their heads were taken and made public examples of justice, the rest being pardoned at the humble request of Thomas Hickathrift and the tinker.

The king, being truly informed of the faithful services performed by these his loving subjects, Thomas Hickathrift and the tinker, he was pleased to send for them to his palace, where a royal banquet was prepared for their entertainment, most of the nobility being present. Now after the banquet was over, the king said unto all that were there—

"These are my trusty and well-beloved subjects, men of approved courage and valour. They are the men that overcame and conquered ten thousand, which were got together to disturb the peace of my realm. According to the character that hath been given to Thomas Hickathrift and Henry Nonsuch, persons here present, they cannot be matched in any other kingdom in the world. Were it possible to have an army of twenty thousand such as these, I dare venture to act the part of Alexander the Great over again, yet, in the meanwhile, as a proof of my royal favour, kneel down and receive the ancient order of knighthood, Mr. Hickathrift," which was instantly performed.

"And as for Henry Nonsuch, I will settle upon him, as a reward for his great service, the sum of forty shillings a year, during life," which said, the king withdrew, and Sir Thomas Hickathrift and Henry Nonsuch, the tinker, returned home, attended by many persons of quality some miles from the court. But, to the great grief of Sir Thomas, at his return from the court, he found his aged mother drawing to her end, who, in a few days after, died, and was buried in the Isle of Ely.

Tom's mother being dead, and he left alone in a large and spacious house, he found himself strange and uncouth, therefore he began to consider with himself that it would not be amiss to seek out for a wife. Hearing of a young rich widow, not far from Cambridge, to her he went and made his addresses, and, at the first coming, she seemed to show him much favour and countenance, but between this and his coming again she had given some entertainment to a more genteel and airy spark, who happened likewise to come while honest Tom was there the second time. He looked wistfully at Tom, and he stared as wistfully at him again. At last the young spark began with abuseful language to affront Tom, telling him that he was a great lubberly whelp, adding that such a one as he should not pretend to make love to a lady, as he was but a brewer's servant.

"Scoundrel!" quoth Tom, "better words should become you, and if you do not mend your manners you shall not fail to feel my sharp correction."

At which the young spark challenged him forth into the back-yard, for, as he said, he did not question but to make a fool of Tom in a trice. Into the yard they both walk together, the young spark with a naked sword, and Tom with neither stick nor staff in his hand nor any other weapon.

"What!" says the spark, "have you nothing to

defend yourself? Well, I shall the sooner despatch you."

Which said, he ran furiously forward, making a pass at Tom, which he put by, and then, wheeling round, Tom gave him such a swinging kick as sent the spark, like a crow, up into the air, from whence he fell upon the ridge of a thatched house, and then came down into a large fish-pond, and had been certainly drowned if it had not been for a poor shepherd who was walking that way, and, seeing him float upon the water, dragged him out with his hook, and home he ran, like a drowned rat, while Tom returned to the lady.

This young gallant being tormented in his mind to think how Tom had conquered and shamed him before his mistress, he was now resolved for speedy revenge, and knowing that he was not able to cope with a man of Tom's strength and activity, he, therefore, hired two lusty troopers to lie in ambush in a thicket which Tom was to pass through from his home to the young lady. Accordingly they attempted to set upon him.

"How, now," quoth Tom, "rascals, what would you be at? Are you, indeed, weary of the world that you so unadvisedly set upon one who is able to crush you in like a cucumber?"

The troopers, laughing at him, said that they were not to be daunted at his high words.

"High words," quoth Tom. "No, I will come to

action," and with that he ran in between these armed troopers, catching them under his arm, horse and men, with as much ease as if they had been but a couple of baker's babbins, steering his course with them hastily towards his own home. As he passed through a meadow, in which there were many haymakers at work, the poor distressed troopers cried out—

"Stop him! stop him! He runs away with two of the king's troopers."

The haymakers laughed heartily to see how Tom hugged them along. Ever and anon he upbraided them for their baseness, and declared that he would make minced meat of them to feed the crows and jackdaws about his house and habitation. This was such a dreadful lecture to them that the poor rogues begged that he would be merciful and spare their lives, and they would discover the whole plot, and who was the person that employed them. This accordingly they did, and gained favour in the sight of Tom, who pardoned them upon promise that they would never be concerned in such a villainous action for the time to come.

In regard Tom had been hindered by these troopers, he delayed his visit to his lady till the next day, and then, coming to her, gave her a full account of what had happened. She was pleased at heart at this wonderful relation, knowing it was safe for a woman to marry with a man who was able to defend her against all assaults whatsoever, and such a one she found Tom to be. The day of marriage was accordingly appointed, and friends and relations invited, yet secret malice, which is never satisfied without sweet revenge, had like to have prevented the solemnity, for, having three miles to go to church, where they were to be married, the aforesaid gentleman had provided a second time Russians in armour, to the number of twenty-one, he himself being then present, either to destroy the life of Tom, or put them into strange consternation. However, thus it happened. In a lonesome place they rolled out upon them, making their first assault upon Tom, and, with a spear, gave him a slight wound, at which his love and the rest of the women shrieked and cried like persons out of their wits. Tom endeavoured all that he could to pacify them, saying—

"Stand you still and I will show you pleasant sport."

With that he caught a back-sword from the side of a gentleman in his own company, with which he so bravely behaved himself that at every stroke he cut off a joint. Loath he was to touch the life of any, but, aiming at their legs and arms, he lopped them off so fast that, in less than a quarter of an hour, there was not one in the company but what had lost a limb, the green grass being stained with their purple gore, and the ground strewn with legs and arms, as 'tis with tiles from the tops of the houses after a dreadful storm—his love and the rest of the company standing all the while as joyful spectators, laughing one at another, saying—

"What a company of cripples has he made, as it were in the twinkling of an eye!"

"Yes," quoth Tom, "I believe that for every drop of blood that I lost, I have made the rascals pay me a limb as a just tribute."

This done, he stept to a farmer's hard by, and hired there a servant, giving him twenty shillings to carry these cripples home to their respective habitations in his cart. Then did he hasten with his love to the church to be married, and then returned home, where they were heartily merry with their friends, after their fierce and dreadful encounter.

Now, Tom being married, he made a plentiful feast, to which he invited all the poor widows in four or five parishes, for the sake of his mother, whom he had lately buried. This feast was kept in his own house, with all manner of varieties that the country could afford, for the space of four days, in honour likewise of the four victories which he had lately obtained. Now, when the time of feasting was ended, a silver cup was missing, and, being asked about it, they every one denied they knew anything about it. At length it was agreed that they should all stand the search, which they did, and the cup was found on a certain old woman, named the widow Stumbelow. Then were all the rest in a rage. Some were for hanging her, others were for chopping the old woman in pieces for her ingratitude to such a generous soul as Sir Thomas Hickathrift, but he entreated them all to be quiet, saying they should not murder the old woman, for he would appoint a punishment for her himself, which was this—he bored a hole through her nose, and, tying a string therein, then ordered her to be led by the nose through all the streets and lanes in Cambridge.

The tidings of Tom's wedding were soon noised in the court, so that the king sent them a royal invitation to the end that he might see his lady. They immediately went, and were received with all demonstrations of joy and triumph, but while they were in their mirth a dreadful cry approached the court, which proved to be the commons of Kent who were come thither to complain of a dreadful giant that was landed in one of the islands, and brought with him abundance of bears and young lions, likewise a dreadful dragon, on which he himself rode, which monster and ravenous beasts had frightened all the inhabitants out of the island. Moreover, they said, if speedy course was not taken to suppress them in time, they might overrun the whole island. The king, hearing this dreadful relation, was a little startled, yet he persuaded them to return home and make the best defence they could for themselves at present, assuring them that he should not forget them, and so they departed.

The king, hearing the aforesaid dreadful tidings, immediately sat in council to consider what was to be done for the overcoming this monstrous giant, and barbarous savage lions and beasts, that with him had invaded his princely territories. At length it was agreed upon that Thomas Hickathrift was the most likely man in the whole kingdom for undertaking of so dangerous an enterprise, he being not only a fortunate man of great strength, but likewise a true and trusty subject, one that was always ready and willing to do his king and country service. For which reason it was thought necessary to make him governor of the aforesaid island, which place of trust and honour he readily received, and accordingly he forthwith went down with his wife and family, attended by a hundred knights and gentlemen, who conducted him to the entrance of the island which he was to govern. A castle in those days there was, in which he was to take up his head-quarters, the same being situated with that advantage that he could view the island for several miles upon occasion. The knights and gentlemen, at last taking their leave of him, wished him all happy success and prosperity. Many days he had not been there when it was his fortune to behold this monstrous giant, mounted upon a dreadful dragon, bearing upon his shoulder a club of iron, having but one eye, the which was placed in his forehead, and larger in compass than a barber's basin, and seemed to appear like a flaming fire. His visage was dreadful, grim and tawny; the hair of his head hanging down his back and shoulders like snakes of a prodigious length; the bristles of his beard being like rusty wire. Lifting up his blare eye, he happened to discover Sir Thomas Hickathrift, who was looking upon him from one of his windows of the castle. The giant then began to knit his brow and breathe forth threatening words to the governor, who, indeed, was a little surprised at the approach of so monstrous a brute. The giant, finding that Tom did not make much haste down to meet him, alighted from the back of the dragon, and chained the same to an oak-tree. Then, marching furiously to the castle, he set his broad shoulder against a corner of the stone walls, as if he intended to overthrow the whole building at once, which Tom perceiving, said—

"Is this the game you would be at? Faith, I shall spoil your sport, for I have a delicate tool to pick your teeth withal."

Then, taking his two-handed sword of five foot long, a weapon which the king had given him to govern with,—taking this, I say, down he went, and flinging open the gates, he there found the giant, who, by an unfortunate slip in his thrusting, was fallen all along, where he lay and could not help himself.

"What!" quoth Tom, "do you come here to take up your lodging? This is not to be suffered."

With that he ran his long broad-sword into the giant's body, which made the monstrous brute give such a terrible groan that it seemed like roaring thunder, making the very neighbouring trees to tremble. Then Tom, pulling out his sword again, at six or seven blows separated his head from his unconscionable trunk, which head, when it was off, seemed like the root of a mighty oak. Then turning to the dragon, which was all this while chained to a tree, without any further discourse, with four blows with his two-handed sword, he cut off his head also. This fortunate adventure being over, he sent immediately for a team of horses and a wagon, which he loaded with these heads. Then, summoning all the constables in the country for a guard, he sent them to the court, with a promise to his majesty that he would rid the whole island likewise of bears and lions before he left it. Tom's victories rang so long that they reached the ears of his old acquaintance the tinker, who, desirous of honour, resolved to go down and visit Tom in his new government. Coming there, he met with kind and loving entertainment, for they were very joyful to see one another. Now, after three or four days' enjoyment of one another's company, Tom told the tinker that he must needs go forth in search after wild bears and lions, in order to rout them out of the island.

"Well," quoth the tinker, "I would gladly take my fortune with you, hoping that I may be serviceable to you upon occasion."

"Well," quoth Tom, "with all my heart, for I must needs acknowledge I shall be right glad of your company."

This said, they both went forward, Tom with his two-handed sword, and the tinker with his long pikestaff. Now, after they had travelled about four or five hours, it was their fortune to light on the whole knot of wild beasts together, of which six of them were bears, the other eight young lions. Now, when they had fastened their eyes on Tom and the tinker, these ravenous beasts began to roar and run furiously, as if they would have devoured them at a mouthful. Tom and the tinker stood, side by side, with their backs against an oak, and as the lions and bears came within their reach, Tom, with his long sword, clove their heads asunder till they were all destroyed, saving one lion who, seeing the rest of his fellows slain, was endeavouring to escape. Now the tinker, being somewhat too venturous, ran too hastily after him, and, having given the lion one blow, he turned upon him again, seizing him by the throat with that violence that the poor tinker fell dead to the ground. Tom Hickathrift, seeing this, gave the lion such a blow that it ended his life.

Now was his joy mingled with sorrow, for though he had cleared the island of those ravenous savage beasts, yet his grief was intolerable for the loss of his old friend. Home he returned to his lady, where, in token of joy for the wonderful success which he had in his dangerous enterprises, he made a very noble and splendid feast, to which he invited most of his best friends and acquaintances, to whom he made the following promise—

"My friends, while I have strength to stand,
    Most manfully I will pursue
All dangers, till I clear this land
    Of lions, bears, and tigers too.
This you'll find true, or I'm to blame,
    Let it remain upon record,
Tom Hickathrift's most glorious fame,
    Who never yet has broke his word.

The man who does his country bless
    Shall merit much from this fair land;
He who relieved them in distress
    His fame upon record shall stand.
And you, my friends, who hear me now,
    Let honest Tom for ever dwell
Within your minds and thoughts, I trow,
    Since he has pleased you all so well."

# THE SPECTRE COACH.

COBBLERS are a thoughtful race of men, and Tom Shanks was one of their number. He lived in the little village of Acton, in Suffolk, and it was there that an adventure befell him, which, as I am informed by a grandson of his, "had an effect on him from that day to this"—though the "this" in the present case is of a somewhat vague meaning, seeing that Tom has unfortunately been dead some twenty years at least. The terrible adventure that befell him was so much the subject of Tom's talk, that if ever tale could be handed down by means of oral tradition sure Tom's story should be intact in every detail.

It seems that one day Tom left Acton on a journey—quite a remarkable event for him, for he was a quiet-going fellow, not given to running away from his last, but sitting contentedly in his little shop, busily employed in providing his neighbours with good foot-gear. On this day, however, Tom was called away by the intelligence that a sister of his, who was in service in a town some little distance away, was ill and wished to see him. The little cobbler was a man with a warm heart, and as soon as he received this ill news he laid aside a pair of shoes he was on for the parson, and which he was very anxious to finish, for the sooner he touched the money the better for him and his; put on his best coat, took his stick in his hand, and, having bid farewell to his wife and three little ones, went on his way, looking back now and then to shake his stick to them, till he came to the turn in the road by the side of the high trees when he could see them no more.

Well, he walked on, and being a stout-hearted little fellow without much flesh to carry, for cobbling did not even in those days bring in a fortune, and Tom and his folk often had hard times of it; he, in the course of the morning, with a slice out of the afternoon, arrived at his destination. There, thank God, he found his sister much better than he might have expected, judging from the account he had heard of her, and having stayed an hour or two to rest his legs, and recruit his stomach with some beef and a pint of ale, he set out on his way homeward.

The way back seemed much longer than it ought to have been, and Tom cleared the ground very slowly. Before he had gone far the night closed in; but what was that to him, for he knew every inch of the road; and as to thieves, why, he had little enough in his pocket to tempt them, and if need be—

and Tom was not for his size deficient in courage—he had a good stout stick to defend himself with. Still it was dismal work that tramp through lonely lanes, with the trees standing on each side—not bright and lively as they had been in the day-time, with the sun shining on their leaves, and the wind rustling amongst them, but drawn up, still and dark, like sentinels watching in big cloaks. The day had closed in with clouds, which threatened to make the cobbler's journey more miserable with a down-pour of rain. But this fortunately kept off, and the moon, having risen, looked out now and then between the clouds, and a star or two winked in a style which brought comfort to Tom's heart—they seemed so companionable.

So he went on and on, till at length he came to the neighbourhood of Acton again; and glad enough he was once more to find himself in quarters where the very trees and gates and stiles seemed, as it were, to be old friends—Tom having been used to the sight of them daily for as many years as had passed since he was born, and those were not a few, for he was not exactly a chicken.

Well, he came at length to the park gates, and was hurrying past them, for the spot had no particularly good name, and he remembered that he had heard some queer tales concerning sights folk had chanced to see there which they would very much sooner have escaped, when on a sudden his legs seemed, as it were, to refuse to stir, and with his heart thumping against his ribs, as if it would beat a way out for itself, Tom came to a dead stand. What was it that he heard? It seemed like a rushing and grinding of stones, with a cracking like a body of men walking over dry sticks. It could not be the wind, for there was not a breath stirring, and the leaves on the trees lay perfectly still. The noise came nearer and nearer, and the next thought of Tom was that he would like to hide himself in some of the dark shadows around him. But his legs would not stir, and it was as much as he could do, with the aid of his stick, to hold himself up on them. To make matters worse, the moon now, just as the cobbler was wishing for darkness, broke out from a cloud, and cast its light all about him, as if with the very object of showing him up. It is true the light enabled him to have a good look about him, but that was not a thing Tom very much cared about just then.

He stood there a few moments, with the sound coming louder and louder, till it seemed to be just at hand. It was evidently in the park itself. Now it was at the gate. Then, all of a sudden, the gates swung back with a terrible clang, and there issued as strange a procession as Tom's, or indeed mortal's, eyes ever set on. First there came two grooms on horses, and then a carriage drawn by four large steeds, while two men rode behind. They were all goodly looking men enough, and the horses were, as Tom saw at a glance, as pretty pieces of flesh as any man might wish to throw leg across, but one thing struck horror to the cobbler's heart as he looked, for he saw that none of the horsemen had a head on him. On they dashed at a break-neck speed, their horses' hoofs seeming to dash fire from the stones on the road, while the wheels of the coach looked like four bright circles, so fast was it drawn over the ground. Cracking their whips, as if to urge the steeds on to even greater speed, the men rode on, nor did Tom hear them utter a word as they swept past him.

As the coach went by him, and his eyes were glued upon it, the interior of the carriage seemed to him to be lighted up in some mysterious manner, and inside, Tom said, he clearly saw a gentleman and a lady, for such they evidently were by their dress, sitting side by side, but without heads like their attendants.

Another minute and all was gone. Tom rubbed his eyes and wondered if he had not been asleep, but who ever heard of a man falling asleep standing up with no better prop than a stick in his hand? He looked at the gates. They were closed and fast. He looked down the road, but could distinguish nothing. In the distance, however, he could hear the sound of, as it were, a big gust of wind gradually travelling away, while all around him was still.

It did not take him long to get home after that, you may be sure, and when he told his story, though there were some that laughed and hinted that Tom was trying to make a hero of himself by pretending that he had seen what no one else of those he told the story to had set eyes on, yet the old folk remembered that they themselves had spoken with folk who had seen the very same sight for themselves, so I think that Tom Shanks has the very best claim to be considered the last man in the place who ever witnessed the progress of the spectre coach.

## THE BAKER'S DAUGHTER.

A VERY long time ago, I cannot tell you when, it is so long since, there lived in a town in Herefordshire a baker who used to sell bread to all the folk around. He was a mean, greedy man, who sought in every way to put money by, and who did not scruple to cheat such people as he was able when they came to his shop.

He had a daughter who helped him in his business, being unmarried and living with him, and seeing how her father treated the people, and how he succeeded in getting money by his bad practices, she, too, in time came to do the like.

One day when her father was away, and the girl remained alone in the shop, an old woman came in—

"My pretty girl," said she, "give me a bit of dough I beg of you, for I am old and hungry."

The girl at first told her to be off, but as the old woman would not go, and begged harder than before for a piece of bread, at last the baker's daughter took up a piece of dough, and giving it to her, says—

"There now, be off, and do not trouble me any more."

"My dear," says the woman, "you have given me a piece of dough, let me bake it in your oven, for I have no place of my own to bake it in."

"Very well," replied the girl, and, taking the dough, she placed it in the oven, while the old woman sat down to wait till it was baked.

When the girl thought the bread should be ready she looked in the oven expecting to find there a small cake, and was very much amazed to find instead a very large loaf of bread. She pretended to look about the oven as if in search of something.

"I cannot find the cake," said she. "It must have tumbled into the fire and got burnt."

"Very well," said the old woman, "give me another piece of dough instead and I will wait while it bakes."

So the girl took another piece of dough, smaller than the first piece, and having put it in the oven, shut to the door. At the end of a few minutes or so she looked in again, and found there another loaf, larger than the last.

"Dear me," said she, pretending to look about her, "I have surely lost the dough again. There's no cake here."

"'Tis a pity," said the old woman, "but never mind. I will wait while you bake me another piece."

So the baker's daughter took a piece of dough as small as one of her fingers and put it in the oven, while the old woman sat near. When she thought it ought to be baked, she looked into the oven and there saw a loaf, larger than either of the others.

"That is mine," said the old woman.

"No," replied the girl. "How could such a large loaf have grown out of a little piece of dough?"

"It is mine, it is sure," said the woman.

"It is not," said the girl, "and you shall not have it."

Well, when the old woman saw that the girl would not give her the loaf, and saw how she had tried to cheat her, for she was a fairy, and knew all the tricks that the baker's daughter had put upon her, she draws out from under her cloak a stick, and just touches the girl with it. Then a wonderful thing occurred, for the girl became all of a sudden changed into an owl, and flying about the room, at last, made for the door, and, finding it open, she flew out and was never seen again.

## THE FAIRY CHILDREN.

"Another wonderful thing," says Ralph of Coggeshall, "happened in Suffolk, at St. Mary's of the Wolf-pits.

A boy and his sister were found by the inhabitants of that place near the mouth of a pit which is there, who had the form of all their limbs like to those of other men, but they were different in the colour of their skin from all the people of our habitable world, for the whole surface of their skin was tinged of a green colour. No one could understand their speech.

When they were brought as curiosities to the house of a certain knight, Sir Richard de Calne, at Wikes, they wept bitterly. Bread and victuals were set before them, but they would touch none of them, though they were tormented by great hunger, as the girl afterwards acknowledged. At length when some beans, just cut, with their stalks, were brought into the house, they made signs, with great avidity, that they should be given to them. When they were brought they opened the stalks instead of the pods, thinking the beans were in the hollow of them.

But not finding them there, they began to weep anew. When those who were present saw this, they opened the pods, and showed them the naked beans. They fed on these with great delight, and for a long time tasted no other food. The boy, however, was always languid and depressed, and he died within a short time.

The girl enjoyed continual good health, and, becoming accustomed to various kinds of food, lost completely that green colour, and gradually recovered the sanguine habit of her entire body. She was afterwards regenerated by the laver of holy baptism, and lived for many years in the service of that knight, as I have frequently heard from him and his family.

Being frequently asked about the people of her country, she asserted that the inhabitants, and all they had in that country, were of a green colour, and that they saw no sun, but enjoyed a degree of light like what is after sunset. Being asked how she came into this country with the aforesaid boy, she replied, that, as they were following their flocks, they came to a certain cavern, on entering which they heard a delightful sound of bells, ravished by whose sweetness they went on for a long time wandering on through the cavern, until they came to its mouth. When they came out of it, they were struck senseless by the excessive light of the sun, and the unusual temperature of the air, and they thus lay for a long time. Being terrified by the noise of those who came on them, they wished to fly, but they could not find the entrance of the cavern before they were caught."

This story is also told by William of Newbury, who places it in the reign of King Stephen. He says he long hesitated to believe it, but was at length overcome by the weight of evidence. According to him, the place where the children appeared, was about four or five miles from Bury-St.-Edmund's. They came in harvest-time out of the Wolf-pits. They both lost their green hue, and were baptized, and learned English. The boy, who was the younger, died, but the girl married a man at Lenna, and lived many years. They said their country was called St. Martin's Land, as that saint was chiefly worshipped there; that the people were Christians, and had churches; that the sun did not rise there, but that there was a bright country which could be seen from theirs, being divided from it by a very broad river.

## THE HISTORY OF JACK AND THE BEANSTALK.

[From a Chap-book printed at Paisley, by G. Caldwell, bookseller. Probable date, 1810.]

In the days of King Alfred there lived a poor woman whose cottage was situated in a remote country village, a great many miles from London.

She had been a widow some years, and had an only child named Jack, whom she indulged to a fault. The consequence of her blind partiality was, that Jack did not pay the least attention to anything she said, but was indolent, careless, and extravagant. His follies were not owing to a bad disposition, but that his mother had never checked him. By degrees she disposed of all she possessed —scarcely anything remained but a cow.

The poor woman one day met Jack with tears in her eyes. Her distress was great, and, for the first time in her life, she could not help reproaching him, saying—

"O you wicked child! by your ungrateful course of life you have at last brought me to beggary and ruin. Cruel, cruel boy! I have not money enough to purchase even a bit of bread for another day. Nothing now remains to sell but my poor cow. I am sorry to part with her. It grieves me sadly, but we must not starve."

For a few minutes Jack felt a degree of remorse, but it was soon over, and he began teasing his mother to let him sell the cow at the next village so much, that she at last consented.

As he was going along he met a butcher, who inquired why he was driving the cow from home. Jack replied he was going to sell it. The butcher held some curious beans in his hat that were of various colours and attracted Jack's notice. This did not pass unnoticed by the butcher, who, knowing Jack's easy temper, thought now was the time to take advantage of it, and, determined not to let slip so good an opportunity, asked what was the price of the cow, offering at the same time all the beans in his hat for her. The silly boy could not conceal the pleasure he felt at what he supposed so great an offer. The bargain was struck instantly, and the cow exchanged for a few paltry beans. Jack made the best of his way home, calling aloud to his mother before he reached the house, thinking to surprise her.

When she saw the beans and heard Jack's account, her patience quite forsook her. She kicked the beans away in a passion—they flew in all directions —some were scattered in the garden. Not having anything to eat, they both went supperless to bed.

Jack awoke very early in the morning, and seeing something uncommon from the window of his bed-chamber, ran downstairs into the garden, where he soon discovered that some of the beans had taken root and sprung up surprisingly. The stalks were of an immense thickness, and had so entwined that they formed a ladder nearly like a chain in appearance.

Looking upwards, he could not discern the top. It appeared to be lost in the clouds. He tried the stalk, found it firm, and not to be shaken. He quickly formed the resolution of endeavouring to climb up to the top in order to seek his fortune, and ran to communicate his intention to his mother, not doubting but she would be equally pleased with himself. She declared he should not go; said it would break her heart if he did; entreated and threatened, but all in vain.

Jack set out, and, after climbing for some hours, reached the top of the beanstalk, fatigued and quite exhausted. Looking around, he found himself in a strange country. It appeared to be a desert, quite barren, not a tree, shrub, house, or living creature to be seen. Here and there were scattered fragments of stone, and at unequal distances small heaps of earth were loosely thrown together.

Jack seated himself, pensively, upon a block of stone, and thought of his mother. He reflected with sorrow on his disobedience in climbing the beanstalk against her will, and concluded that he must die of hunger.

However, he walked on, hoping to see a house where he might beg something to eat and drink. Presently a handsome young woman appeared at a distance. As she approached Jack could not help admiring how beautiful and lively she looked. She was dressed in the most elegant manner, and had a small white wand in her hand, on the top of which was a peacock of pure gold.

While Jack was looking, with the greatest surprise, at this charming female, she came up to him, and, with a smile of the most bewitching sweetness, inquired how he came there. Jack related the circumstance of the beanstalk. She asked him if he recollected his father. He replied he did not, and added there must be some mystery relating to him, because if he asked his mother who his father was she always burst into tears and appeared to be violently agitated, nor did she recover herself for some days after. One thing, however, he could not avoid observing on these occasions, which was, that she always carefully avoided answering him, and even seemed afraid of speaking, as if there were some secret connected with his father's history which she must not disclose.

The young woman replied—

"I will reveal the whole story. Your mother

must not do so. But before I begin I require a solemn promise on your part to do what I command. I am a fairy, and, if you do not perform exactly what I desire, you will be destroyed."

Jack was frightened at her menaces, and promised to fulfil her injunctions exactly, and the fairy thus addressed him—

"Your father was a rich man. His disposition was very benevolent. He was very good to the poor, and constantly relieved them. He made it a rule never to let a day pass without doing good to some person. On one particular day in the week he kept open house, and invited only those who were reduced and had lived well. He always presided himself, and did all in his power to render his guests comfortable. The rich and the great were next invited. The servants were all happy and greatly attached to their master and mistress. Your father, though only a private gentleman, was as rich as a prince, and he deserved all he possessed, for he only lived to do good. Such a man was soon known and talked of. A giant lived a great many miles off. This man was altogether as wicked as your father was good. He was, in his heart, envious, covetous, and cruel, but he had the art of concealing those vices. He was poor, and wished to enrich himself at any rate.

"Hearing your father spoken of, he formed the design of becoming acquainted with him, hoping to ingratiate himself into your father's favour. He removed quickly into your neighbourhood, and caused it to be reported that he was a gentleman who had just lost all he possessed by an earthquake and had found it difficult to escape with his life. His wife was with him. Your father gave credit to his story and pitied him. He gave him handsome apartments in his own house, and caused him and his wife to be treated like visitors of consequence, little imagining that the giant was undertaking a horrid return for all his favours.

"Things went on this way for some time, the giant becoming daily more impatient to put his plan in execution. At last a favourable opportunity presented itself. Your father's house was at some distance from the sea-shore, but with a glass the coast could be seen distinctly. The giant was one day using the telescope; the wind was very high, and he saw a fleet of ships in distress off the rocks. He hastened to your father, mentioned the circumstance, and eagerly requested he would send all the servants he could spare to relieve the sufferers.

"Every one was instantly despatched, except the porter and your nurse. The giant then joined your father in the study, and appeared to be delighted. He really was so. Your father recommended a favourite book, and was handing it down, when the giant, taking the opportunity, stabbed him, and he instantly fell down dead. The giant left the body, found the porter and nurse, and presently despatched them, being determined to have no living witnesses of his crimes.

"You were then only three months old. Your mother had you in her arms in a remote part of the house, and was ignorant of what was going on. She went into the study, but how was she shocked on discovering your father dead. She was stupefied with horror and grief, and was motionless. The giant, who was seeking her, found her in that state, and hastened to serve her and you as he had done your father, but she fell at his feet, and, in a pathetic manner, besought him to spare her life and yours.

"Remorse, for a moment, seemed to touch the barbarian's heart. He granted your lives, but first he made her take a most solemn oath never to inform you who your father was, or to answer any questions concerning him, assuring her that if she did he would certainly discover her and put both of you to death in the most cruel manner. Your mother took you in her arms and fled as quickly as possible. She was scarcely gone when the giant repented he had suffered her to escape. He would have pursued her instantly, but he had to provide for his own safety, as it was necessary he should be gone before the servants returned. Having gained your father's confidence he knew where to find all his treasure. He soon loaded himself and his wife, set the house on fire in several places, and, when the servants returned, the house was burnt quite down to the ground.

"Your poor mother, forlorn, abandoned, and forsaken, wandered with you a great many miles from this scene of desolation. Fear added to her haste. She settled in the cottage where you were brought up, and it was entirely owing to her fear of the giant that she never mentioned your father to you.

"I became your father's guardian at his birth, but fairies have laws to which they are subject as well as mortals. A short time before the giant went to your father's I transgressed. My punishment was a suspension of power for a limited time—an unfortunate circumstance—for it totally prevented my succouring your father.

"The day on which you met the butcher, as you went to sell your mother's cow, my power was restored. It was I who secretly prompted you to take the beans in exchange for the cow.

"By my power the beanstalk grew to so great a height and formed a ladder. I need not add I inspired you with a strong desire to ascend the ladder.

"The giant lives in this country, and you are the person appointed to punish him for all his wickedness. You will have dangers and difficulties to encounter, but you must persevere in avenging the death of your father, or you will not prosper in any of your undertakings, but be always miserable.

"As to the giant's possessions, you may seize on all you can, for everything he has is yours though now you are unjustly deprived of it. One thing I desire. Do not let your mother know you are acquainted with your father's history till you see me again.

"Go along the direct road, and you will soon see the house where your cruel enemy lives. While you do as I order you I will protect and guard you, but, remember, if you dare disobey my commands, a most dreadful punishment awaits you."

When the fairy had concluded, she disappeared leaving Jack to pursue his journey. He walked on till after sunset when, to his great joy, he espied a large mansion. This agreeable sight revived his drooping spirits, and he redoubled his speed, and soon reached the house. A plain-looking woman was at the door, and Jack accosted her, begging she would give him a morsel of bread and a night's lodging.

She expressed the greatest surprise at seeing him, and said it was quite uncommon to see a human being near their house, for it was well known her husband was a large and very powerful giant, and that he would never eat anything but human flesh, if he could possibly get it; that he did not think anything of walking fifty miles to procure it, usually being out the whole day for that purpose.

This account greatly terrified Jack, but still he

hoped to elude the giant, and therefore he again entreated the woman to take him in for one night only, and hide him where she thought proper. The good woman at last suffered herself to be persuaded, for she was of a compassionate and generous disposition, and took him into the house.

First they entered a fine large hall, magnificently furnished. They then passed through several spacious rooms, all in the same style of grandeur, but they appeared to be quite forsaken and desolate.

A long gallery was next. It was very dark, with just light enough to show that, instead of a wall, on one side there was a grating of iron which parted off a dismal dungeon, from whence issued the groans of those poor victims whom the cruel giant reserved in confinement for his own voracious appetite.

Poor Jack was half dead with fear, and would have given the world to have been with his mother again, for he now began to fear that he should never see her more, and gave himself up for lost. He even mistrusted the good woman, and thought she had let him into the house for no other purpose than to lock him up among the unfortunate people in the dungeon.

At the further end of the gallery there was a spacious kitchen, and a very excellent fire was burning in the grate. The good woman bade Jack sit down, and gave him plenty to eat and drink. Jack, not seeing anything here to make him uncomfortable, soon forgot his fear, and was just beginning to enjoy himself when he was aroused by a loud knocking at the street-door, which made the whole house shake. The giant's wife ran to secure Jack in the oven and then went to let her husband in.

Jack heard him accost her in a voice like thunder, saying—

"Wife, I smell fresh meat."

"Oh, my dear," replied she, "it is nothing but the people in the dungeon."

The giant appeared to believe her, and walked into the very kitchen where poor Jack was concealed, who shook, trembled, and was more terrified than he had yet been.

At last the monster seated himself quietly by the fireside, whilst his wife prepared supper. By degrees Jack recovered himself sufficiently to look at the giant through a small crevice. He was quite astonished to see what an amazing quantity he devoured, and thought he would never have done eating and drinking. When supper was ended the giant desired his wife to bring him his hen. A very beautiful hen was brought and placed on the table before him. Jack's curiosity was very great to see what would happen. He observed that every time the giant said "Lay," the hen laid an egg of solid gold.

The giant amused himself a long while with his

hen, and meanwhile his wife went to bed. At length the giant fell asleep by the fireside and snored like the roaring of a cannon. At daybreak Jack, finding the giant still asleep, and not likely to awaken soon, crept softly out of his hiding-place, seized the hen, and ran off with her.

He met with some difficulty in finding his way out of the house, but, at last, he reached the road in safety. He easily found his way to the beanstalk and descended it better and quicker than he had expected. His mother was overjoyed to see him. He found her crying bitterly, and lamenting his hard fate, for she concluded he had come to some shocking end through his rashness.

Jack was impatient to show his hen, and inform his mother how valuable it was.

"And now, mother," said Jack, "I have brought home that which will make us rich, and I hope to make some amends for the affliction I have caused you through my idleness, extravagance, and folly."

The hen produced as many golden eggs as they desired, which Jack and his mother sold, and so in a little time became possessed of as much riches as they wanted.

For some months Jack and his mother lived very happily together, but he, being very desirous of travelling, recollecting the fairy's commands, and fearing that if he delayed she would put her threats into execution, longed to climb the beanstalk and pay the giant another visit, in order to carry away some more of his treasure, for, during the time that Jack was in the giant's mansion, while he lay concealed in the oven, he learned, from the conversation that took place between the giant and his wife, that he possessed some wonderful curiosities. Jack thought of his journey again and again, but still he could not summon resolution enough to break it to his mother, being well assured she would endeavour to prevent his going. However, one day he told her boldly that he must take a journey up the beanstalk. His mother begged and prayed him not to think of it, and tried all in her power to dissuade him. She told him that the giant's wife would certainly know him again, and the giant would desire nothing better than to get him into his power, that he might put him to a cruel death in order to be revenged for the loss of his hen.

Jack, finding that all his arguments were useless, pretended to give up the point, though he was resolved to go at all events. He had a dress prepared which would disguise him, and something to colour his skin, and he thought it impossible for any one to recollect him in this dress.

In a few mornings after this, he rose very early, changed his complexion, and, unperceived by any one, climbed the beanstalk a second time. He was greatly fatigued when he reached the top, and very hungry.

Having rested some time on on of the stones, he pursued his journey to the giant's mansion. He reached it late in the evening, and found the woman at the door as before. Jack addressed her, at the same time telling her a pitiful tale, and requesting she would give him some victuals and drink, and also a night's lodging.

She told him (what he knew very well before) about her husband's being a powerful and cruel giant and also how she one night admitted a poor, hungry, friendless boy, who was half dead with travelling, and that the ungrateful fellow had stolen one of the giant's treasures, ever since which her husband had been worse than before, had used her very cruelly, and continually upbraided her with being the cause of his loss.

Jack was at no loss to discover that he was attending to the account of a story in which he was the principal actor. He did his best to persuade the old woman to admit him, but found it a very hard task.

At last she consented, and as she led the way Jack observed that everything was just as he had found it before. She took him into the kitchen, and after he had done eating and drinking, she hid him in an old lumber closet. The giant returned at the usual time, and walked in so heavily that the house was shaken to the foundation. He seated himself by the fire, and, soon after, exclaimed—

"Wife, I smell fresh meat."

The wife replied it was the crows, which had brought a piece of raw meat and left it on the top of the house.

Whilst supper was preparing, the giant was very ill-tempered and impatient, frequently lifting up his hand to strike his wife for not being quick enough, but she was always so fortunate as to elude the blow. The giant was also continually upbraiding her with the loss of his wonderful hen.

The giant's wife, having set supper on the table, went to another apartment and brought from it a huge pie which she also placed before him.

When he had ended his plentiful supper and eaten till he was quite satisfied, he said to his wife—

"I must have something to amuse me, either my bags of money or my harp."

After a good deal of ill-humour, and after having teased his wife for some time, he commanded her to bring down his bags of gold and silver. Jack, as before, peeped out of his hiding place, and presently the wife brought two bags into the room. They were of a very large size. One was filled with new guineas, and the other with new shillings. They were placed before the giant, who began reprimanding his poor wife most severely for staying so long. She replied, trembling with fear, that they were so heavy she could scarcely lift them, and concluded by saying she would never again bring them downstairs, adding that she had nearly fainted owing to their weight.

This so exasperated the giant that he raised his hand to strike her, but she escaped and went to bed, leaving him to count over his treasure by way of amusement.

The giant took his bags, and after turning them over and over to see they were in the same state he had left them, began to count their contents. First the bag which contained the silver was emptied, and the contents placed upon the table. Jack viewed the glittering heaps with delight, and most heartily wished them in his own possession. The giant (little thinking he was so narrowly watched) reckoned the silver over several times, and then, having satisfied himself that all was safe, put it into the bags again, which he made very secure.

The other bag was opened next, and the guineas placed upon the table. If Jack was pleased at the sight of the silver, how much more delighted must he have felt when he saw such a heap of glittering gold? He even had the boldness to think of gaining both bags, but, suddenly recollecting himself, he began to fear that the giant would sham sleep, the better to entrap any one who might be concealed.

When the giant had counted over the gold till he was tired, he put it up, if possible more secure than he had put up the silver before, and he then fell back on his chair by the fireside and fell asleep.

He snored so loud that Jack compared his noise to the roaring of the sea in a high wind, when the tide is coming in. At last Jack concluded him to be asleep and therefore secure. He stole out of his hiding-place and approached the giant, in order to carry off the two bags of money. Just as he laid his hand upon one of the bags a little dog, which he had not observed before, started from under the giant's chair and barked at Jack most furiously, who now gave himself up for lost. Fear rivetted him to the spot, and instead of endeavouring to escape he stood still, though expecting his enemy to awake every instant. Contrary, however, to his expectation the giant continued in a sound sleep, and the dog grew weary of barking. Jack now began to recollect himself, and, on looking around, saw a large piece of meat. This he threw to the dog, who instantly seized it, and took it into the lumber-closet which Jack had just left.

Finding himself delivered from a noisy and troublesome enemy, and seeing the giant did not awake, Jack boldly seized the bags, and, throwing them over his shoulders, ran out of the kitchen. He reached the street-door in safety, and found it quite daylight. On his way to the top of the beanstalk he found himself greatly incommoded with the weight of the money bags, and, really, they were so heavy he could scarcely carry them.

Jack was overjoyed when he found himself near

the beanstalk. He soon reached the bottom and ran to meet his mother. To his great surprise the cottage was deserted. He ran from one room to another without being able to find any one. He then hastened into the village, hoping to see some of his neighbours, who could inform him where he could find her.

An old woman at last directed him to a neighbouring house, where his mother was ill of a fever. He was greatly shocked on finding her apparently dying, and could scarcely bear his own reflections on knowing himself to be the cause of it.

On being informed of our hero's safe return, his mother, by degrees, revived, and gradually recovered. Jack presented her his two valuable bags, and they lived happy and comfortably. The cottage was rebuilt and well furnished.

For three years Jack heard no more of the beanstalk, but he could not forget it, though he feared making his mother unhappy. She would not mention the hated beanstalk, lest her doing so should remind him of taking another journey.

Notwithstanding the comforts Jack enjoyed at home, his mind continually dwelt upon the beanstalk, for the fairy's menaces in case of his disobedience were ever present to his mind and prevented him from being happy. He could think of nothing else. It was in vain he endeavoured to amuse himself. He became thoughtful, would arise at the first dawn of day, and would view the beanstalk for hours together.

His mother discovered that something preyed heavily upon his mind, and endeavoured to discover the cause, but Jack knew too well what the consequence would be should he discover the cause of his melancholy to her. He did his utmost, therefore, to conquer the great desire he had for another journey up the beanstalk. Finding, however, that his inclination grew too powerful for him, he began to make secret preparations for his journey, and, on the longest day, arose as soon as it was light, ascended the beanstalk, and reached the top with some little trouble. He found the road, journey, etc., much as it was on the two former times. He arrived at the giant's mansion in the evening, and found his wife standing, as usual, at the door. Jack had disguised himself so completely that she did not appear to have the least recollection of him. However, when he pleaded hunger and poverty in order to gain admittance, he found it very difficult, indeed, to persuade her. At last he prevailed, and was concealed in the copper.

When the giant returned, he said—

"I smell fresh meat," but Jack felt composed, for the giant had said so before, and had been soon satisfied; however, the giant started up suddenly and searched all round the room. Whilst this was going forward Jack was exceedingly terrified, and ready to die with fear, wishing himself at home a thousand times, but when the giant approached the copper, and put his hand upon the lid, Jack thought his death was certain. The giant ended his search there without moving the lid, and seated himself quietly by the fireside.

The giant at last ate a hearty supper, and when he had finished, he commanded his wife to fetch down his harp. Jack peeped under the copper lid and soon saw the most beautiful harp that could be imagined. It was placed by the giant on the table, who said—

"Play," and it instantly played of its own accord, without being touched. The music was uncommonly fine. Jack was delighted, and felt more anxious to get the harp into his possession than either of the former treasures.

The giant's soul was not attuned to harmony, and the music soon lulled him into a sound sleep. Now, therefore, was the time to carry off the harp. As the giant appeared to be in a more profound sleep than usual, Jack, soon determined, got out of the copper and seized the harp. The harp, however, was enchanted by a fairy, and it called out loudly—

"Master, master!"

The giant awoke, stood up, and tried to pursue Jack, but he had drunk so much that he could hardly stand. Poor Jack ran as fast as he could, and, in a little time, the giant recovered sufficiently to walk slowly, or rather, to reel after him. Had he been sober he must have overtaken Jack instantly, but as he then was, Jack contrived to be first at the top of the beanstalk. The giant called after him in a voice like thunder, and sometimes was very near him.

The moment Jack got down the beanstalk he called out for a hatchet, and one was brought him directly. Just at that instant the giant was beginning to descend, but Jack with his hatchet cut the beanstalk close off at the root, which made the giant fall headlong into the garden. The fall killed him, thereby releasing the world from a barbarous enemy.

Jack's mother was delighted when she saw the beanstalk destroyed. At this instant the fairy appeared. She first addressed Jack's mother, and explained every circumstance relating to the journeys up the beanstalk. The fairy then charged Jack to be dutiful to his mother, and to follow his father's good example, which was the only way to be happy. She then disappeared. Jack heartily begged his mother's pardon for all the sorrow and affliction he had caused her, promising most faithfully to be very dutiful and obedient to her for the future.

## JOHNNY REED'S CAT.

"YES, cats are queer folk, sure enough, and often know more than a simple beast ought to by knowledge that's rightly come by. There's that cat there, you've been looking at, will stand at a door on its hind legs with its front paws on the handle trying like a Christian to open the door, and mewling in a manner that's almost like talking. He's a London cat, he is, being brought me by a cousin who lives there, and is called Gilpin, after, I'm told, a mayor who was christened the same. He's a knowing cat, sure enough; but it's not the London cats that are cleverer than the country ones. Who knows, he may be a relative of Johnny Reed's own tom-cat himself."

"And who was Johnny Reed? and what was there remarkable about his cat?"

"Have you never heard tell of Johnny Reed's cat? It's an old tale they have in the north country, and it's true enough, though folk may not believe it in these days when the Bible's not gospel enough for some of them. I've heard my father often tell the story, and he came from Newcastle way, which is the very part where Johnny Reed used to live, being a parish sexton in a village not far away.

"Well, Johnny Reed was the sexton, as I've already said, and he and his wife kept a cat, a well enough behaved creature, sure enough, and a beast as he had no fault to set on, saving a few of the tricks which all cats play at times, and which seem born in the blood of the creatures. It was all black except one white paw, and seemed as honest and decent a beast as could be, and Tom would as soon have suspected it of being any more than it really seemed to be as he would one of his own children themselves, like many other folk, perhaps, who, may be, have cats of the same kind, little thinking it.

"Well, the cat had been with him some years when a strange thing occurred.

"One night Johnny was going home late from the churchyard, where he had been digging a grave for a person who had died on a sudden, throwing the grave on Johnny's hands unexpectedly, so that he had to stop working at it by the light of a lantern to have it ready for the next day's burying. Well, having finished his work, and having put his tools in the shed in a corner of the yard, and having locked them up safe, he began to walk home pretty brisk, thinking would his wife be up and have a bit of fire for him, for the night was cold, a keen wind blowing over the fields.

"He hadn't gone far before he comes to a gate at the roadside, and there seemed to be a strange shadow about it, in which Johnny saw, as it might be, a lot of little gleaming fires dancing about, while some stood steady, just like flashes of light from little windows in buildings all on fire inside. Says Johnny to himself, for he was not a man to be easily frightened, being accustomed by his calling to face things which might upset other folk—

"'Hullo! What's here? Here's a thing I never saw before,' and with that he walks straight up to the gate, while the shadow got deeper and the fires brighter the nearer he came to it.

"Well, when he came right up to the gate he finds that the shadow was just none at all, but nine black cats, some sitting and some dancing about, and the lights were the flashes from their eyes. When he came nearer he thought to scare them off, and he calls out—

"'Sh—sh—sh,' but never a cat stirs for all of it.

"'I'll soon scatter you, you ugly varmin,' says Johnny, looking about him for a stone, which was not to be found, the night being dark and preventing him seeing one. Just then he hears a voice calling—

"'Johnny Reed!'

"'Hullo!' says he, 'who's that wants me?'

"'Johnny Reed,' says the voice again.

"'Well,' says Johnny, 'I'm here,' and looking round and seeing no one, for no one was about 'tis true. 'Was it one of you,' says he, joking like, to the cats, 'as was calling me?'

"'Yes, of course,' answers one of them, as plain as ever Christian spoke. 'It's me as has called you these three times.'

"Well, with that, you may be sure, Johnny begins to feel curious, for 'twas the first time he had ever been spoken to by a cat, and he didn't know what it might lead to exactly. So he takes off his hat to the cat, thinking that it was, perhaps, best to show it respect, and, seeing that he was unable to guess with whom he was dealing, hoping to come off all the better for a little civility.

"'Well, sir,' says he, 'what can I do for you?'

"'It's not much as I want with you,' says the cat, 'but it's better it'll be with you if you do what I tell you. Tell Dan Ratcliffe that Peggy Poyson's dead.'

"'I will, sir,' says Johnny, wondering at the same time how he was to do it, for who Dan Ratcliffe was he knew no more than the dead. Well, with that all the cats vanished, and Johnny, running the rest of the way home, rushes into his house, smoking hot from the fright and the distance he had to go over.

"'Nan,' says he to his wife, the first words he spoke, 'who's Dan Ratcliffe?'

"'Dan Ratcliffe,' says she. 'I never heard of him,

and don't know there's any one such living about here.'

"'No more do I,' says he, 'but I must find him wherever he is.'

"Then he tells his wife all about how he had met the cats, and how they had stopped him and given him the message. Well, his cat sits there in front of the fire looking as snug and comfortable as a cat could be, and nearly half-asleep, but when Johnny comes to telling his wife the message the cats had given him, then it jumped up on its feet, and looks at Johnny, and says—

"'What! is Peggy Poyson dead? Then it's no time for me to be here;' and with that it springs through the door and vanishes, nor was ever seen again from that day to this."

"And did the sexton ever find Dan Ratcliffe," I asked.

"Never. He searched high and low for him about, but no one could tell him of such a person, though Johnny looked long enough, thinking it might be the worse for him if he didn't do his best to please the cats. At last, however, he gave the matter up."

"Then, what was the meaning of the cat's message?"

"It's hard to tell; but many folk thought, and I'm inclined to agree with them, that Dan Ratcliffe was Johnny's own cat, and no one else, looking at the way he acted, and no other of the name being known. Who Peggy Poyson was no one could tell, but likely enough it was some relative of the cat, or may be some one it was interested in, for it's little we know concerning the creatures and their ways, and with whom and what they're mixed up."

## LAME MOLLY.

Two Devonshire serving-maids declared, as an excuse perhaps for spending more money than they ought upon finery, that the pixies were very kind to them, and would often drop silver for their pleasure into a bucket of fair water, which they placed for the accommodation of those little beings every night in the chimney-corner before they went to bed. Once, however, it was forgotten; and the pixies, finding themselves disappointed by an empty bucket, whisked up-stairs to the maids' bedroom, popped through the keyhole, and began, in a very audible tone, to exclaim against the laziness and neglect of the damsels.

One of them, who lay awake and heard all this, jogged her fellow-servant, and proposed getting up immediately to repair the fault of omission; but the lazy girl, who liked not being disturbed out of a comfortable nap, pettishly declared "That, for her part, she would not stir out of bed to please all the pixies in Devonshire." The good-humoured damsel, however, got up, filled the bucket, and was rewarded by a handful of silver pennies found in it the next morning. But, ere that time had arrived, what was her alarm, as she crept towards the bed, to hear all the elves in high and stern debate consulting as to what punishment should be inflicted on the lazy lass who would not stir for their pleasure.

Some proposed "pinches, nips, and bobs," others to spoil her new cherry-coloured bonnet and ribands. One talked of sending her the toothache, another of giving her a red nose, but this last was voted too severe and vindictive a punishment for a pretty young woman. So, tempering mercy with justice, the pixies were kind enough to let her off with a lame leg, which was so to continue only for seven years, and was alone to be cured by a certain herb, growing on Dartmoor, whose long and learned and very difficult name the elfin judge pronounced in a high and audible voice. It was a name of seven syllables, seven being also the number of years decreed for the chastisement.

The good-natured maid, wishing to save her fellow-damsel so long a suffering, tried with might and main to bear in mind the name of this potent herb. She said it over and over again, tied a knot in her garter at every syllable, in order to assist her memory, and thought she had the word as sure as her own name, and very possibly felt much more anxious about retaining the one than the other. At length she dropped asleep, and did not wake till the morning. Now, whether her head might be like a sieve, that lets out as fast as it takes in, or whether the over-exertion to remember caused her to forget, cannot be determined, but certain it is when she opened her eyes, she knew nothing at all about the matter, excepting that Molly was to go lame on her right leg for seven long years, unless a herb with a strange name could be got to cure her. And lame she went for nearly the whole of that period.

At length (it was about the end of the time) a merry, squint-eyed, queer-looking boy started up one fine summer day, just as she went to pluck a mushroom, and came tumbling, head over heels, towards her. He insisted on striking her leg with a plant which he held in his hand. From that moment she got well, and lame Molly, as a reward for her patience in suffering, became the best dancer in the whole town at the celebrated festivities of May-day on the green.

# THE BROWN MAN OF THE MOORS.

In the year before the great rebellion two young men from Newcastle were sporting on the high moors above Elsdon, and, after pursuing their game several hours, sat down to dine in a green glen, near one of the mountain streams. After their repast, the younger lad ran to the brook for water, and, after stooping to drink, was surprised, on lifting his head again, by the appearance of a brown dwarf, who stood on a crag covered with brackens across the burn. This extraordinary personage did not appear to be above half the stature of a common man, but was uncommonly stout and broad-built, having the appearance of vast strength. His dress was entirely brown, the colour of the brackens, and his head covered with frizzled red hair. His countenance was expressive of the most savage ferocity, and his eyes glared like those of a bull.

It seems he addressed the young man, first threatening him with his vengeance for having trespassed on his demesnes, and asking him if he knew in whose presence he stood. The youth replied that he supposed him to be the lord of the moors; that he had offended through ignorance; and offered to bring him the game he had killed. The dwarf was a little mollified by this submission, but remarked that nothing could be more offensive to him than such an offer, as he considered the wild animals as his subjects, and never failed to avenge their destruction. He condescended further to inform the young man that he was, like himself, mortal, though of years far exceeding the lot of common humanity, and that he hoped for salvation. He never, he added, fed on anything that had life, but lived in the summer on whortle berries, and in winter on nuts and apples, of which he had great store in the woods. Finally, he invited his new acquaintance to accompany him home and partake his hospitality, an offer which the youth was on the point of accepting, and was just going to spring across the brook (which if he had done, the dwarf would certainly have torn him to pieces) when his foot was arrested by the voice of his companion, who thought he had tarried long. On his looking round again "the wee brown man was fled."

The story adds that the young man was imprudent enough to slight the admonition, and to sport over the moors on his way homewards, but soon after his return he fell into a lingering disorder, and died within a year.

# HOW THE COBBLER CHEATED THE DEVIL.

IT chanced that once upon a time long years ago, in the days when strange things used to happen in the world, and the devil himself used sometimes to walk about in it in a bare-faced fashion, to the distraction of all good and bad folk alike, he came to a very small town where he resolved to stay a while to play some of his tricks. How it was, whether the people were better or were worse than he expected to find them, whether they would not give way to him, or whether they went beyond him and outwitted him, I don't know, and so cannot say; but sure it is that in a short while he became terribly angry with the folk, and at length was so disgusted that he threatened he would make them repent their treatment of him, for he would punish them in a manner which should show them his power. With that he flew off in a fury, and the folk, knowing with whom they had to deal, were very sad thinking what terrible thing would overtake them, and at their wits' end to imagine how they might manage to escape the claws of the Evil One.

Accordingly it was decided to call a meeting of the townsfolk, to which all, old and young, should come to deliver their opinion as to the best course to be pursued, only those too old to walk, the sick, and the foolish, being not called to the council.

Very many different courses were proposed, and while these were being debated a man rushed into the hall where the council was held, and informed them that their enemy was coming, for he had himself seen him making his way to the town, bearing on his shoulder a stone almost big enough to bury the place under it. He reported that the devil was yet a long way off, for his load hampered him sadly and he could not travel fast.

What to do the councillors did not know, when suddenly there came amongst them a poor cobbler, whom they had forgot to call to the meeting, for he was, indeed, looked upon as only half-witted.

"I will go and meet him," said he, "and stop him coming here."

"You stop him!" cried they all; "it's mad you must be to think of it."

"I'll go all the same," said the cobbler, and without saying a word more he goes out and begins to make ready for his journey.

First of all he collected together as many old boots and shoes as he could find, and when he had got them all in a bundle, he finds out the man who had seen the devil coming on, and inquired of him the way he should go to meet him. The man told him the road, and the cobbler set out. He walked, and walked, and walked, till at last he came to the devil, who was sitting by the roadside resting himself and trying to get cool, for the day was warm, and he was nearly worn out with carrying the big rock which lay beside him.

"Do you know such-and-such a place?" asks he of the man, naming the town he would be at.

"I do, indeed," says the man, "for I ought to, seeing I have lived in its neighbourhood these many years, and have only left there to travel here."

"And how many days have you been getting here?" asked the devil anxiously, for he had hoped he was near the end of his journey.

"Oh, days and days," replies the man. "See here," and he opens his bundle of old boots that he had ready,—" see here," says he, "these are the boots I've worn out on the hard road in coming from the place here."

"Have you, indeed!" says the devil, looking at them amazed, little thinking that the man was lying as he showed him pair after pair, all in holes and shreds. "Well, indeed, it must be a long way off," and he looks around him, and then at the rock, and thinks what a terrible long way he has had to bring it, and begins to doubt whether, after all, since he's still got so far to go, it's worth all the trouble.

"If it had been near," says he, "it would have

been a different thing, and I would have shown them what it is to treat me as they did, but as it's so far off it's another matter, and I don't think it's worth the trouble."

So he just takes up the rock and flings it aside in a field, and goes off back again. So the cobbler came home, and told all the townsfolk what he had done, and how he had cheated the devil, and I can assure you that they all admired his cleverness, and the joke of tricking the devil as he had, nor did they allow him to lose in consequence of missing his day's work.

## THE TAVISTOCK WITCH.

An old witch in days of yore lived in the neighbourhood of Tavistock, and whenever she wanted money she would assume the shape of a hare, and would send out her grandson to tell a certain huntsman, who lived hard by, that he had seen a hare sitting at such a particular spot, for which he always received the reward of sixpence. After this deception had been practised many times, the dogs turned out' the hare pursued, often seen but never caught, a sportsman of the party began to suspect "that the devil was in the dance," and there would be no end to it. The matter was discussed, a justice consulted, and a clergyman to boot, and it was thought that however clever the devil might be, law and church combined would be more than a match for him. It was therefore agreed that, as the boy was singularly regular in the hour at which he came to announce the sight of the hare, all should be in readiness for a start the instant such information was given, and a neighbour of the witch, nothing friendly to her, promised to let the parties know directly that the old woman and her grandson left the cottage and went off together, the one to be hunted, and the other to set on the hunt.

The news came, the hounds were unkennelled, and huntsmen and sportsmen set off with surprising speed. The witch, now a hare, and her little colleague in iniquity, did not expect so very speedy a turn out, so that the game was pursued at a desperate rate, and the boy, forgetting himself in a moment of alarm, was heard to exclaim—

"Run, granny, run; run for your life!"

At last the pursuers lost the hare, and she once more got safe into the cottage by a little hole in the bottom of the door, but not large enough to admit a hound in chase. The huntsman and the squires, with their train, lent a hand to break open the door, but could not do it till the parson and the justice came up, but as law and church were certainly designed to break through iniquity, even so did they now succeed in bursting the magic bonds that opposed them. Up-stairs they all went. There they found the old hag, bleeding and covered with wounds, and still out of breath. She denied she was a hare, and railed at the whole party.

"Call up the hounds," said the huntsman, "and let us see what they take her to be. Maybe we may yet have another hunt."

On hearing this, the old woman cried quarter. The boy dropped on his knees and begged hard for mercy. Mercy was granted on condition of its being received with a good whipping, and the huntsman, having long practised amongst the hounds, now tried his hand on their game. Thus the old woman escaped a worse fate for the time being, but on being afterwards put on trial for bewitching a young woman, and making her spit pins, the above was given as evidence against her, and the old woman finished her days, like a martyr, at the stake.

# THE WORM OF LAMBTON.

THE young heir of Lambton led a dissolute and evil course of life, equally regardless of the obligations of his high estate, and the sacred duties of religion. According to his profane custom, he was fishing on a Sunday, and threw his line into the river to catch fish, at a time when all good men should have been engaged in the solemn observance of the day. After having toiled in vain for some time, he vented his disappointment at his ill success, in curses loud and deep, to the great scandal of all who heard him, on their way to Holy Mass, and to the manifest peril of his own soul.

At length he felt something extraordinary tugging at his line, and, in the hope of catching a large fish, he drew it up with the utmost skill and care, yet it required all his strength to bring the expected fish to land.

What was his surprise and mortification, when, instead of a fish, he found that he had only caught a worm of most unseemly and disgusting appearance. He hastily tore it from his hook and threw it into a well hard by.

He again threw in his line, and continued to fish, when a stranger of venerable appearance, passing by, asked him—

"What sport?"

To which he replied—

"I think I've caught the devil;" and directed the inquirer to look into the well.

The stranger saw the worm, and remarked that he had never seen the like of it before—that it was like an eft, but that it had nine holes on each side of its mouth, and tokened no good.

The worm remained neglected in the well, but soon grew so large that it became necessary to seek another abode. It usually lay in the day-time coiled round a rock in the middle of the river, and at night frequented a neighbouring hill, twining itself around the base; and it continued to increase in length until it could lap itself three times around the hill.

It now became the terror of the neighbourhood, devouring lambs, sucking the cow's milk, and committing every species of injury on the cattle of the affrighted peasantry.

The immediate neighbourhood was soon laid waste, and the worm, finding no further support on the north side of the river, crossed the stream towards Lambton Hall, where the old lord was then living in grief and sorrow, the young heir of Lambton having repented him of his former sins, and gone to the wars in a far distant land.

The terrified household assembled in council, and it was proposed by the stewart, a man far advanced in years and of great experience, that the large trough which stood in the courtyard should be filled with milk. The monster approached and, eagerly drinking the milk, returned without inflicting further injury, to repose around its favourite hill.

The worm returned the next morning, crossing the stream at the same hour, and directing its way to the hall. The quantity of milk to be provided was soon found to be the product of nine cows, and if any portion short of this quantity was neglected or forgotten the worm showed the most violent signs of rage, by lashing its tail around the trees in the park, and tearing them up by the roots.

Many a gallant knight of undoubted fame and prowess sought to slay this monster which was the terror of the whole country side, and it is related that in these mortal combats, although the worm had been frequently cut asunder, yet the several parts had immediately reunited, and the valiant assailant never escaped without the loss of life or limb, so that, after many fruitless and fatal attempts to destroy the worm, it remained, at length, in tranquil possession of its favourite hill—all men fearing to encounter so deadly an enemy.

At length, after seven long years, the gallant heir of Lambton returned from the wars of Christendom, and found the broad lands of his ancestors laid waste and desolate. He heard the wailings of the people, for their hearts were filled with terror and alarm. He hastened to the hall of his ancestors, and received the embraces of his aged father, worn out with sorrow and grief, both for the absence of his son, whom he had considered dead, and for the dreadful waste inflicted on his fair domain by the devastations of the worm.

He took no rest until he crossed the river to examine the worm, as it lay coiled around the base of the hill, and being a knight of tried valour and sound discretion, and hearing the fate of all those who had fallen in the strife, he consulted a Sibyl on the best means to be pursued to slay the monster.

He was told that he himself had been the cause of all the misery which had been brought upon the country, which inceased his grief and strengthened his resolution. He was also told that he must have his best suit of mail studded with spear-blades, and, taking his stand on the rock in the middle of the river, commend himself to Providence and the might of his sword, first making a solemn vow, if successful, to slay the first living thing he met, or, if he failed to do so, the Lords of Lambton for nine generations would never die in their beds.

He made the solemn vow in the chapel of his forefathers, and had his coat studded with the blades of the sharpest spears. He took his stand on the rock in the middle of the river, and unsheathing his trusty sword, which had never failed him in time of need, he commended himself to the will of Providence.

At the accustomed hour the worm uncoiled its lengthened folds, and, leaving the hill, took its usual course towards Lambton Hall, and approached the rock where it sometimes reposed. The knight, nothing dismayed, struck the monster on the head with all his might and main, but without producing any other visible effect than irritating and vexing the worm, which, closing on the knight, clasped its frightful coils around him, and endeavoured to strangle him in its poisonous embrace.

The knight was, however, provided against this dangerous extremity, for, the more closely he was pressed by the worm, the more deadly were the wounds inflicted by his coat of spear-blades, until the river ran with gore.

The strength of the worm diminished as its efforts increased to destroy the knight, who, seizing a favourable opportunity, made such a good use of his sword that he cut the monster in two. The severed part was immediately carried away by the current, and the worm, being thus unable to reunite itself, was, after a long and desperate conflict, destroyed by the gallantry and courage of the knight of Lambton.

The afflicted household were devoutly engaged in prayer during the combat, but on the fortunate issue, the knight, according to promise, blew a blast on his bugle to assure his father of his safety, and that he might let loose his favourite hound which was destined to be the sacrifice. The aged father, forgetting everything but his parental feelings, rushed forward to embrace his son.

When the knight beheld his father he was overwhelmed with grief. He could not raise his arm against his parent, but, hoping that his vow might be accomplished, and the curse averted by destroying the next living thing he met, he blew another blast on his bugle.

His favourite hound broke loose and bounded to receive his caresses, when the gallant knight, with grief and reluctance, once more drew his sword, still reeking with the gore of the monster, and plunged it into the heart of his faithful companion. But in vain—the prediction was fulfilled, and the Sibyl's curse pressed heavily on the house of Lambton for nine generations.

# THE OLD WOMAN AND THE CROOKED SIXPENCE.

An old woman was sweeping her house, and she found a crooked sixpence.

"What," says she, "shall I do with this sixpence? I will go to the market and buy a pig with it."

She went; and as she was coming home she came to a stile. Now the pig would not go over the stile. The woman went on a little further and met a dog—

"Dog," said she, "bite pig. Piggy won't go over the stile, and I shan't get home to-night."

But the dog would not bite the pig. The woman went on a little further, and she met a stick.

"Stick," said she, "beat dog. Dog won't bite pig, piggy won't go over stile, and I shan't get home to-night."

But the stick would not. The woman went on a little further, and she met a fire.

"Fire," said she, "burn stick. Stick won't beat dog, dog won't bite pig, piggy won't go over the stile, and I shan't get home to-night."

## THE OLD WOMAN AND THE CROOKED SIXPENCE.

But the fire would not. The woman went on a little further and she met some water.

"Water," said she, "quench fire. Fire won't burn stick, stick won't beat dog," etc.

But the water would not. The woman went on a little further, and she met an ox.

"Ox," said she, "drink water. Water won't quench fire," etc.

But the ox would not. The woman went on again, and she met a butcher.

"Butcher," said she, "kill ox. Ox won't drink water," etc.

But the butcher would not. The woman went on a little further, and met a rope.

"Rope," said she, "hang butcher. Butcher won't kill ox," etc.

But the rope would not. Again the woman went on, and she met a rat.

"Rat," said she, "gnaw rope. Rope won't hang butcher," etc.

But the rat would not. The woman went on a little further, and met a cat.

"Cat," said she, "kill rat. Rat won't gnaw rope," etc.

"Oh," said the cat, "I will kill the rat if you will fetch me a basin of milk from the cow over there."

The old woman went to the cow and asked her to let her have some milk for the cat.

"No," said the cow; "I will let you have no milk unless you bring me a mouthful of hay from yonder stack."

Away went the old woman to the stack and fetched the hay and gave it to the cow. Then the cow gave her some milk, and the old woman took it to the cat.

When the cat had lapped the milk, the cat began to kill the rat, the rat began to gnaw the rope, the rope began to hang the butcher, the butcher began to kill the ox, the ox began to drink the water, the water began to quench the fire, the fire began to burn the stick, the stick began to beat the dog, the dog began to bite the pig, and piggy, in a fright, jumped over the stile, and so, after all, the old woman got safe home that night.

## THE YORKSHIRE BOGGART.

A BOGGART intruded himself, upon what pretext or by what authority is unknown, into the house of a quiet, inoffensive, and laborious farmer; and, when once it had taken possession, it disputed the right of domicile with the legal mortal tenant, in a very unneighbourly and arbitrary manner. In particular, it seemed to have a great aversion to children. As there is no point on which a parent feels more acutely than that of the maltreatment of his off-spring, the feelings of the father, and more particularly of his good dame, were daily, ay, and nightly, harrowed up by the malice of this malignant and invisible boggart (a boggart is seldom visible to the human eye, though it is frequently seen by cattle, particularly by horses, and then they are said to "take the *boggle*," a Yorkshireism for a shying horse). The children's bread and butter would be snatched away, or their porringers of bread and milk would be dashed down by an invisible hand; or if they were left alone for a few minutes, they were sure to be found screaming with terror on the return of the parents, like the farmer's children in the tale of the *Field of Terror*, whom the "drudging goblin" used to torment and frighten when he was left alone with them.

The stairs led up from the kitchen; a partition of boards covered the ends of the steps, and formed a closet beneath the staircase; a large round knot was accidentally displaced from one of the boards of this partition. One day the farmer's youngest boy was playing with the shoe-horn, and, as children will do, he stuck the horn into this knot-hole. Whether the aperture had been found by the boggart as a peep-hole to watch the motions of the family, or whether he wished to amuse himself, is uncertain, but sure it is the horn was thrown back with surprising precision at the head of the child. It was found that as often as the horn was replaced in the hole, so surely it was ejected with a straight aim at the offender's head. Time at length made familiar this wonderful occurrence, and that which at the first was regarded with terror, became at length a kind of amusement with the more thoughtless and daring of the family. Often was the horn slipped slyly into the hole, and the boggart never failed to dart it out at the head of one or the other, but most commonly he or she who placed it there was the mark at which the invisible foe launched the offending horn. They used to call this, in their provincial dialect, "laking wit boggart," *i.e.*, playing with the boggart. As if enraged at these liberties taken with his boggartship, the goblin commenced a series of night disturbances. Heavy steps, as of a person in wooden clogs, were often heard clattering down the stairs in the dead hour of darkness, and the pewter and earthen dishes appeared to be dashed on the kitchen floor, though, in the morning, all were found uninjured on their respective shelves.

The children were chiefly marked out as objects of dislike by their unearthly tormenter. The curtains of their beds would be violently pulled backward and forward. Anon, a heavy weight, as of a human being, would press them nearly to suffocation. They would then scream out for their "daddy" and "mammy," who occupied the adjoining room, and thus the whole family was disturbed night after night. Things could not long go on after this fashion. The farmer and his good dame resolved to leave a place where they had not the least shadow of rest or comfort.

The farmer, whose name was George Gilbertson, was following, with his wife and family, the last load of furniture, when they met a neighbouring farmer, whose name was John Marshall, between whom and the unhappy tenant the following colloquy took place—

"Well, George, and soa you're leaving t' ould hoose at last?"

"Heigh, Johnny, ma lad, I'm forc'd till it, for that boggart torments us soa we can neither rest neet nor day for 't. It seems loike to have such a malice again't poor bairns. It ommost kills my poor dame here at thoughts on 't, and soa, ye see, we 're forc'd to flitt like."

He had got thus far in his complaint when, behold! a shrill voice, from a deep upright churn, called out—

"Ay, ay, George, we 're flitting, you see."

"Confound thee," says the poor farmer, "if I 'd known thou 'd been there I wadn't ha stirrid a peg. Nay, nay, it 's to na use, Mally," turning to his wife, "we may as weel turn back again to t' ould hoose, as be tormented in another that 's not sa convenient."

They are said to have turned back, but the boggart and they afterwards came to a better understanding, though it long continued its trick of shooting the horn from the knot-hole.

# THE DUERGAR.

THE following encounters with the *duergar*, a species of mischievous elves, are said to have taken place on Simonside Hills, a mountainous district between Rothbury and Elsdon in Northumberland.

A person well acquainted with the locality went out one night to amuse himself with the pranks of these mysterious beings. When he had wandered a considerable time, he shouted loudly—

"Tint! tint!" and a light appeared before him, like a burning candle in the window of a shepherd's cottage. Thither, with great caution, he bent his steps, and speedily approached a deep slough, from whence a quantity of moss or peat had been excavated, and which was now filled with mud and water. Into this he threw a piece of turf which he raised at his feet, and when the sound of the splash echoed throughout the surrounding stillness, the decoying light was extinguished. The adventurer retraced his steps, overjoyed at his dexterity in outwitting the fiendish imps, and in a moment of exultation, as if he held all the powers of darkness in defiance, he again cried to the full extent of his voice—

"Tint! tint!"

His egotism subsided, however, more quickly than it arose, when he observed three of the little demons, with hideous visages, approach him, carrying torches in their diminutive hands, as if they wished to inspect the figure of their enemy. He now betook himself to the speed of his heels for safety, but found that an innumerable multitude of the same species were gathering round him, each with a torch in one hand and a short club in the other, which they brandished with such gestures, as if they were resolved to oppose his flight, and drive him back into the morass. Like a knight of romance he charged with his oaken staff the foremost of his foes, striking them, as it seemed, to the earth, for they disappeared, but his offensive weapon encountered in its descent no substance of flesh or bone, and beyond its sweep the demons appeared to augment both in size and number. On witnessing so much of the unearthly, his heart failed him. He sank down in a state of stupor, nor was he himself again till the gray light of the morning dispersed his unhallowed opponents, and revealed before him the direct way to his own dwelling.

Another time, a traveller, wandering over these mountain solitudes, had the misfortune to be benighted, and, perceiving near him a glimmering light, he hastened thither and found what appeared to be a hut, on the floor of which, between two rough, gray stones, the embers of a fire, which had been supplied with wood, were still glowing and unconsumed. He entered, and the impression on his mind was that the place had been deserted an hour or two previously by gipsies, for on one side lay a couple of old gate-posts ready to be split up for fuel, and a quantity of refuse brush-wood, such as is left from besom making, was strewn upon the floor. With this material he trimmed the fire, and had just seated himself on one of the stones, when a diminutive figure in human shape, not higher than his knee, came waddling in at the door, and took possession of the other. The traveller, being acquainted with the manner in which things of this description ought to be regarded, retained his self-possession, kept his seat, and remained silent, knowing that if he rose up or spoke, his danger would be redoubled, and as the flame blazed up he examined minutely the hollow eyes, the stern vindictive features, and the short, strong limbs, of the visitor before him. By degrees he perceived that the hut afforded little or no shelter from the cold night air, and as the energy of the fire subsided he lifted from the floor a piece of wood, broke it over his knee, and laid the fragments upon the red-hot embers. Whether this operation was regarded by his strange neighbour as a species of insult we cannot say, but the demon seized, as if in bitter mockery, one of the gate-posts, broke it likewise over its knee, and laid the pieces on the embers in the same manner. The other having no wish to witness a further display of such marvellous agency, thenceforth permitted the fire to die away, and kept his position in darkness and silence, till the fair dawn of returning day made him aware of the extreme danger to which he was exposed. He saw a quantity of white ashes before him, but the grim dwarfish intruder, with the roof and walls of the hut, were gone, and he himself, sat upon a stone, sure enough, but it formed one of the points of a deep, rugged precipice, over which the slightest inadvertent movement had been the means of dashing him to pieces.

# THE BARN ELVES.

An honest Hampshire farmer was sore distressed by the nightly unsettling of his barn. However straightly, over night, he laid his sheaves on the threshing floor, for the application of the morning's flail, when morning came all was topsy-turvy, higgledy-piggledy, though the door remained locked, and there was no sign whatever of irregular entry.

Resolved to find out who played him these mischievous pranks, Hodge couched himself one night deeply among the sheaves, and watched for the enemy. At length midnight arrived. The barn was illuminated as if by moonbeams of wonderful brightness, and through the keyhole came thousands of elves, the most diminutive that could be imagined. They immediately began their gambols among the straw, which was soon in the most admired disorder. Hodge wondered, but interfered not, but at last the supernatural thieves began to busy themselves in a way still less to his taste, for each elf set about conveying the crop away, a straw at a time, with astonishing activity and perseverance. The keyhole was still their port of egress and regress, and it resembled the aperture of a beehive, on a sunny day in June. The farmer was rather annoyed at seeing his grain vanish in this fashion, when one of the fairies, while hard at work, said to another, in the tiniest voice that ever was heard—

"I weat; you weat?" (I sweat; do you sweat?)

Hodge could contain himself no longer. He leapt out, crying—

"The deuce sweat ye! Let me get among ye."

The fairies all flew away so frightened that they never disturbed the barn any more.

# LEGENDS OF KING ARTHUR.

IMMEMORIAL tradition has asserted that King Arthur, his queen Guinevere, court of lords and ladies, and his hounds, were enchanted in some cave of the crags, or in a hall below the castle of Sewingshields, and would continue entranced there till some one should first blow a bugle-horn that lay on a table near the entrance into the hall, and then " with the sword of stone" cut a garter, also placed there beside it. But none had ever heard where the entrance to this enchanted hall was, till a farmer at Sewingshields, about fifty years since, was sitting knitting on the ruins of the castle, and his clew fell and ran downwards through a bush of briars and nettles, as he supposed, into a deep subterranean passage. Full in the faith that the entrance into King Arthur's hall was now discovered, he cleared the briary portal of its weeds and rubbish, and entering a vaulted passage, followed, in his darkling way, the web of his clew. The floor was infested with toads and lizards, and the dark wings of bats, disturbed by his unhallowed intrusion, flitted fearfully around him. At length his sinking faith was strengthened by a dim, distant light, which, as he advanced, grew gradually lighter, till, all at once, he entered a vast and vaulted hall, in the centre of which a fire without fuel, from a broad crevice in the floor, blazed with a high and lambent flame, that showed all the carved walls and fretted roof, and the monarch and his queen and court reposing around in a theatre of thrones and costly couches. On the floor, beyond the fire, lay the faithful and deep-toned pack of thirty couple of hounds, and on the table, before it, the spell-dissolving horn, sword, and garter. The farmer reverently but firmly grasped the sword, and as he drew it leisurely from its rusty scabbard, the eyes of the monarch and his courtiers began to open, and they rose till they sat upright. He cut the garter, and, as the sword was being slowly sheathed, the spell assumed its ancient power, and they all gradually sank to rest, but not before the monarch lifted up his eyes and hands, and exclaimed—

"O woe betide that evil day
On which this witless wight was born
Who drew the sword—the garter cut,
But never blew the bugle-horn."

Of this favourite tradition, the most remarkable variation is respecting the place where the farmer descended. Some say that after the king's denunciation, terror brought on loss of memory, and the farmer was unable to give any correct account of his adventure, or the place where it occurred. All agree that Mrs. Spearman, the wife of another and more recent occupier of the estate, had a dream in which she saw a rich hoard of treasure among the ruins of the castle, and that for many days together she stood over workmen employed in searching for it, but without success.

Another version of the story has less of "the pomp of sceptred state" than the preceding, and has evidently sprung from a baser original, but its verity is not the less to be depended upon.

A shepherd one day, in quest of a strayed sheep on the crags, had his attention aroused by the scene around him assuming an appearance he had never before witnessed. There seemed to be about it a more than wonted vividness, and such a deep solemnity hung over its aspect, that its features became, as it were, palpably impressed upon his mind. While he was musing upon this unexpected occurrence, his steps were arrested by a ball of thread. This he laid hold of, and, pursuing the path it pointed out, found it led into a cavern, in the recesses of which, as the guiding line used by miners in their explorations of devious passages, it appeared to lose itself. As he approached, he felt perforce constrained to follow the strange conductor, that had so marvellously come into his hands. After passing through a long and dreary vestibule, he entered into an apartment in the interior. An immense fire blazed on the hearth, and cast its broad flashes with a wild, unearthly glare, to the remotest corner of the chamber. Over it was placed a huge caldron, as if preparations were being made for a feast on an extensive scale. Two hounds lay couchant on either side of the fire-place, in the stillness of unbroken slumber. The only remarkable piece of furniture in the apartment was a table covered with green cloth. At the head of the table, a being, considerably advanced in years, of a dignified mien, and clad in the habiliments of war, sat, as it were, fast asleep, in an arm-chair. At the other end of the table lay a horn and a sword. Notwithstanding these signs of life, there prevailed a dead silence throughout the chamber, the very feeling of which made the shepherd reflect that he had advanced far beyond the limits of human experience, and that he was now in the presence of objects that belonged more to death than to life. The very idea made his flesh creep. He, however, had sufficient fortitude to advance to the table and lift the horn. The hounds pricked up their ears most fearfully, and the grisly veteran started up on his elbow, and raising his half-unwilling eyes, told the staggered hind that if he would blow the horn and draw the sword, he would confer upon him the honours of knighthood to last through time. Such unheard-of dignities, from a source so ghastly, either met with no appreciation from the awe-stricken swain, or the terror of finding himself alone in the company, it might be of malignant phantoms, who were only tempting him to his ruin, became too urgent to be resisted, and, therefore, proposing to divide the peril with a comrade, he groped his darkling way, as best his quaking limbs could support him, back to the blessed daylight. On his return, with a reinforcement of strength and courage, all traces of the former scene had disappeared. The crags presented their usual cheerful and quiet aspect, and every vestige of the opening of a cavern was obliterated. Thus failed another of the repeated opportunities for releasing the spellbound king of Britain from the " charmed sleep of ages." Within his rocky chamber he still sleeps on, as tradition tells, till the appointed hour; or if invited by his enchantress to participate in the illusions of the fairy festival, it has charms for him no longer. " Wasted with care," he sits beside her —the banquet untasted—the pageantry unmasked—

> ". . . By constraint
> Her guest, and from his native land withheld
> By sad necessity."

## SILKY.

ABOUT the commencement of the present century the inhabitants of the quiet village of Black Heddon, near Stamfordham, and of its vicinity, who lived, as most other villagers do, with all possible harmony amongst themselves, and relishing no more external disturbance than was consistent with their gentle and sequestered mode of existence, were dreadfully annoyed by the pranks of a preternatural being called Silky. This name it had obtained from its manifesting a marked predilection to make itself visible in the semblance of a female dressed in silk. Many a time, when one of the more timorous of the community had a night journey to perform, have they unawares and invisibly been dogged and watched by this spectral tormentor, who, at the dreariest part of the road—the most suitable for thrilling surprises—would suddenly break forth in dazzling splendour. If the person happened to be on horseback, a sort of exercise for which she evinced a strong partiality, she would unexpectedly seat herself behind, "rattling in her silks." There, after enjoying a comfortable ride, with instantaneous abruptness she would, like a thing destitute of continuity, dissolve away and become incorporate with the nocturnal shades, leaving the bewildered horseman in blank amazement.

At Belsay, some two or three miles from Black Heddon, she had a favourite resort. This was a romantic crag finely studded with trees, under the gloomy umbrage of which, "like one forlorn," she loved to wander all the live-long night. Here often has the belated peasant, with awe-stricken vision, beheld her dimly through the sombre twilight as if engaged in splitting great stones, or hewing with many a repeated stroke some stately "monarch of the grove." While he thus stood and gazed, and listened to intimations, impossible to be misapprehended, of the dread reality of that mysterious being, concerning whom so various conjectures were awake, all at once, excited by that wondrous agency, he would hear the howling of a resistless tempest rushing through the woodland—the branches creaking in violent concussion, or rent into pieces by the impetuous fury of the blast—while, to the eye, not a leaf was seen to quiver, or a pensile spray to bend. The bottom of this crag is washed by a picturesque lake or fish-pond, at whose outlet is a waterfall, over which a venerable tree, sweeping its leafy arms, adds impressiveness to the scene. Amid the complicated and contorted limbs of this tree, Silky possessed a rude chair, where she was wont, in her moody moments, to sit—wind-rocked—enjoying the rustling of the storm in the dark woods, or the gush of the cascade. The tree, so consecrated in the sympathies and terrors of the people of the vicinity, has been preserved. Though now (1842) no longer tenanted by its aerial visitant, it yet spreads majestically its time-hallowed canopy over the spot, awakening in the love-versed rustic, when the winter's wind waves gusty and sonorous through its leafless boughs, the soul-harrowing recollection of the exploits of the ancient fay,—but in the spring-time, beautiful with the full-flushed verdure of that exuberant season, recipient of the kindling emotions of reverence and affection. It still bears the name of "Silky's seat," in memory of its once wonderful occupant.

Silky exercised a marvellous influence over the brute creation. Horses, which indisputably possess a discernment of spirits superior to that of man, and are more sharp-sighted in the dark, were in an extraordinary degree sensitive of her presence and control. Having once perceived the effects of her power she seems to have had a perverse pleasure in meddling with and arresting those poor defenceless animals, while engaged in the most exemplary performance of their labours. When this misfortune occurred there was no remedy that brute-force could devise. Expostulation, soothing, whipping, and kicking, were all exerted in vain to make the restive beast resume the proper and intended direction. The ultimate resource, unless it might be the whim of Silky to revoke the spell, was the magic dispelling witchwood, which, it is satisfactory to learn, was of unfailing efficacy. One poor wight, a farm-servant, was once the selected victim of her mischievous frolics. He had to go to a colliery at some distance for coals, and it was late in the evening before he could return. Silky, with spirit-like prescience, having intimation of the circumstance, waylaid him at a bridge—a "ghastly, ghost-alluring edifice," since called "Silky's Brig," lying a little to the south of Black Heddon, on the road between that place and Stamfordham. Just as he had arrived at "the height of that bad eminence," the keystone, horses and cart became fixed and immovable as fate. In that melancholy plight might both man and horses have continued—quaking, and sweating, and paralysed—till the morning light had thrown around them its mantle of protection—had not a neighbour's servant come to the rescue, who opportunely carried some of the potent witchwood (mountain-ash) about his person. On the arrival of this seasonable aid, the perplexed driver rallied his scattered senses, and the helpless animals, being duly seasoned after the fashion prescribed on such occasions, he had the heart-felt satisfaction of seeing them apply themselves, with the customary alacrity, to the draught. The charm was effectually overcome, and in a short time both the man and the coals reached home in safety. Ever afterwards, however, as long as he lived, he took the precaution of rendering himself spell-proof, by being furnished with a sufficient quantity of witchwood, being by no means disposed that Silky should a second time amuse herself at his expense and that of his team.

She was wayward and capricious. Sometimes she installed herself in the office of that old familiar Lar—Brownie, but, with characteristic misdirection, in a manner exactly the reverse of that useful species of hobgoblin. Here it may be remarked that, throughout her disembodied career, she can scarcely be said to have performed one benevolent action for the sake of its moral qualities. She had, from first to last, a perpetual latent hankering for mischief, and gloried in withering surprises and unforeseen movements. As is customary with that "sturdy fairy," as she is designated by the great English Lexicographer, her works were performed at night, or between the hours of sunset and day-dawn. If the good old dames had thoroughly cleaned their houses, which country people make a practice of doing, especially on Saturdays, so that they may have a comfortable and decent appearance on the Sabbath-day, after they had retired to rest, Silky would silently turn everything topsy-turvy, and the morning presented a scene of indescribable confusion.

On the contrary, if the house had been left in a disorderly state, a plan which the folk generally found it best to adopt, everything would have been arranged with the greatest nicety.

At length a term had arrived to her erratic course, and both she and the peaceably disposed inhabitants whom she disquieted obtained the repose so long mutually desired. She abruptly disappeared. It had long been surmised, by those who paid attention to those dark matters, that she was the troubled phantom of some person, who had died very miserable, in consequence of having great treasure, which, before being taken by her mortal agony, had not been disclosed, and on that account Silky could not rest in her grave. About the period referred to a domestic female servant being alone in one of the rooms of a house in Black Heddon, was frightfully alarmed by the ceiling above suddenly giving way, and from it there dropped, with a prodigious clash, something quite black, shapeless, and uncouth. The servant did not stop to scrutinise an object so hideous and startling, but fled to her mistress, screaming at the pitch of her voice—

"The deevil's in the house! The deevil's in the house! He's come through the ceiling!"

With this terrible announcement the whole family were speedily convoked, and great was the consternation at the idea of the foe of mankind being amongst them in visible form. In this appalling extremity, a considerable time elapsed before any one could brace up courage to face the enemy, or be prevailed on to go and inspect the cause of their alarm. At last the mistress, who chanced to be the most stout-hearted, ventured into the room when, instead of the personage, on account of whom such awful apprehensions were entertained, a great dog or calf-skin lay on the floor, sufficiently black and uncomely, but filled with gold.

After this Silky was never more heard or seen. Her destiny was accomplished, her spirit laid, and she now sleeps with her ancestors.

# CONTENTS

|  | PAGE |
|---|---|
| Canobie Dick and Thomas of Ercildoun, | 1 |
| Coinnach Oer, | 5 |
| Elphin Irving, | 9 |
| The Ghosts of Craig-Aulnaic, | 32 |
| The Doomed Rider, | 39 |
| Whippety Stourie, | 43 |
| The Weird of the Three Arrows, | 46 |
| The Laird of Balmachie's Wife, | 52 |
| Michael Scott, | 55 |
| The Minister and the Fairy, | 63 |
| The Fisherman and the Merman, | 66 |
| The Laird o' Co', | 70 |
| Ewen of the Little Head, | 72 |
| Jock and his Mother, | 76 |
| Saint Columba, | 80 |
| The Mermaid Wife, | 86 |
| The Fiddler and the Bogle of Bogandoran, | 89 |
| Thomas the Rhymer, | 93 |

## CONTENTS.

| | PAGE |
|---|---|
| Fairy Friends, | 98 |
| The Seal-catcher's Adventure, | 101 |
| The Fairies of Merlin's Craig, | 106 |
| Rory Macgillivray, | 109 |
| The Haunted Ships, | 114 |
| The Brownie, | 140 |
| Mauns' Stane, | 143 |
| "Horse and Hattock," | 151 |
| Secret Commonwealth, | 154 |
| The Fairy Boy of Leith, | 170 |
| The Dracæ, | 173 |
| Lord Tarbat's Relations, | 175 |
| The Bogle, | 184 |
| Daoine Shie, or the Men of Peace, | 185 |
| The Death "Bree," | 189 |

# CANOBIE DICK AND THOMAS OF ERCILDOUN.

Now it chanced many years since that there lived on the Borders a jolly rattling horse-cowper, who was remarkable for a reckless and fearless temper, which made him much admired and a little dreaded amongst his neighbours. One moonlight night, as he rode over Bowden Moor, on the west side of the Eildon Hills, the scene of Thomas the Rhymer's prophecies, and often mentioned in his history, having a brace of horses along with him, which he had not been able to dispose of, he met a man of venerable appearance and singularly antique dress, who, to his great surprise, asked the price of his horses, and began to chaffer with him on the subject. To Canobie Dick, for so shall we call our Border dealer, a chap was a chap, and he would have sold a horse to the devil himself, without minding his cloven hoof, and would have probably cheated Old Nick into the bargain. The stranger paid the price they agreed on, and all that puzzled Dick in the transaction was, that the gold which he received was

*Scotch.*

in unicorns, bonnet-pieces, and other ancient coins, which would have been invaluable to collectors, but were rather troublesome in modern currency. It was gold, however, and therefore Dick contrived to get better value for the coin than he perhaps gave to his customer. By the command of so good a merchant, he brought horses to the same spot more than once; the purchaser only stipulating that he should always come by night and alone. I do not know whether it was from mere curiosity, or whether some hope of gain mixed with it, but after Dick had sold several horses in this way, he began to complain that dry bargains were unlucky, and to hint, that since his chap must live in the neighbourhood, he ought, in the courtesy of dealing, to treat him to half a mutchkin.

"You may see my dwelling if you will," said the stranger; "but if you lose courage at what you see there, you will rue it all your life."

Dickon, however, laughed the warning to scorn, and having alighted to secure his horse, he followed the stranger up a narrow footpath, which led them up the hills to the singular eminence stuck betwixt the most southern and the centre peaks, and called, from its resemblance to such an animal in its form, the Lucken Hare. At the foot of this eminence, which is almost as famous for witch-meetings as the neighbouring windmill of Kippilaw, Dick was somewhat startled to observe that his conductor entered the hillside by a passage or cavern, of which he himself, though well acquainted with the spot, had never seen nor heard.

"You may still return," said his guide, looking ominously back upon him; but Dick scorned to show the white feather, and on they went. They entered a very long range of stables; in every stall stood a coal-black horse; by every horse lay a knight in coal-black armour, with a drawn sword in his hand; but all were as silent, hoof and limb, as if they had been cut out of marble. A great number of torches lent a gloomy lustre to the hall, which, like those of the Caliph Vathek, was of large dimensions. At the upper end, however, they at length arrived, where a sword and horn lay on an antique table.

"He that shall sound that horn and draw that sword," said the stranger, who now intimated that he was the famous Thomas of Ercildoun, "shall, if his heart fail him not, be king over all broad Britain. So speaks the tongue that cannot lie. But all depends on courage, and much on your taking the sword or horn first."

Dick was much disposed to take the sword, but his bold spirit was quailed by the supernatural terrors of the hall, and he thought to unsheathe the sword first might be construed into defiance, and give offence to the powers of the mountain. He took the bugle with a trembling hand, and blew a feeble note, but loud enough to produce a terrible answer. Thunder rolled in stunning peals through the immense hall; horses and men started to life; the steeds snorted, stamped, ground their bits, and tossed their heads; the warriors sprang to their feet, clashed their armour, and brandished their swords. Dick's terror was extreme at seeing the whole army, which had been so lately silent as the grave, in uproar, and about to rush on him. He dropped the horn, and made a feeble attempt to seize the enchanted sword; but at the same moment a voice pronounced aloud the mysterious words—

"Woe to the coward, that ever he was born,
Who did not draw the sword before he blew the horn!"

At the same time a whirlwind of irresistible fury howled through the long hall, bore the unfortunate horse-jockey clear out of the mouth of the cavern, and precipitated him over a steep bank of loose stones, where the shepherds found him the next morning, with just breath sufficient to tell his fearful tale, after concluding which he expired.

# COINNACH OER.

COINNACH OER, which means Dun Kenneth, was a celebrated man in his generation. He has been called the Isaiah of the North. The prophecies of this man are very frequently alluded to and quoted in various parts of the Highlands; although little is known of the man himself, except in Ross-shire. He was a small farmer in Strathpeffer, near Dingwall, and for many years of his life neither exhibited any talents, nor claimed any intelligence above his fellows. The manner in which he obtained the prophetic gift was told by himself in the following manner :—

As he was one day at work in the hill casting (digging) peats, he heard a voice which seemed to call to him out of the air. It commanded him to dig under a little green knoll which was near, and to gather up the small white stones which he would discover beneath the turf. The voice informed him, at the same time, that while he kept these stones in his possession, he should be endued with the power of supernatural foreknowledge.

Kenneth, though greatly alarmed at this aerial conversation, followed the directions of his invisible instructor, and turning up the turf on the hillock, in a little time discovered the talismans. From that day forward, the mind of Kenneth was illuminated by gleams of unearthly light; and he made many predictions, of which the credulity of the people, and the coincidence of accident, often supplied confirmation; and he certainly became the most notable of the Highland prophets. The most remarkable and well known of his vaticinations is the following:—"Whenever a M'Lean with long hands, a Fraser with a black spot on his face, a M'Gregor with a black knee, and a club-footed M'Leod of Raga, shall have existed; whenever there shall have been successively three M'Donalds of the name of John, and three M'Kinnons of the same Christian name,—oppressors will appear in the country, and the people will change their own land for a strange one." All these personages have appeared since; and it is the common opinion of the peasantry, that the consummation of the prophecy was fulfilled, when the exaction of the exorbitant rents reduced the Highlanders to poverty, and the introduction of the sheep banished the people to America.

Whatever might have been the gift of Kenneth Oer, he does not appear to have used it with an extraordinary degree of discretion; and the last time he exercised it, he was very near paying dear for his divination.

On this occasion he happened to be at some high festival of the M'Kenzies at Castle Braan. One of the guests was so exhilarated by the scene of gaiety, that he could not forbear an eulogium on the gallantry of the feast, and the nobleness of the guests. Kenneth, it appears, had no regard for the M'Kenzies, and was so provoked by this sally in their praise, that he not only broke out into a severe satire against their whole race, but gave vent to the prophetic denunciation of wrath and confusion upon their posterity. The guests being informed (or having overheard a part) of this rhapsody, instantly rose up with one accord to punish the contumely of the prophet. Kenneth, though he foretold the fate of others, did not in any manner look into that of himself; for this reason, being doubtful of debating the propriety of his prediction upon such unequal terms, he fled with the greatest precipitation. The M'Kenzies followed with infinite zeal; and more than one ball had whistled over the head of the seer before he reached Loch Ousie. The consequences of this prediction so disgusted Kenneth with any further exercise of his prophetic calling, that, in the anguish of his flight, he solemnly renounced all communication with its power; and, as he ran along the margin of Loch Ousie, he took out the wonderful pebbles, and cast them in a fury into the water. Whether his evil genius had now forsaken him, or his condition was better than that of his pursuers, is unknown, but certain it is, Kenneth, after the sacrifice of the pebbles, outstripped his enraged enemies, and never, so far as I have heard, made any attempt at prophecy from the hour of his escape.

Kenneth Oer had a son, who was called Ian Dubh Mac Coinnach (Black John, the son of Kenneth), and lived in the village of Miltoun, near Dingwall. His chief occupation was brewing whisky; and he was killed in a fray at Miltoun, early in the present century. His exit would not have formed the catastrophe of an epic poem, and appears to have been one of those events of which his father had no intelligence, for it happened in the following manner :—

Having fallen into a dispute with a man with whom he had previously been on friendly terms, they proceeded to blows; in the scuffle, the boy, the son of Ian's adversary, observing the two combatants locked in a close and firm gripe of eager contention, and being doubtful of the event, ran into the house and brought out the iron pot-crook, with which he saluted the head of the unfortunate Ian so severely, that he not only relinquished his combat, but departed this life on the ensuing morning.

# ELPHIN IRVING,

## THE FAIRIES' CUPBEARER.

> " The lady kilted her kirtle green
>   A little aboon her knee,
> The lady snooded her yellow hair
>   A little aboon her bree,
> And she's gane to the good greenwood
>   As fast as she could hie.
>
> And first she let the black steed pass,
>   And syne she let the brown,
> And then she flew to the milk-white steed,
>   And pulled the rider down :
> Syne out then sang the queen o' the fairies,
>   Frae midst a bank of broom,
> She that has won him, young Tamlane,
>   Has gotten a gallant groom."
>
>   *Old Ballad.*

"THE romantic vale of Corriewater, in Annandale, is regarded by the inhabitants, a pastoral and unmingled people, as the last border refuge of those beautiful and capricious beings, the fairies. Many old people yet living imagine they have had intercourse of good words and good deeds with the 'good folk'; and continue to tell that in the ancient days the fairies danced on the hill, and revelled in the glen, and showed themselves, like the mysterious children of the deity of old, among the sons and daughters of men. Their visits to the earth were periods of joy and mirth to mankind, rather than of sorrow and apprehension. They played on musical instruments of wonderful sweetness and variety of note, spread unexpected feasts, the supernatural flavour of which overpowered on many occasions the religious scruples of the Presbyterian shepherds, performed wonderful deeds of horsemanship, and marched in midnight processions, when the sound of their elfin minstrelsy charmed youths and maidens into love for their persons and pursuits; and more than one family of Corriewater have the fame of augmenting the numbers of the elfin chivalry. Faces of friends and relatives, long since doomed to the battle-trench or the deep sea, have been recognised by those who dared to gaze on the fairy march. The maid has seen her lost lover, and the mother her stolen child; and the courage to plan and achieve their deliverance has been possessed by, at least, one border maiden. In the legends of the people of Corrievale, there is a singular mixture of elfin and human adventure, and the traditional story of the Cupbearer to the Queen of the Fairies appeals alike to our domestic feelings and imagination.

"In one of the little green loops or bends on the banks of Corriewater, mouldered walls, and a few stunted wild plum-trees and vagrant roses, still point out the site of a cottage and garden. A well of pure spring-water leaps out from an old tree-root before the door; and here the shepherds, shading themselves in summer from the influence of the sun, tell to their children the wild tale of Elphin Irving and his sister Phemie; and, singular as the story seems, it has gained full credence among the people where the scene is laid."

"I ken the tale and the place weel," interrupted an old Scottish woman, who, from the predominance of scarlet in her apparel, seemed to have been a follower of the camp,—"I ken them weel, and the tale's as true as a bullet to its aim and a spark to powder. O bonnie Corriewater, a thousand times have I pulled gowans on its banks wi' ane that lies stiff and stark on a foreign shore in a bloody grave;" and, sobbing audibly, she drew the remains of a military cloak over her face, and allowed the story to proceed.

"When Elphin Irving and his sister Phemie were in their sixteenth year, for tradition says they were twins, their father was drowned in Corriewater, attempting to save his sheep from a sudden swell, to which all mountain streams are liable; and their mother, on the day of her husband's burial, laid down her head on the pillow, from which, on the seventh day, it was lifted to be dressed for the same grave. The inheritance left to the orphans may be briefly described: seventeen acres of plough and pasture land, seven milk cows, and seven pet sheep (many old people take delight in odd numbers); and to this may be added seven bonnet-pieces of Scottish gold, and a broadsword and spear, which their ancestor had wielded with such strength and courage in the battle of Dryfe Sands, that the minstrel who sang of that deed of arms ranked him only second to the Scotts and Johnstones.

"The youth and his sister grew in stature and in beauty. The brent bright brow, the clear blue eye, and frank and blithe deportment of the former gave him some influence among the young women of the valley; while the latter was no less the admiration of the young men, and at fair and dance, and at bridal, happy was he who touched but her hand, or received the benediction of her eye. Like all other Scottish beauties, she was the theme of many a song; and while tradition is yet busy with the singular history of her brother, song has taken all the care that rustic minstrelsy can of the gentleness of her spirit and the charms of her person."

"Now I vow," exclaimed a wandering piper, "by mine own honoured instrument, and by all other instruments that ever yielded music for the joy and delight of mankind, that there are more bonnie songs made about fair Phemie Irving than about all other dames of Annandale, and many of them are both high and bonnie. A proud lass maun she be if her spirit hears; and men say the dust lies not insensible of beautiful verse; for her charms are breathed through a thousand sweet lips, and no further gone than yestermorn I heard a lass singing on a green hillside what I shall not readily forget. If ye like to listen, ye shall judge; and it will not stay the story long, nor mar it much, for it is short, and about Phemie Irving." And, accordingly, he chanted the following rude verses, not unaccompanied by his honoured instrument, as he called his pipe, which chimed in with great effect, and gave richness to a voice which felt better than it could express :—

### FAIR PHEMIE IRVING.

Gay is thy glen, Corrie,
  With all thy groves flowering;
Green is thy glen, Corrie,
  When July is showering;
And sweet is yon wood where
  The small birds are bowering,
And there dwells the sweet one
  Whom I am adoring.

Her round neck is whiter
  Than winter when snowing;
Her meek voice is milder
  Than Ae in its flowing;
The glad ground yields music
  Where she goes by the river;
One kind glance would charm me
  For ever and ever.

The proud and the wealthy
  To Phemie are bowing;
No looks of love win they
  With sighing or suing;

> Far away maun I stand
>   With my rude wooing,
> She's a flow'ret too lovely
>   Too bloom for my pu'ing.
>
> Oh were I yon violet
>   On which she is walking;
> Oh were I yon small bird
>   To which she is talking;
> Or yon rose in her hand,
>   With its ripe ruddy blossom;
> Or some pure gentle thought
>   To be blest with her bosom.

This minstrel interruption, while it established Phemie Irving's claim to grace and to beauty, gave me additional confidence to pursue the story.

"But minstrel skill and true love-tale seemed to want their usual influence when they sought to win her attention; she was only observed to pay most respect to those youths who were most beloved by her brother; and the same hour that brought these twins to the world seemed to have breathed through them a sweetness and an affection of heart and mind which nothing could divide. If, like the virgin queen of the immortal poet, she walked 'in maiden meditation fancy free,' her brother Elphin seemed alike untouched with the charms of the fairest virgins in Corrie. He ploughed his field, he reaped his grain, he leaped, he ran, and wrestled, and danced, and sang, with more skill and life and grace than all other youths of the district; but he had no twilight and stolen interviews; when all other young men had their loves by their side, he was single, though not unsought, and his joy seemed never perfect save when his sister was near him. If he loved to share his time with her, she loved to share her time with him alone, or with the beasts of the field, or the birds of the air. She watched her little flock late, and she tended it early; not for the sordid love of the fleece, unless it was to make mantles for her brother, but with the look of one who had joy in its company. The very wild creatures, the deer and the hares, seldom sought to shun her approach, and the bird forsook not its nest, nor stinted its song, when she drew nigh; such is the confidence which maiden innocence and beauty inspire.

"It happened one summer, about three years after they became orphans, that rain had been for a while withheld from the earth, the hillsides began to parch, the grass in the vales to wither, and the stream of Corrie was diminished between its banks to the size of an ordinary rill. The shepherds drove their flocks to moorlands, and marsh and tarn had their reeds invaded by the scythe to supply the cattle with food. The sheep of his sister were Elphin's constant care; he drove them to the moistest pastures during the day, and he often watched them at midnight, when flocks, tempted by the sweet dewy grass, are known to browse eagerly, that he might guard them from the fox, and lead them to the choicest herbage. In these nocturnal watchings he sometimes drove his little flock over the water of Corrie, for the fords were hardly ankle-deep; or permitted his sheep to cool themselves in the stream, and taste the grass which grew along the brink. All this time not a drop of rain fell, nor did a cloud appear in the sky.

"One evening, during her brother's absence with the flock, Phemie sat at her cottage-door, listening to the bleatings of the distant folds and the lessened murmur of the water of Corrie, now scarcely audible beyond its banks. Her eyes, weary with watching along the accustomed line of road for the return of Elphin, were turned on the pool beside her, in which the stars were glimmering fitful and faint. As she looked she imagined the water grew brighter and brighter; a wild illumination presently shone upon the pool, and leaped from bank to bank, and suddenly changing into a human form, ascended the margin, and, passing her, glided swiftly into the cottage. The visionary form was so like her brother in shape and air, that, starting up, she flew into the house, with the hope of finding him in his customary seat. She found him not, and, impressed with the terror which a wraith or apparition seldom fails to inspire, she uttered a shriek so loud and so piercing as to be heard at Johnstone Bank, on the other side of the vale of Corrie."

An old woman now rose suddenly from her seat

in the window-sill, the living dread of shepherds, for she travelled the country with a brilliant reputation for witchcraft, and thus she broke in upon the narrative: "I vow, young man, ye tell us the truth upset and down-thrust. I heard my douce grandmother say that on the night when Elphin Irving disappeared—disappeared I shall call it, for the bairn can but be gone for a season, to return to us in his own appointed time—she was seated at the fireside at Johnstone Bank; the laird had laid aside his bonnet to take the Book, when a shriek mair loud, believe me, than a mere woman's shriek—and they can shriek loud enough, else they're sair wranged—came over the water of Corrie, so sharp and shrilling, that the pewter plates dinneled on the wall; such a shriek, my douce grandmother said, as rang in her ear till the hour of her death, and she lived till she was aughty-and-aught, forty full ripe years after the event. But there is another matter, which, doubtless, I cannot compel ye to believe: it was the common rumour that Elphin Irving came not into the world like the other sinful creatures of the earth, but was one of the kane-bairns of the fairies, whilk they had to pay to the enemy of man's salvation every seventh year. The poor lady-fairy—a mother's aye a mother, be she elves' flesh or Eve's flesh—hid her elf son beside the christened flesh in Marion Irving's cradle, and the auld enemy lost his prey for a time. Now, hasten on with your story, which is not a bodle the waur for me. The maiden saw the shape of her brother, fell into a faint, or a trance, and the neighbours came flocking in—gang on with your tale, young man, and dinna be affronted because an auld woman helped ye wi't."

"It is hardly known," I resumed, "how long Phemie Irving continued in a state of insensibility. The morning was far advanced, when a neighbouring maiden found her seated in an old chair, as white as monumental marble; her hair, about which she had always been solicitous, loosened from its curls, and hanging disordered over her neck and bosom, her hands and forehead. The maiden touched the one, and kissed the other; they were as cold as snow; and her eyes, wide open, were fixed on her brother's empty chair, with the intensity of gaze of one who had witnessed the appearance of a spirit. She seemed insensible of any one's presence, and sat fixed and still and motionless. The maiden, alarmed at her looks, thus addressed her:—'Phemie, lass, Phemie Irving! Dear me, but this be awful! I have come to tell ye that seven of your pet sheep have escaped drowning in the water; for Corrie, sae quiet and sae gentle yestreen, is rolling and dashing frae bank to bank this morning. Dear me, woman, dinna let the loss of the world's gear bereave ye of your senses. I would rather make ye a present of a dozen mugewes of the Tinwald brood myself; and now I think on 't, if ye'll send over Elphin, I will help him hame with them in the gloaming myself. So, Phemie, woman, be comforted.'

"At the mention of her brother's name she cried out, 'Where is he? Oh, where is he?' gazed wildly round, and, shuddering from head to foot, fell senseless on the floor. Other inhabitants of the valley, alarmed by the sudden swell of the river, which had augmented to a torrent, deep and impassable, now came in to inquire if any loss had been sustained, for numbers of sheep and teds of hay had been observed floating down about the dawn of the morning. They assisted in reclaiming the unhappy maiden from her swoon; but insensibility was joy compared to the sorrow to which she awakened. 'They have ta'en him away, they have ta'en him away,' she chanted, in a tone of delirious pathos; 'him that was whiter and fairer than the lily on Lyddal Lee. They have long sought, and they have long sued, and they had the power to prevail against my prayers at last. They have ta'en him away; the flower is plucked from among the weeds, and the dove is slain amid a flock of ravens. They came with shout, and they came with song, and they spread the charm, and they placed the spell, and the baptised brow has been bowed down to the unbaptised hand. They have ta'en him away, they have ta'en him away; he was too lovely, and too good, and too noble, to bless us with his continuance on earth; for what are the sons of men compared to him?—the light of the moonbeam to the morning sun, the glowworm to the eastern star. They have ta'en him away, the invisible dwellers of the earth. I saw them come on him with shouting and with singing, and they charmed him where he sat, and away they bore him; and the horse he rode was never shod with iron, nor owned before the mastery of human hand. They have ta'en him away over the water, and over the wood, and over the hill. I got but ae look of his bonnie blue ee, but ae, ae look. But as I have endured what never maiden endured, so will I undertake what never maiden undertook, I will win him from them all. I know the invisible ones of the earth; I have heard their wild and wondrous music in the wild woods, and there shall a christened maiden seek him, and achieve his deliverance.' She paused, and glancing around a circle of condoling faces, down which the tears were dropping like rain, said, in a calm and altered but still delirious tone: 'Why do you weep, Mary Halliday? and why do you weep, John Graeme? Ye think that Elphin Irving—oh, it's a bonnie, bonnie name, and dear to many a maiden's heart as well as mine—ye think he is drowned in Corrie; and ye will seek in the deep, deep pools for the bonnie, bonnie corse, that ye may weep over it, as it lies in its last linen, and lay it, amid weeping and wailing in the dowie kirkyard.

Ye may seek, but ye shall never find; so leave me to trim up my hair, and prepare my dwelling, and make myself ready to watch for the hour of his return to upper earth.' And she resumed her household labours with an alacrity which lessened not the sorrow of her friends.

"Meanwhile the rumour flew over the vale that Elphin Irving was drowned in Corriewater. Matron and maid, old man and young, collected suddenly along the banks of the river, which now began to subside to its natural summer limits, and commenced their search; interrupted every now and then by calling from side to side, and from pool to pool, and by exclamations of sorrow for this misfortune. The search was fruitless: five sheep, pertaining to the flock which he conducted to pasture, were found drowned in one of the deep eddies; but the river was still too brown, from the soil of its moorland sources, to enable them to see what its deep shelves, its pools, and its overhanging and hazelly banks concealed. They remitted further search till the stream should become pure; and old man taking old man aside, began to whisper about the mystery of the youth's disappearance; old women laid their lips to the ears of their coevals, and talked of Elphin Irving's fairy parentage, and his having been dropped by an unearthly hand into a Christian cradle. The young men and maids conversed on other themes; they grieved for the loss of the friend and the lover, and while the former thought that a heart so kind and true was not left in the vale, the latter thought, as maidens will, on his handsome person, gentle manners, and merry blue eye, and speculated with a sigh on the time when they might have hoped a return for their love. They were soon joined by others who had heard the wild and delirious language of his sister: the old belief was added to the new assurance, and both again commented upon by minds full of superstitious feeling, and hearts full of supernatural fears, till the youths and maidens of Corrievale held no more love trysts for seven days and nights, lest, like Elphin Irving, they should be carried away to augment the ranks of the unchristened chivalry.

"It was curious to listen to the speculations of the peasantry. 'For my part,' said a youth, 'if I were sure that poor Elphin escaped from that perilous water, I would not give the fairies a pound of hiplock wool for their chance of him. There has not been a fairy seen in the land since Donald Cargil, the Cameronian, conjured them into the Solway for playing on their pipes during one of his nocturnal preachings on the hip of the Burnswark hill.'

"'Preserve me, bairn,' said an old woman, justly exasperated at the incredulity of her nephew, 'if ye winna believe what I both heard and saw at the moonlight end of Craigyburnwood on a summer night, rank after rank of the fairy folk, ye'll at least believe a douce man and a ghostly professor, even the late minister of Tinwaldkirk. His only son—I mind the lad weel, with his long yellow locks and his bonnie blue eyes—when I was but a gilpie of a lassie, *he* was stolen away from off the horse at his father's elbow, as they crossed that false and fearsome water, even Locherbriggflow, on the night of the Midsummer fair of Dumfries. Ay, ay, who can doubt the truth of that? Have not the godly inhabitants of Almsfieldtown and Tinwaldkirk seen the sweet youth riding at midnight, in the midst of the unhallowed troop, to the sound of flute and of dulcimer, and though meikle they prayed, naebody tried to achieve his deliverance?'

"'I have heard it said by douce folk and sponsible,' interrupted another, 'that every seven years the elves and fairies pay kane, or make an offering of one of their children, to the grand enemy of salvation, and that they are permitted to purloin one of the children of men to present to the fiend—a more acceptable offering, I'll warrant, than one of their own infernal brood that are Satan's sib allies, and drink a drop of the deil's blood every May morning. And touching this lost lad, ye all ken his mother was a hawk of an uncanny nest, a second cousin of Kate Kimmer, of Barfloshan, as rank a witch as ever rode on ragwort. Ay, sirs, what's bred in the bone is ill to come out of the flesh.'

"On these and similar topics, which a peasantry full of ancient tradition and enthusiasm and superstition readily associate with the commonest occurrences of life, the people of Corrievale continued to converse till the fall of evening, when each, seeking their home, renewed again the wondrous subject, and illustrated it with all that popular belief and poetic imagination could so abundantly supply.

"The night which followed this melancholy day was wild with wind and rain; the river came down broader and deeper than before, and the lightning, flashing by fits over the green woods of Corrie, showed the ungovernable and perilous flood sweeping above its banks. It happened that a farmer, returning from one of the border fairs, encountered the full swing of the storm; but mounted on an excellent horse, and mantled from chin to heel in a good grey plaid, beneath which he had the further security of a thick greatcoat, he sat dry in his saddle, and proceeded in the anticipated joy of a subsided tempest and a glowing morning sun. As he entered the long grove, or rather remains of the old Galwegian forest, which lines for some space the banks of the Corriewater, the storm began to abate, the wind sighed milder and milder among the trees, and here and there a star, twinkling momentarily through the sudden rack of the clouds, showed the river raging from bank to brae. As he shook the moisture from his clothes, he was not without a wish that the day would dawn, and that he might be preserved on a road which his imagination beset with greater perils than the raging river; for his superstitious feeling let loose upon his path elf and goblin, and the current traditions of the district supplied very largely to his apprehension the ready materials of fear.

"Just as he emerged from the wood, where a fine sloping bank, covered with short greensward, skirts the limit of the forest, his horse made a full pause, snorted, trembled, and started from side to side, stooped his head, erected his ears, and seemed to scrutinise every tree and bush. The rider, too, it may be imagined, gazed round and round, and peered warily into every suspicious-looking place. His dread of a supernatural visitation was not much allayed when he observed a female shape seated on the ground at the root of a huge old oak-tree, which stood in the centre of one of those patches of verdant sward, known by the name of 'fairy rings,' and avoided by all peasants who wish to prosper. A long thin gleam of eastern daylight enabled him to examine accurately the being who, in this wild place and unusual hour, gave additional terror to this haunted spot. She was dressed in white from the neck to the knees; her arms, long and round and white, were perfectly bare; her head, uncovered, allowed her long hair to descend in ringlet succeeding ringlet, till the half of her person was nearly concealed in the fleece. Amidst the whole, her hands were constantly busy in shedding aside the tresses which interposed between her steady and uninterrupted gaze down a line of old road which wound among the hills to an ancient burial-ground.

"As the traveller continued to gaze, the figure suddenly rose, and, wringing the rain from her long locks, paced round and round the tree, chanting in a wild and melancholy manner an equally wild and delirious song.

### THE FAIRY OAK OF CORRIEWATER.

 The small bird's head is under its wing,
  The deer sleeps on the grass;
 The moon comes out, and the stars shine down,
  The dew gleams like the glass:
 There is no sound in the world so wide,
  Save the sound of the smitten brass,
 With the merry cittern and the pipe
  Of the fairies as they pass.
 But oh! the fire maun burn and burn,
 And the hour is gone, and will never return.

 The green hill cleaves, and forth, with a bound,
  Comes elf and elfin steed;
 The moon dives down in a golden cloud,
  The stars grow dim with dread;
 But a light is running along the earth,
  So of heaven's they have no need:
 O'er moor and moss with a shout they pass,
  And the word is spur and speed—
 But the fire maun burn, and I maun quake,
 And the hour is gone that will never come back.

And when they came to Craigyburnwood,
　　The Queen of the Fairies spoke :
"Come, bind your steeds to the rushes so green,
　　And dance by the haunted oak :
I found the acorn on Heshbon Hill,
　　In the nook of a palmer's poke,
A thousand years since ; here it grows !"
　　And they danced till the greenwood shook :
But oh ! the fire, the burning fire,
The longer it burns, it but blazes the higher.


" I have won me a youth," the Elf Queen said,
　　" The fairest that earth may see ;
This night I have won young Elph Irving
　　My cupbearer to be.
His service lasts but seven sweet years,
　　And his wage is a kiss of me."
And merrily, merrily, laughed the wild elves
　　Round Corris's greenwood tree.
But oh ! the fire it glows in my brain,
And the hour is gone, and comes not again.


The Queen she has whispered a secret word,
　　" Come hither my Elphin sweet,
And bring that cup of the charmèd wine,
　　Thy lips and mine to weet."
But a brown elf shouted a loud, loud shout,
　　" Come, leap on your coursers fleet,
For here comes the smell of some baptised flesh,
　　And the sounding of baptised feet."
But oh ! the fire that burns, and maun burn ;
For the time that is gone will never return.


On a steed as white as the new-milked milk,
　　The Elf Queen leaped with a bound,
And young Elphin a steed like December snow
　　'Neath him at the word he found.
But a maiden came, and her christened arms
　　She linked her brother around,

And called on God, and the steed with a snort
   Sank into the gaping ground.
But the fire maun burn, and I maun quake,
And the time that is gone will no more come back.

And she held her brother, and lo ! he grew
   A wild bull waked in ire ;
And she held her brother, and lo ! he changed
   To a river roaring higher ;
And she held her brother, and he became
   A flood of the raging fire ;
She shrieked and sank, and the wild elves laughed
   Till the mountain rang and mire.
But oh ! the fire yet burns in my brain,
And the hour is gone, and comes not again.

"O maiden, why waxed thy faith so faint,
   Thy spirit so slack and slaw ?
Thy courage kept good till the flame waxed wud,
   Then thy might begun to thaw ;
Had ye kissed him with thy christened lip,
   Ye had wan him frae 'mang us a'.
Now bless the fire, the elfin fire,
   That made thee faint and fa' ;
Now bless the fire, the elfin fire,
The longer it burns it blazes the higher."

"At the close of this unusual strain, the figure sat down on the grass, and proceeded to bind up her long and disordered tresses, gazing along the old and unfrequented road. 'Now God be my helper,' said the traveller, who happened to be the laird of Johnstone Bank, 'can this be a trick of the fiend, or can it be bonnie Phemie Irving who chants this dolorous sang? Something sad has befallen that makes her seek her seat in this eerie nook amid the darkness and tempest ; through might from aboon I will go on and see.' And the horse, feeling something of the owner's reviving spirit in the application of spur-steel, bore him at once to the foot of the tree. The poor delirious maiden uttered a yell of piercing joy as she beheld him, and, with the swiftness of a creature winged, linked her arms round the rider's waist, and shrieked till the woods rang. 'Oh, I have ye now, Elphin, I have ye now,' and she strained him to her bosom with a convulsive grasp. 'What ails ye, my bonnie lass?' said the laird of Johnstone Bank, his fears of the supernatural vanishing when he beheld her sad and bewildered look. She raised her eyes at the sound, and seeing a strange face, her arms slipped their hold, and she dropped with a groan on the ground.

"The morning had now fairly broke; the flocks shook the rain from their sides, the shepherds hastened to inspect their charges, and a thin blue smoke began to stream from the cottages of the valley into the brightening air. The laird carried Phemie Irving in his arms, till he observed two shepherds ascending from one of the loops of Corriewater, bearing the lifeless body of her brother. They had found him whirling round and round in one of the numerous eddies, and his hands, clutched and filled with wool, showed that he had lost his life in attempting to save the flock of his sister. A plaid was laid over the body, which, along with the unhappy maiden in a half-lifeless state, was carried into a cottage, and laid in that apartment distinguished among the peasantry by the name of the chamber. While the peasant's wife was left to take care of Phemie, old man and matron and maid had collected around the drowned youth, and each began to relate the circumstances of his death, when the door suddenly opened, and his sister, advancing to the corpse, with a look of delirious serenity, broke out into a wild laugh and said: 'Oh, it is wonderful, it's truly wonderful! That bare and death-cold body, dragged from the darkest pool of Corrie, with its hands filled with fine wool, wears the perfect similitude of my own Elphin! I'll tell ye—the spiritual dwellers of the earth, the fairyfolk of our evening tale, have stolen the living body, and fashioned this cold and inanimate clod to mislead your pursuit. In common eyes this seems all that Elphin Irving would be, had he sunk in Corriewater; but so it seems not to me. Ye have sought the living soul, and ye have found only its garment. But oh, if ye had beheld him, as I beheld him to-night, riding among the elfin troop, the fairest of them all; had you clasped him in your arms, and wrestled for him with spirits and terrible shapes from the other world, till your heart quailed and your flesh was subdued, then would ye yield no credit to the semblance which this cold and apparent flesh bears to my brother. But hearken! On Hallowmass Eve, when the spiritual people are let loose on earth for a season, I will take my stand in the burial-ground of Corrie; and when my Elphin and his unchristened troop come past, with the sound of all their minstrelsy, I will leap on him and win him, or perish for ever.'

"All gazed aghast on the delirious maiden, and many of her auditors gave more credence to her distempered speech than to the visible evidence before them. As she turned to depart, she looked round, and suddenly sank upon the body, with tears streaming from her eyes, and sobbed out, " My brother! Oh, my brother!' She was carried out insensible, and again recovered; but relapsed into her ordinary delirium, in which she continued till the Hallow Eve after her brother's burial. She was found seated in the ancient burial-ground, her back against a broken gravestone, her locks white with frost-rime, watching with intensity of look the road to the kirkyard; but the spirit which gave life to the fairest form of all the maids of Annandale was fled for ever."

Such is the singular story which the peasants know by the name of "Elphin Irving, the Fairies' Cupbearer"; and the title, in its fullest and most supernatural sense, still obtains credence among the industrious and virtuous dames of the romantic vale of Corrie.

# THE GHOSTS OF CRAIG-AULNAIC.

Two celebrated ghosts existed, once on a time, in the wilds of Craig-Aulnaic, a romantic place in the district of Strathdown, Banffshire. The one was a male and the other a female. The male was called Fhuna Mhoir Ben Baynac, after one of the mountains of Glenavon, where at one time he resided; and the female was called Clashnichd Aulnaic, from her having had her abode in Craig-Aulnaic. But although the great ghost of Ben Baynac was bound by the common ties of nature and of honour to protect and cherish his weaker companion, Clashnichd Aulnaic, yet he often treated her in the most cruel and unfeeling manner. In the dead of night, when the surrounding hamlets were buried in deep repose, and when nothing else disturbed the solemn stillness of the midnight scene, oft would the shrill shrieks of poor Clashnichd burst upon the slumberer's ears, and awake him to anything but pleasant reflections.

But of all those who were incommoded by the noisy and unseemly quarrels of these two ghosts, James Owre or Gray, the tenant of the farm of

Balbig of Delnabo, was the greatest sufferer. From the proximity of his abode to their haunts, it was the misfortune of himself and family to be the nightly audience of Clashnichd's cries and lamentations, which they considered anything but agreeable entertainment.

One day as James Gray was on his rounds looking after his sheep, he happened to fall in with Clashnichd, the ghost of Aulnaic, with whom he entered into a long conversation. In the course of it he took occasion to remonstrate with her on the very disagreeable disturbance she caused himself and family by her wild and unearthly cries—cries which, he said, few mortals could relish in the dreary hours of midnight. Poor Clashnichd, by way of apology for her conduct, gave James Gray a sad account of her usage, detailing at full length the series of cruelties committed upon her by Ben Baynac. From this account, it appeared that her living with the latter was by no means a matter of choice with Clashnichd; on the contrary, it seemed that she had, for a long time, lived apart with much comfort, residing in a snug dwelling, as already mentioned, in the wilds of Craig-Aulnaic; but Ben Baynac having unfortunately taken into his head to pay her a visit, took a fancy, not to herself, but her dwelling, of which, in his own name and authority, he took immediate possession, and soon after he expelled poor Clashnichd, with many stripes, from her natural inheritance. Not satisfied with invading and depriving her of her just rights, he was in the habit of following her into her private haunts, not with the view of offering her any endearments, but for the purpose of inflicting on her person every torment which his brain could invent.

Such a moving relation could not fail to affect the generous heart of James Gray, who determined from that moment to risk life and limb in order to vindicate the rights and avenge the wrongs of poor Clashnichd, the ghost of Craig-Aulnaic. He, therefore, took good care to interrogate his new *protégée* touching the nature of her oppressor's constitution, whether he was of that *killable* species of ghost that could be shot with a silver sixpence, or if there was any other weapon that could possibly accomplish his annihilation. Clashnichd informed him that she had occasion to know that Ben Baynac was wholly invulnerable to all the weapons of man, with the exception of a large mole on his left breast, which was no doubt penetrable by silver or steel; but that, from the specimens she had of his personal prowess and strength, it were vain for mere man to attempt to combat him. Confiding, however, in his expertness as an archer—for he was allowed to be the best marksman of the age— James Gray told Clashnichd he did not fear him with all his might,—that *he* was a man; and desired her, moreover, next time the ghost chose to repeat his incivilities to her, to apply to him, James Gray, for redress.

It was not long ere he had an opportunity of fulfilling his promises. Ben Baynac having one night, in the want of better amusement, entertained himself by inflicting an inhuman castigation on Clashnichd, she lost no time in waiting on James Gray, with a full and particular account of it. She found him smoking his *cutty*, for it was night when she came to him; but, notwithstanding the inconvenience of the hour, James needed no great persuasion to induce him to proceed directly along with Clashnichd to hold a communing with their friend, Ben Baynac, the great ghost. Clashnichd was stout and sturdy, and understood the knack of travelling much better than our women do. She expressed a wish that, for the sake of expedition, James Gray would suffer her to bear him along, a motion to which the latter agreed; and a few minutes brought them close to the scene of Ben Baynac's residence. As they approached his haunt, he came forth to meet them, with looks and gestures which did not at all indicate a cordial welcome. It was a fine moonlight night, and they could easily observe his actions. Poor Clashnichd was now sorely afraid of the great ghost. Apprehending instant destruction from his fury, she exclaimed to James Gray that they would be both dead people, and that immediately, unless James Gray hit with an arrow the mole which covered Ben

Baynac's heart. This was not so difficult a task as James had hitherto apprehended it. The mole was as large as a common bonnet, and yet nowise disproportioned to the natural size of the ghost's body, for he certainly was a great and a mighty ghost. Ben Baynac cried out to James Gray that he would soon make eagle's meat of him; and certain it is, such was his intention, had not the shepherd so effectually stopped him from the execution of it. Raising his bow to his eye when within a few yards of Ben Baynac, he took deliberate aim; the arrow flew—it hit—a yell from Ben Baynac announced the result. A hideous howl re-echoed from the surrounding mountains, responsive to the groans of a thousand ghosts; and Ben Baynac, like the smoke of a shot, vanished into air.

Clashnichd, the ghost of Aulnaic, now found herself emancipated from the most abject state of slavery, and restored to freedom and liberty, through the invincible courage of James Gray. Overpowered with gratitude, she fell at his feet, and vowed to devote the whole of her time and talents towards his service and prosperity. Meanwhile, being anxious to have her remaining goods and furniture removed to her former dwelling, whence she had been so iniquitously expelled by Ben Baynac, the great ghost, she requested of her new master the use of his horses to remove them. James observing on the adjacent hill a flock of deer, and wishing to have a trial of his new servant's sagacity or expertness, told her those were his horses—she was welcome to the use of them; desiring that when she had done with them, she would inclose them in his stable. Clashnichd then proceeded to make use of the horses, and James Gray returned home to enjoy his night's rest.

Scarce had he reached his arm-chair, and reclined his cheek on his hand, to ruminate over the bold adventure of the night, when Clashnichd entered, with her "breath in her throat," and venting the bitterest complaints at the unruliness of his horses, which had broken one-half of her furniture, and caused her more trouble in the stabling of them than their services were worth.

"Oh! they are stabled, then?" inquired James Gray. Clashnichd replied in the affirmative. "Very well," rejoined James, "they shall be tame enough to-morrow."

From this specimen of Clashnichd, the ghost of Craig-Aulnaic's expertness, it will be seen what a valuable acquisition her service proved to James Gray and his young family. They were, however, speedily deprived of her assistance by a most unfortunate accident. From the sequel of the story, from which the foregoing is an extract, it appears that poor Clashnichd was deeply addicted to propensities which at that time rendered her kin so obnoxious to their human neighbours. She was constantly in the habit of visiting her friends much oftener than she was invited, and, in the course of such visits, was never very scrupulous in making free with any eatables which fell within the circle of her observation.

One day, while engaged on a foraging expedition of this description, she happened to enter the Mill of Delnabo, which was inhabited in those days by the miller's family. She found his wife engaged in roasting a large gridiron of fine savoury fish, the agreeable smell proceeding from which perhaps occasioned her visit. With the usual inquiries after the health of the miller and his family, Clashnichd proceeded with the greatest familiarity and good-humour to make herself comfortable at their expense. But the miller's wife, enraged at the loss of her fish, and not relishing such unwelcome familiarity, punished the unfortunate Clashnichd rather too severely for her freedom. It happened that there was at the time a large caldron of boiling water suspended over the fire, and this caldron the enraged wife overturned in Clashnichd's bosom!

Scalded beyond recovery, she fled up the wilds of Craig-Aulnaic, uttering the most melancholy lamentations, nor has she been ever heard of since.

# THE DOOMED RIDER.

"The Conan is as bonny a river as we hae in a' the north country. There's mony a sweet sunny spot on its banks, an' mony a time an' aft hae I waded through its shallows, whan a boy, to set my little scautling-line for the trouts an' the eels, or to gather the big pearl-mussels that lie sae thick in the fords. But its bonny wooded banks are places for enjoying the day in—no for passing the nicht. I kenna how it is; it's nane o' your wild streams that wander desolate through a desert country, like the Aven, or that come rushing down in foam and thunder, ower broken rocks, like the Foyers, or that wallow in darkness, deep, deep in the bowels o' the earth, like the fearfu' Auldgraunt; an' yet no ane o' these rivers has mair or frightfuller stories connected wi' it than the Conan. Ane can hardly saunter ower half-a-mile in its course, frae where it leaves Coutin till where it enters the sea, without passing ower the scene o' some frightful auld legend o' the kelpie or the waterwraith. And ane o' the most frightful looking o' these places is to be found among the woods of Conan House. Ye enter a swampy meadow that waves wi' flags an' rushes like a corn-field in harvest, an' see a hillock covered wi' willows rising like an island in the midst. There are thick mirkwoods on ilka side; the river, dark an' awesome, an' whirling round an' round in mossy eddies, sweeps away behind it; an' there is an auld burying-ground, wi' the broken ruins o' an auld Papist kirk, on the tap. Ane can see amang the rougher stanes the rose-wrought mullions of an arched window, an' the trough that ance held the holy water. About twa hunder years ago—a wee mair maybe, or a wee less, for ane canna be very sure o' the date o' thae old stories—the building was entire; an' a spot near it, whar the wood now grows thickest, was laid out in a corn-field. The marks o' the furrows may still be seen amang the trees.

"A party o' Highlanders were busily engaged, ae day in harvest, in cutting down the corn o' that field; an' just aboot noon, when the sun shone brightest an' they were busiest in the work, they heard a voice frae the river exclaim :—'The hour but not the man has come.' Sure enough, on looking round, there was the kelpie stan'in' in what they ca' a fause ford, just fornent the auld kirk. There is a deep black pool baith aboon an' below, but i' the ford there's a bonny ripple, that shows, as ane might think, but little depth o' water; an' just i' the middle o' that, in a place where a horse might swim, stood the kelpie. An' it again repeated its words:—'The hour but not the man has come,' an' then flashing through the water like a drake, it disappeared in the lower pool. When the folk stood wondering what the creature might mean, they saw a man on horseback come spurring down the hill in hot haste, making straight for the fause ford. They could then understand her words at ance; an' four o' the stoutest o' them sprang oot frae amang the corn to warn him o' his danger, an' keep him back. An' sae they tauld him what they had seen an' heard, an' urged him either to turn back an' tak' anither road, or stay for an hour or sae where he was. But he just wadna hear them, for he was baith unbelieving an' in haste, an' wauld hae taen the ford for a' they could say, hadna the Highlanders, determined on saving him whether he would or no, gathered round him an' pulled him frae his horse, an' then, to mak' sure o' him, locked him up in the auld kirk. Weel, when the hour had gone by—the fatal hour o' the kelpie—they flung open the door, an' cried to him that he might noo gang on his journey. Ah! but there was nae answer, though; an' sae they cried a second time, an' there was nae answer still; an' then they went in, an' found him lying stiff an' cauld on the floor, wi' his face buried in the water o' the very stone trough that we may still see amang the ruins.

His hour had come, an' he had fallen in a fit, as 'twould seem, head-foremost amang the water o' the trough, where he had been smothered,—an' sae ye see, the prophecy o' the kelpie availed naething."

# WHIPPETY STOURIE.

There was once a gentleman that lived in a very grand house, and he married a young lady that had been delicately brought up. In her husband's house she found everything that was fine—fine tables and chairs, fine looking-glasses, and fine curtains; but then her husband expected her to be able to spin twelve hanks o' thread every day, besides attending to her house; and, to tell the even-down truth, the lady could not spin a bit. This made her husband glunchy with her, and, before a month had passed, she found hersel' very unhappy.

One day the husband gaed away upon a journey, after telling her that he expected her, before his return, to have not only learned to spin, but to have spun a hundred hanks o' thread. Quite downcast, she took a walk along the hillside, till she cam' to a big flat stane, and there she sat down and grat. By and by she heard a strain o' fine sma' music, coming as it were frae aneath the stane, and, on turning it up, she saw a cave below, where there were sitting six wee ladies in green gowns, ilk ane o' them spinning on a little wheel, and singing,

> "Little kens my dame at hame
> That Whippety Stourie is my name."

The lady walked into the cave, and was kindly asked by the wee bodies to take a chair and sit down, while they still continued their spinning. She observed that ilk ane's mouth was thrawn away to ae side, but she didna venture to speer the reason. They asked why she looked so unhappy, and she telt them that it was she was expected by her husband to be a good spinner, when the plain truth was that she could not spin at all, and found herself quite unable for it, having been so delicately brought up; neither was there any need for it, as her husband was a rich man.

"Oh, is that a'?" said the little wifies, speaking out of their cheeks alike.

"Yes, and is it not a very good a' too?" said the lady, her heart like to burst wi' distress.

"We could easily quit ye o' that trouble," said the wee women. "Just ask us a' to dinner for the day when your husband is to come back. We'll then let you see how we'll manage him."

So the lady asked them all to dine with herself and her husband, on the day when he was to come back.

When the gudeman came hame, he found the

house so occupied with preparations for dinner, that he had nae time to ask his wife about her thread; and, before ever he had ance spoken to her on the subject, the company was announced at the hall door. The six ladies all came in a coach-and-six, and were as fine as princesses, but still wore their gowns of green. The gentleman was very polite, and showed them up the stair with a pair of wax candles in his hand. And so they all sat down to dinner, and conversation went on very pleasantly, till at length the husband, becoming familiar with them, said—

"Ladies, if it be not an uncivil question, I should like to know how it happens that all your mouths are turned away to one side?"

"Oh," said ilk ane at ance, "it's with our constant *spin-spin-spinning*."

"Is that the case?" cried the gentleman; "then, John, Tam, and Dick, fie, go haste and burn every rock, and reel, and spinning-wheel in the house, for I'll not have my wife to spoil her bonnie face with *spin-spin-spinning*."

And so the lady lived happily with her gudeman all the rest of her days.

# THE WEIRD OF THE THREE ARROWS.

Sir James Douglas, the companion of Bruce, and well known by his appellation of the "Black Douglas," was once, during the hottest period of the exterminating war carried on by him and his colleague Randolph, against the English, stationed at Linthaughlee, near Jedburgh. He was resting, himself and his men after the toils of many days' fighting-marches through Teviotdale; and, according to his custom, had walked round the tents, previous to retiring to the unquiet rest of a soldier's bed. He stood for a few minutes at the entrance to his tent contemplating the scene before him, rendered more interesting by a clear moon, whose silver beams fell, in the silence of a night without a breath of wind, calmly on the slumbers of mortals destined to mix in the melée of dreadful war, perhaps on the morrow. As he stood gazing, irresolute whether to retire to rest or indulge longer in a train of thought not very suitable to a warrior who delighted in the spirit-stirring scenes of his profession, his eye was attracted by the figure of an old woman, who approached him with a trembling step, leaning on a staff, and holding in her left hand three English cloth-shaft arrows.

"You are he who is ca'ed the guid Sir James?" said the old woman.

"I am, good woman," replied Sir James. "Why hast thou wandered from the sutler's camp?"

"I dinna belang to the camp o' the hoblers," answered the woman. "I hae been a residenter in Linthaughlee since the day when King Alexander passed the door o' my cottage wi' his bonny French bride, wha was terrified awa' frae Jedburgh by the death's-head whilk appeared to her on the day o' her marriage. What I hae suffered sin' that day" (looking at the arrows in her hand) "lies between me an' heaven."

"Some of your sons have been killed in the wars, I presume?" said Sir James.

"Ye hae guessed a pairt o' my waes," replied the woman. "That arrow" (holding out one of the three) "carries on its point the bluid o' my first born; that is stained wi' the stream that poured frae the heart o' my second; and that is red wi' the gore in which my youngest weltered, as he gae up the life that made me childless. They were a' shot by English hands, in different armies, in different battles. I am an honest woman, and wish to return to the English what belongs to the English; but that in the same fashion in which they were sent.

The Black Douglas has the strongest arm an' the surest ee in auld Scotland; an' wha can execute my commission better than he?"

"I do not use the bow, good woman," replied Sir James. "I love the grasp of the dagger or the battle-axe. You must apply to some other individual to return your arrows."

"I canna tak' them hame again," said the woman, laying them down at the feet of Sir James. "Ye'll see me again on St. James' E'en."

The old woman departed as she said these words. Sir James took up the arrows, and placed them in an empty quiver that lay amongst his baggage. He retired to rest, but not to sleep. The figure of the old woman and her strange request occupied his thoughts, and produced trains of meditation which ended in nothing but restlessness and disquietude. Getting up at daybreak, he met a messenger at the entrance of his tent, who informed him that Sir Thomas de Richmont, with a force of ten thousand men, had crossed the Borders, and would pass through a narrow defile, which he mentioned, where he could be attacked with great advantage. Sir James gave instant orders to march to the spot; and, with that genius for scheming, for which he was so remarkable, commanded his men to twist together the young birch-trees on either side of the passage to prevent the escape of the enemy. This finished, he concealed his archers in a hollow way, near the gorge of the pass.

The enemy came on; and when their ranks were embarrassed by the narrowness of the road, and it was impossible for the cavalry to act with effect, Sir James rushed upon them at the head of his horsemen; and the archers, suddenly discovering themselves, poured in a flight of arrows on the confused soldiers, and put the whole army to flight. In the heat of the onset, Douglas killed Sir Thomas de Richmont with his dagger.

Not long after this, Edmund de Cailon, a knight of Gascony, and Governor of Berwick, who had been heard to vaunt that he had sought the famous Black Knight, but could not find him, was returning to England, loaded with plunder, the fruit of an inroad on Teviotdale. Sir James thought it a pity that a Gascon's vaunt should be heard unpunished in Scotland, and made long forced marches to satisfy the desire of the foreign knight, by giving him a sight of the dark countenance he had made a subject of reproach. He soon succeeded in gratifying both himself and the Gascon. Coming up in his terrible manner, he called to Cailon to stop, and, before he proceeded into England, receive the respects of the Black Knight he had come to find, but hitherto had not met. The Gascon's vaunt was now changed; but shame supplied the place of courage, and he ordered his men to receive Douglas's attack. Sir James assiduously sought his enemy. He at last succeeded; and a single combat ensued, of a most desperate character. But who ever escaped the arm of Douglas when fairly opposed to him in single conflict? Cailon was killed; he had met the Black Knight at last.

"So much," cried Sir James, "for the vaunt of a Gascon!"

Similar in every respect to the fate of Cailon, was that of Sir Ralph Neville. He, too, on hearing the great fame of Douglas's prowess, from some of Cailon's fugitive soldiers, openly boasted that he would fight with the Scottish Knight, if he would come and show his banner before Berwick. Sir James heard the boast and rejoiced in it. He marched to that town, and caused his men to ravage the country in front of the battlements, and burn the villages. Neville left Berwick with a strong body of men; and, stationing himself on a high ground, waited till the rest of the Scots should disperse to plunder; but Douglas called in his detachment and attacked the knight. After a desperate conflict, in which many were slain, Douglas, as was his custom, succeeded in bringing the leader to a personal encounter, and the skill of the Scottish knight was again successful. Neville was slain, and his men utterly discomfited.

Having retired one night to his tent to take some rest after so much pain and toil, Sir James Douglas was surprised by the reappearance of the old woman whom he had seen at Linthaughlee.

"This is the feast o' St. James," said she, as she approached him. "I said I would see ye again this nicht, an' I'm as guid's my word. Hae ye returned the arrows I left wi' ye to the English wha sent them to the hearts o' my sons?"

"No," replied Sir James. "I told ye I did not fight with the bow. Wherefore do ye importune me thus?"

"Give me back the arrows then," said the woman.

Sir James went to bring the quiver in which he had placed them. On taking them out, he was surprised to find that they were all broken through the middle.

"How has this happened?" said he. "I put these arrows in this quiver entire, and now they are broken."

"The weird is fulfilled!" cried the old woman, laughing eldrichly, and clapping her hands. "That broken shaft cam' frae a soldier o' Richmont's; that frae ane o' Cailon's, and that frae ane o' Neville's. They are a' dead, an' I am revenged!"

The old woman then departed, scattering, as she went, the broken fragments of the arrows on the floor of the tent.

# THE LAIRD OF BALMACHIE'S WIFE.

In the olden times, when it was the fashion for gentlemen to wear swords, the Laird of Balmachie went one day to Dundee, leaving his wife at home ill in bed. Riding home in the twilight, he had occasion to leave the high road, and when crossing between some little romantic knolls, called the Cur-hills, in the neighbourhood of Carlungy, he encountered a troop of fairies supporting a kind of litter, upon which some person seemed to be borne. Being a man of dauntless courage, and, as he said, impelled by some internal impulse, he pushed his horse close to the litter, drew his sword, laid it across the vehicle, and in a firm tone exclaimed—

"In the name of God, release your captive."

The tiny troop immediately disappeared, dropping the litter on the ground. The laird dismounted, and found that it contained his own wife, dressed in her bedclothes. Wrapping his coat around her, he placed her on the horse before him, and, having only a short distance to ride, arrived safely at home.

Placing her in another room, under the care of an attentive friend, he immediately went to the chamber where he had left his wife in the morning, and there to all appearance she still lay, very sick of a fever. She was fretful, discontented, and complained much of having been neglected in his absence, at all of which the laird affected great concern, and pretending much sympathy, insisted upon her rising to have her bed made. She said that she was unable to rise, but her husband was peremptory, and having ordered a large wood fire to warm the room, he lifted the impostor from the bed, and bearing her across the floor as if to a chair, which had been previously prepared, he threw her on the fire, from which she bounced like a sky-rocket, and went through the ceiling, and out at the roof of the house, leaving a hole among the slates. He then brought in his own wife, a little recovered from her alarm, who said, that sometime after sunset, the nurse having left her for the purpose of preparing a little candle, a multitude of elves came in at the window, thronging like bees from a hive. They filled the room, and having lifted her from the bed carried her through the window, after which she recollected nothing further, till she saw her husband standing over her on the Cur-hills, at the back of

Carlungy. The hole in the roof, by which the female fairy made her escape, was mended, but could never be kept in repair, as a tempest of wind happened always once a year, which uncovered that particular spot, without injuring any other part of the roof.

# MICHAEL SCOTT.

In the early part of Michael Scott's life he was in the habit of emigrating annually to the Scottish metropolis, for the purpose of being employed in his capacity of mason. One time as he and two companions were journeying to the place of their destination for a similar object, they had occasion to pass over a high hill, the name of which is not mentioned, but which is supposed to have been one of the Grampians, and being fatigued with climbing, they sat down to rest themselves. They had no sooner done so than they were warned to take to their heels by the hissing of a large serpent, which they observed revolving itself towards them with great velocity. Terrified at the sight, Michael's two companions fled, while he, on the contrary, resolved to encounter the reptile. The appalling monster approached Michael Scott with distended mouth and forked tongue; and, throwing itself into a coil at his feet, was raising its head to inflict a mortal sting, when Michael, with one stroke of his stick, severed its body into three pieces. Having rejoined his affrighted comrades, they resumed their journey; and, on arriving at the next public-house, it being late, and the travellers being weary, they took up their quarters at it for the night. In the course of the night's conversation, reference was naturally made to Michael's recent exploit with the serpent, when the landlady of the house, who was remarkable for her "arts," happened to be present. Her curiosity appeared much excited by the conversation; and, after making some inquiries regarding the colour of the serpent, which she was told was white, she offered any of them that would procure her the middle piece such a tempting reward, as induced one of the party instantly to go for it. The distance was not very great; and on reaching the spot, he found the middle and tail piece in the place where Michael left them, but the head piece was gone

The landlady on receiving the piece, which still vibrated with life, seemed highly gratified at her acquisition; and, over and above the promised reward, regaled her lodgers very plentifully with the choicest dainties in her house. Fired with curiosity to know the purpose for which the serpent was intended, the wily Michael Scott was immediately seized with a severe fit of indisposition, which caused him to prefer the request that he might be allowed to sleep beside the fire, the warmth of which, he affirmed, was in the highest degree beneficial to him.

Never suspecting Michael Scott's hypocrisy, and naturally supposing that a person so severely indisposed would feel very little curiosity about the contents of any cooking utensils which might lie around the fire, the landlady allowed his request. As soon as the other inmates of the house were retired to bed, the landlady resorted to her darling occupation; and, in his feigned state of indisposition, Michael had a favourable opportunity of watching most scrupulously all her actions through the keyhole of a door leading to the next apartment where she was. He could see the rites and ceremonies with which the serpent was put into the oven, along with many mysterious ingredients. After which the unsuspicious landlady placed the dish by the fireside, where lay the distressed traveller, to stove till the morning.

Once or twice in the course of the night the "wife of the change-house," under the pretence of inquiring for her sick lodger, and administering to him some renovating cordials, the beneficial effects of which he gratefully acknowledged, took occasion to dip her finger in her saucepan, upon which the cock, perched on his roost, crowed aloud. All Michael's sickness could not prevent him considering very inquisitively the landlady's cantrips, and particularly the influence of the sauce upon the crowing of the cock. Nor could he dissipate some inward desires he felt to follow her example. At the same time, he suspected that Satan had a hand in the pie, yet he thought he would like very much to be at the bottom of the concern; and thus his reason and his curiosity clashed against each other for the space of several hours. At length passion, as is too often the case, became the conqueror. Michael, too, dipped his finger in the sauce, and applied it to the tip of his tongue, and immediately the cock perched on the *spardan* announced the circumstance in a mournful clarion. Instantly his mind received a new light to which he was formerly a stranger, and the astonished dupe of a landlady now found it her interest to admit her sagacious lodger into a knowledge of the remainder of her secrets.

Endowed with the knowledge of "good and evil," and all the "second sights" that can be acquired, Michael left his lodgings in the morning, with the philosopher's stone in his pocket. By daily perfecting his supernatural attainments, by new series of discoveries, he became more than a match for Satan himself. Having seduced some thousands of Satan's best workmen into his employment, he trained them up so successfully to the architective business, and inspired them with such industrious habits, that he was more than sufficient for all the architectural work of the empire. To establish this assertion, we need only refer to some remains of his workmanship still existing north of the Grampians, some of them, stupendous bridges built by him in one short night, with no other visible agents than two or three workmen.

On one occasion work was getting scarce, as might have been naturally expected, and his workmen, as they were wont, flocked to his doors, perpetually exclaiming, "Work! work! work!" Continually annoyed by their incessant entreaties, he called out to them in derision to go and make a dry road from Fortrose to Arderseir, over the Moray Firth. Immediately their cry ceased, and as Scott supposed it wholly impossible for them to execute his order, he retired to rest, laughing most heartily at the chimerical sort of employment he had given to his industrious workmen. Early in the morning, however, he got up and took a walk at the break of day down to the shore to divert himself at the fruitless labours of his zealous workmen. But on reaching the spot, what was his astonishment to find the formidable piece of work allotted to them only a few hours before already nearly finished. Seeing the great damage the commercial class of the community would sustain from the operation, he ordered the workmen to demolish the most part of their work; leaving, however, the point of Fortrose to show the traveller to this day the wonderful exploit of Michael Scott's fairies.

On being thus again thrown out of employment, their former clamour was resumed, nor could Michael Scott, with all his sagacity, devise a plan to keep them in innocent employment. He at length discovered one. "Go," says he, "and manufacture me ropes that will carry me to the back of the moon, of these materials—*miller's-sudds* and sea-sand." Michael Scott here obtained rest from his active operators; for, when other work failed them, he always despatched them to their rope manufactory. But though these agents could never make proper ropes of those materials, their efforts to that effect are far from being contemptible, for some of their ropes are seen by the sea-side to this day.

We shall close our notice of Michael Scott by reciting one anecdote of him in the latter part of his life.

In consequence of a violent quarrel which Michael Scott once had with a person whom he conceived to have caused him some injury, he resolved, as the highest punishment he could inflict upon him, to send his adversary to that evil place designed only for Satan and his black companions. He accordingly, by means of his supernatural machinations, sent the poor unfortunate man thither; and had he been sent by any other means than those of Michael Scott, he would no doubt have met with a warm reception. Out of pure spite to Michael, however, when Satan learned who was his billet-master, he would no more receive him than he would receive the Wife of Beth; and instead of treating the unfortunate man with the harshness characteristic of him, he showed him considerable civilities. Introducing him to his "Ben Taigh," he directed her to show the stranger any curiosities he might wish to see, hinting very significantly that he had provided some accommodation for their mutual friend, Michael Scott, the sight of which might afford him some gratification. The polite housekeeper accordingly conducted the stranger through the principal apartments in the house, where he saw fearful sights. But the bed of Michael Scott!—his greatest enemy could not but feel satiated with revenge at the sight of it. It was a place too horrid to be described, filled promiscuously with all the awful brutes imaginable. Toads and lions, lizards and leeches, and, amongst the rest, not the least conspicuous, a large serpent gaping for Michael Scott, with its mouth wide open. This last sight having satisfied the stranger's curiosity, he was led to the outer gate, and came away. He reached his friends, and, among other pieces of news touching his travels, he was not backward in relating the entertainment that awaited his friend Michael Scott, as soon as he would "stretch his foot" for the other world. But Michael did not at all appear disconcerted at his friend's intelligence. He affirmed that he would disappoint all his enemies in their expectations—in proof of which he gave the following signs: "When I am just dead," says he, "open my breast and extract my heart. Carry it to some place where the public may see the result. You will then transfix it upon a long pole, and if Satan will have my soul, he will come in the likeness of a black raven and carry it off; and if my soul will be saved it will be carried off by a white dove."

His friends faithfully obeyed his instructions. Having exhibited his heart in the manner directed, a large black raven was observed to come from the east with great fleetness, while a white dove came from the west with equal velocity. The raven made a furious dash at the heart, missing which, it was unable to curb its force, till it was considerably past it; and the dove, reaching the spot at the same time, carried off the heart amidst the rejoicing and ejaculations of the spectators.

## THE MINISTER AND THE FAIRY.

Not long since, a pious clergyman was returning home, after administering spiritual consolation to a dying member of his flock. It was late of the night, and he had to pass through a good deal of *uncanny* land. He was, however, a good and a conscientious minister of the Gospel, and feared not all the spirits in the country. On his reaching the end of a lake which stretched along the roadside for some distance, he was a good deal surprised at hearing the most melodious strains of music. Overcome by pleasure and curiosity, the minister coolly sat down to listen to the harmonious sounds, and try what new discoveries he could make with regard to their nature and source. He had not sat many minutes before he could distinguish the approach of the music, and also observe a light in the direction from whence it proceeded gliding across the lake towards him. Instead of taking to his heels, as any faithless wight would have done, the pastor fearlessly determined to await the issue of the phenomenon. As the light and music drew near, the clergyman could at

length distinguish an object resembling a human being walking on the surface of the water, attended by a group of diminutive musicians, some of them bearing lights, and others instruments of music, from which they continued to evoke those melodious strains which first attracted his attention. The leader of the band dismissed his attendants, landed on the beach, and afforded the minister the amplest opportunities of examining his appearance. He was a little primitive-looking grey-headed man, clad in the most grotesque habit the clergyman had ever seen, and such as led him at once to suspect his real character. He walked up to the minister, whom he saluted with great grace, offering an apology for his intrusion. The pastor returned his compliments, and, without further explanation, invited the mysterious stranger to sit down by his side. The invitation was complied with, upon which the minister proposed the following question:—
"Who art thou, stranger, and from whence?"

To this question the fairy, with downcast eye, replied that he was one of those sometimes called *Doune Shee,* or men of peace, or good men, though the reverse of this title was a more fit appellation for them. Originally angelic in his nature and attributes, and once a sharer of the indescribable joys of the regions of light, he was seduced by Satan to join him in his mad conspiracies; and, as a punishment for his transgression, he was cast down from those regions of bliss, and was now doomed, along with millions of fellow-sufferers, to wander through seas and mountains, until the coming of the Great Day. What their fate would be then they could not divine, but they apprehended the worst. "And," continued he, turning to the minister, with great anxiety, "the object of my present intrusion on you is to learn your opinion, as an eminent divine, as to our final condition on that dreadful day."

Here the venerable pastor entered upon a long conversation with the fairy, touching the principles of faith and repentance. Receiving rather unsatisfactory answers to his questions, the minister desired the "sheech" to repeat after him the Paternoster, in attempting to do which, it was not a little remarkable that he could not repeat the word "art," but said "*wert*," in heaven. Inferring from every circumstance that their fate was extremely precarious, the minister resolved not to puff the fairies up with presumptuous, and, perhaps, groundless expectations. Accordingly, addressing himself to the unhappy fairy, who was all anxiety to know the nature of his sentiments, the reverend gentleman told him that he could not take it upon him to give them any hopes of pardon, as their crime was of so deep a hue as scarcely to admit of it. On this the unhappy fairy uttered a shriek of despair, plunged headlong into the loch, and the minister resumed his course to his home.

*Scotch.*

# THE FISHERMAN AND THE MERMAN.

Of mermen and merwomen many strange stories are told in the Shetland Isles. Beneath the depths of the ocean, according to these stories, an atmosphere exists adapted to the respiratory organs of certain beings, resembling, in form, the human race, possessed of surpassing beauty, of limited supernatural powers, and liable to the incident of death. They dwell in a wide territory of the globe, far below the region of fishes, over which the sea, like the cloudy canopy of our sky, loftily rolls, and they possess habitations constructed of the pearl and coral productions of the ocean. Having lungs not adapted to a watery medium, but to the nature of atmospheric air, it would be impossible for them to pass through the volume of waters that intervenes between the submarine and supramarine world, if it were not for the extraordinary power they inherit of entering the skin of some animal capable of existing in the sea, which they are enabled to occupy by a sort of demoniacal possession. One shape they put on, is that of an animal human above the waist, yet terminating below in the tail and fins of a fish, but the most favourite form is that of the larger seal or Haaf-fish; for, in possessing an amphibious nature, they are enabled not only to exist in the ocean, but to land on some rock, where they frequently lighten themselves of their sea-dress, resume their proper shape, and with much curiosity examine the nature of the upper world belonging to the human race. Unfortunately, however, each merman or merwoman possesses but one skin, enabling the individual to ascend the seas, and if, on visiting the abode of man, the garb be lost, the hapless being must unavoidably become an inhabitant of the earth.

A story is told of a boat's crew who landed for the purpose of attacking the seals lying in the hollows of the crags at one of the stacks. The men stunned a number of the animals, and while they were in this state stripped them of their skins, with the fat attached to them. Leaving the carcasses on the rock, the crew were about to set off for the shore of Papa Stour, when such a tremendous swell arose that every one flew quickly to the boat. All succeeded in entering it except one man, who had imprudently lingered behind. The crew were unwilling to leave a companion to perish on the skerries, but the surge increased so fast, that after many unsuccessful attempts to bring the boat close in to the stack the unfortunate wight was left to his fate. A stormy night came on, and the deserted

Shetlander saw no prospect before him but that of perishing from cold and hunger, or of being washed into the sea by the breakers which threatened to dash over the rocks. At length, he perceived many of the seals, who, in their flight had escaped the attack of the boatmen, approach the skerry, disrobe themselves of their amphibious hides, and resume the shape of the sons and daughters of the ocean. Their first object was to assist in the recovery of their friends, who having been stunned by clubs, had, while in that state, been deprived of their skins. When the flayed animals had regained their sensibility, they assumed their proper form of mermen or merwomen, and began to lament in a mournful lay, wildly accompanied by the storm that was raging around, the loss of their sea-dress, which would prevent them from again enjoying their native azure atmosphere, and coral mansions that lay below the deep waters of the Atlantic. But their chief lamentation was for Ollavitinus, the son of Gioga. who, having been stripped of his seal's skin, would be for ever parted from his mates, and condemned to become an outcast inhabitant of the upper world. Their song was at length broken off, by observing one of their enemies viewing, with shivering limbs and looks of comfortless despair, the wild waves that dashed over the stack. Gioga immediately conceived the idea of rendering subservient to the advantage of the son the perilous situation of the man-

She addressed him with mildness, proposing to carry him safe on her back across the sea to Papa Stour, on condition of receiving the seal-skin of Ollavitinus. A bargain was struck, and Gioga clad herself in her amphibious garb; but the Shetlander, alarmed at the sight of the stormy main that he was to ride through, prudently begged leave of the matron, for his better preservation, that he might be allowed to cut a few holes in her shoulders and flanks, in order to procure, between the skin and the flesh, a better fastening for his hands and feet. The request being complied with, the man grasped the neck of the seal, and committing himself to her care, she landed him safely at Acres Gio in Papa Stour; from which place he immediately repaired to a skeo at Hamna Voe, where the skin was deposited, and honourably fulfilled his part of the contract, by affording Gioga the means whereby her son could again revisit the ethereal space over which the sea spread its green mantle.

# THE LAIRD O' CO'.

IN the days of yore, the proprietors of Colzean, in Ayrshire (ancestors of the Marquis of Ailsa), were known in that country by the title of Lairds o' Co', a name bestowed on Colzean from some co's (or coves) in the rock beneath the castle.

One morning, a very little boy, carrying a small wooden can, addressed the Laird near the castle gate, begging for a little ale for his mother, who was sick. The Laird directed him to go to the butler and get his can filled; so away he went as ordered. The butler had a barrel of ale on tap, but about half full, out of which he proceeded to fill the boy's can; but to his extreme surprise he emptied the cask, and still the little can was not nearly full. The butler was unwilling to broach another barrel, but the little fellow insisted on the fulfilment of the Laird's order, and a reference was made to the Laird by the butler, who stated the miraculous capacity of the tiny can, and received instant orders to fill it if all the ale in the cellar would suffice. Obedient to this command, he broached another cask, but had scarcely drawn a drop when the can was full, and the dwarf departed with expressions of gratitude.

Some years afterwards the Laird being at the wars in Flanders was taken prisoner, and for some reason or other (probably as a spy) condemned to die a felon's death. The night prior to the day for his execution, being confined in a dungeon strongly barricaded, the doors suddenly flew open, and the dwarf reappeared, saying—

"Laird o' Co',
Rise an' go."

a summons too welcome to require repetition.

On emerging from prison, the boy caused him to mount on his shoulders, and in a short time set him down at his own gate, on the very spot where they had formerly met, saying—

"Ae gude turn deserves anither—
Tak' ye that for being sae kin' to my auld mither,"

and vanished.

# EWEN OF THE LITTLE HEAD.

About three hundred years ago, Ewen Maclaine of Lochbuy, in the island of Mull, having been engaged in a quarrel with a neighbouring chief, a day was fixed for determining the affair by the sword. Lochbuy, before the day arrived, consulted a celebrated witch as to the result of the feud. The witch declared that if Lochbuy's wife should on the morning of that day give him and his men food unasked, he would be victorious, but if not, the result would be the reverse. This was a disheartening response for the unhappy votary, his wife being a noted shrew.

The fatal morning arrived, and the hour for meeting the enemy approached, but there appeared no symptoms of refreshment for Lochbuy and his men. At length the unfortunate man was compelled to ask his wife to supply them with food. She set down before them curds, but without spoons. When the husband inquired how they were to eat them, she replied they should assume the bills of hens. The men ate the curds, as well as they could, with their hands; but Lochbuy himself ate none. After behaving with the greatest bravery in the bloody conflict which ensued, he fell covered with wounds, leaving his wife to the execration of the people. She is still known in that district under the appellation of Corr-dhu, or the Black Crane.

But the miseries brought on the luckless Lochbuy by his wife did not end with his life, for he died fasting, and his ghost is frequently seen to this day riding the very horse on which he was mounted when he was killed. It was a small, but very neat and active pony, dun or mouse-coloured, to which the Laird was much attached, and on which he had ridden for many years before his death. Its appearance is as accurately described in the island of Mull as any steed is at Newmarket. The prints of its shoes are discerned by connoisseurs, and the rattling of its curb is recognised in the darkest night. It is not particular with regard to roads, for it goes up hill and down dale with equal velocity. Its hard-fated rider still wears the same green cloak which covered him in his last battle; and he is particularly distinguished by the small size of his head, a peculiarity which, we suspect, the learned disciples of Spurzheim have never yet had the sagacity to discover as indicative of an extraordinary talent and incomparable perseverance in horsemanship.

It is now above three hundred years since Ewen-a-chin-vig (*Anglice*, Hugh of the Little Head) fell in the field of honour; but neither the vigour of the horse nor of the rider is yet diminished. His mournful duty has always been to attend the dying moments of every member of his own tribe, and to escort the departed spirit on its long and arduous journey. He has been seen in the remotest of the Hebrides; and he has found his way to Ireland on these occasions long before steam navigation was invented. About a century ago he took a fancy for a young man of his own race, and frequently did him the honour of placing him behind himself on horseback. He entered into conversation with him, and foretold many circumstances connected with the fate of his successors, which have undoubtedly since come to pass.

Many a long winter night have I listened to the feats of Ewen-a-chin-vig, the faithful and indefatigable guardian of his ancient family, in the hour of their last and greatest trial, affording an example worthy the imitation of every chief,—perhaps not beneath the notice of Glengarry himself.

About a dozen years since some symptoms of Ewen's decay gave very general alarm to his friends. He accosted one of his own people (indeed he never has been known to notice any other), and, shaking him cordially by the hand, he attempted to place him on the saddle behind him, but the uncourteous dog declined the honour. Ewen struggled hard, but the clown was a great, strong, clumsy fellow, and stuck to the earth with all his might. He candidly acknowledged, however, that his chief would have prevailed, had it not been for a birch-tree which stood by, and which he got within the fold of his left arm. The contest became very warm indeed, and the tree was certainly twisted like an osier, as thousands can testify who saw it as well as myself. At length, however, Ewen lost his seat for the first time, and the instant the pony found he was his own master, he set off with the fleetness of lightning. Ewen immediately pursued his steed, and the wearied rustic sped his way homeward. It was the general opinion that Ewen found considerable difficulty in catching the horse; but I am happy to learn that he has been lately seen riding the old mouse-coloured pony without the least change in either the horse or the rider. Long may he continue to do so!

Those who from motives of piety or curiosity have visited the sacred island of Iona, must remember to have seen the guide point out the tomb of Ewen, with his figure on horseback, very elegantly sculptured in alto-relievo, and many of the above facts are on such occasions related.

## JOCK AND HIS MOTHER.

YE see, there was a wife had a son, and they called him Jock; and she said to him, "You are a lazy fellow; ye maun gang awa' and do something for to help me." "Weel," says Jock, "I'll do that." So awa' he gangs, and fa's in wi' a packman. Says the packman, "If you carry my pack a' day, I'll gie you a needle at night." So he carried the pack, and got the needle; and as he was gaun awa' hame to his mither, he cuts a burden o' brackens, and put the needle into the heart o' them. Awa' he gaes hame. Says his mither, "What hae ye made o' yoursel' the day?" Says Jock, "I fell in wi' a packman, and carried his pack a' day, and he gae me a needle for't, and ye may look for it amang the brackens." "Hout," quo' she, "ye daft gowk, you should hae stuck it into your bonnet, man." "I'll mind that again," quo' Jock.

Next day he fell in wi' a man carrying plough socks. "If ye help me to carry my socks a' day, I'll gie ye ane to yersel' at night." "I'll do that," quo' Jock. Jock carried them a' day, and got a sock, which he stuck in his bonnet. On the way hame, Jock was dry, and gaed away to take a drink out o' the burn; and wi' the weight o' the sock, his bonnet fell into the river, and gaed out o' sight. He gaed hame, and his mither says, "Weel, Jock, what hae you been doing a' day?" And then he tells her. "Hout," quo' she, "you should hae tied the string to it, and trailed it behind you." "Weel," quo' Jock, "I'll mind that again."

Awa' he sets, and he fa's in wi' a flesher. "Weel," says the flesher, "if ye'll be my servant a' day, I'll gie ye a leg o' mutton at night." "I'll be that," quo' Jock. He got a leg o' mutton at night. He ties a string to it, and trails it behind him the hale road hame. "What hae ye been doing?" said his mither. He tells her. "Hout, you fool, ye should hae carried it on your shouther." "I'll mind that again," quo' Jock.

Awa' he gaes next day, and meets a horse-dealer. He says, "If you will help me wi' my horses a' day, I'll give you ane to yoursel' at night." "I'll do that," quo' Jock. So he served him, and got his horse, and he ties its feet; but as he was not able to carry it on his back, he left it lying on the roadside. Hame he comes, and tells his mither. "Hout, ye daft gowk, ye'll ne'er turn wise! Could ye no hae loupen on it, and ridden it?" "I'll mind that again," quo' Jock.

Aweel, there was a grand gentleman, wha had a

daughter wha was very subject to melancholy; and her father gae out that whaever should mak' her laugh would get her in marriage. So it happened that she was sitting at the window ae day, musing in her melancholy state, when Jock, according to the advice o' his mither, cam' flying up on a cow's back, wi' the tail over his shouther. And she burst out into a fit o' laughter. When they made inquiry wha made her laugh, it was found to be Jock riding on the cow. Accordingly, Jock was sent for to get his bride. Weel, Jock was married to her, and there was a great supper prepared. Amongst the rest o' the things, there was some honey, which Jock was very fond o'. After supper, they all retired, and the auld priest that married them sat up a' night by the kitchen fireside. So Jock waukens in the night-time, and says, "Oh, wad ye gie me some o' yon nice sweet honey that we got to our supper last night?" "Oh ay," says his wife, "rise and gang into the press, and ye'll get a pig fou o't." Jock rose, and thrust his hand into the honey-pig for a nievefu' o't, and he could not get it out. So he cam' awa' wi' the pig in his hand, like a mason's mell, and says, "Oh, I canna get my hand out." "Hoot," quo' she, "gang awa' and break it on the cheek-stane." By this time, the fire was dark, and the auld priest was lying snoring wi' his head against the chimney-piece, wi' a huge white wig on. Jock gaes awa', and gae him a whack wi' the honey-pig on the head, thinking it was the cheek-stane, and knocks it a' in bits. The auld priest roars out, "Murder!" Jock tak's doun the stair as hard as he could bicker, and hides himsel' amang the bees' skeps.

That night, as luck wad have it, some thieves cam' to steal the bees' skeps, and in the hurry o' tumbling them into a large grey plaid, they tumbled Jock in alang wi' them. So aff they set, wi' Jock and the skeps on their backs. On the way, they had to cross the burn where Jock lost his bonnet. Ane o' the thieves cries, "Oh, I hae fand a bonnet!" and Jock, on hearing that, cries out, "Oh, that's mine!" They thocht they had got the deil on their backs. So they let a' fa' in the burn; and Jock, being tied in the plaid, couldna get out; so he and the bees were a' drowned thegither.

If a' tales be true, that's nae lee.

## SAINT COLUMBA.

Soon after Saint Columba established his residence in Iona, tradition says that he paid a visit to a great seminary of Druids, then in the vicinity, at a place called Camusnan Ceul, or Bay of Cells, in the district of Ardnamurchan. Several remains of Druidical circles are still to be seen there, and on that bay and the neighbourhood many places are still named after their rites and ceremonies; such as *Ardintibert*, the Mount of Sacrifice, and others. The fame of the Saint had been for some time well known to the people, and his intention of instructing them in the doctrines of Christianity was announced to them. The ancient priesthood made every exertion to dissuade the inhabitants from hearing the powerful eloquence of Columba, and in this they were seconded by the principal man then in that country, whose name was Donald, a son of Connal.

The Saint had no sooner made his appearance, however, than he was surrounded by a vast multitude, anxious to hear so celebrated a preacher; and after the sermon was ended, many persons expressed a desire to be baptized, in spite of the remonstrances of the Druids. Columba had made choice of an eminence centrally situated for performing worship; but there was no water near the spot, and the son of Connal threatened with punishment any who should dare to procure it for his purpose. The Saint stood with his back leaning on a rock; after a short prayer, he struck the rock with his foot, and a stream of water issued forth in great abundance. The miracle had a powerful effect on the minds of his hearers, and many became converts to the new religion. This fountain is still distinguished by the name of Columba, and is considered of superior efficacy in the cure of diseases. When the Catholic form of worship prevailed in that country it was greatly resorted to, and old persons yet remember to have seen offerings left at the fountain in gratitude for benefits received from the benignant influence of the Saint's blessing on the water. At length it is said that a daughter of Donald, the son of Connal, expressed a wish to be baptized, and the father restrained her by violence. He also, with the aid of the Druids, forced Columba to take refuge in his boat, and the holy man departed for Iona, after warning the inhospitable Caledonian to prepare for another world, as his life would soon terminate.

The Saint was at sea during the whole night, which was stormy; and when approaching the shores of his own sacred island the following morning, a vast number of ravens were observed flying over the boat, chasing another of extraordinary large size. The croaking of the ravens awoke the Saint, who had been sleeping; and he instantly exclaimed that the son of Connal had just expired, which was afterwards ascertained to be true.

A very large Christian establishment appears to have been afterwards formed in the Bay of Cells; and the remains of a chapel, dedicated to Saint Kiaran, are still to be seen there. It is the favourite place of interment among the Catholics of this day. Indeed, Columba and many of his successors seem to have adopted the policy of engrafting their institutions on those which had formerly existed in the country. Of this there are innumerable instances, at least we observe the ruins of both still visible in many places; even in Iona we find the burying-ground of the Druids known at the present day. This practice may have had advantages at the time, but it must have been ultimately productive of many corruptions; and, in a great measure, accounts for many superstitious and absurd customs which prevailed among that people to a very recent period, and which are not yet entirely extinct. In a very ancient family in that country two round balls of coarse glass have been carefully preserved from time immemorial, and to these have been ascribed many virtues—amongst others, the cure of any extraordinary disease among cattle. The balls were immersed in cold water for three days and nights, and the water was afterwards sprinkled over all the cattle; this was expected to cure those affected, and to prevent the disease in the rest. From the names and appearance of these balls, there is no doubt that they had been symbols used by the Archdruids.

Within a short distance of the Bay of Cells there is a cave very remarkable in its appearance, and still more so from the purposes to which it has been appropriated. Saint Columba, on one of his many voyages among the Hebrides, was benighted on this rocky coast, and the mariners were alarmed for their own safety. The Saint assured them that neither he nor his crew would ever be drowned. They unexpectedly discovered a light at no great distance, and to that they directed their course. Columba's boat consisted of a frame of osiers, which was covered with hides of leather, and it was received into a very narrow creek close to this cave. After returning thanks for their escape, the Saint and his people had great difficulty in climbing up to the cave, which is elevated considerably above sea. They at length got sight of the fire which had first attracted their attention. Several persons sat around it, and their appearance was not much calculated to please the holy man. Their aspects were fierce, and they had on the fire some flesh roasting over the coals. The Saint gave them his benediction; and he was invited to sit down among them and to share their hurried repast, with which he gladly complied. They were freebooters, who lived by plunder and robbery, and this Columba soon discovered. He advised them to forsake that course, and to be converted to his doctrines, to which they all assented, and in the morning they accompanied the Saint on his voyage homeward. This circumstance created a high veneration for the cave among the disciples and successors of Columba, and that veneration still continues, in some degree. In one side of it there was a cleft of the rock, where lay the water with which the freebooters had been baptized; and this was afterwards formed by art into a basin, which is supplied with water by drops from the roof of the cave. It is alleged never to be empty or to overflow, and the most salubrious qualities are ascribed to it. To obtain the benefit of it, however, the votaries must undergo a very severe ordeal. They must be in the cave before daylight; they stand on the spot where the Saint first landed his boat, and nine waves must dash over their heads; they must afterwards pass through nine openings in the walls of the cave; and, lastly, they must swallow nine mouthfuls out of the holy basin. After invoking the aid of the Saint, the votaries within three weeks are either relieved by death or by recovery. Offerings are left in a certain place appropriated for that purpose; and these are sometimes of considerable value, nor are they ever abstracted. Strangers are always informed that a young man, who had wantonly taken away some of these not many years since, broke his leg before he got home, and this affords the property of the Saint ample protection.

# THE MERMAID WIFE.

A story is told of an inhabitant of Unst, who, in walking on the sandy margin of a voe, saw a number of mermen and mermaids dancing by moonlight, and several seal-skins strewed beside them on the ground. At his approach they immediately fled to secure their garbs, and, taking upon themselves the form of seals, plunged immediately into the sea. But as the Shetlander perceived that one skin lay close to his feet, he snatched it up, bore it swiftly away, and placed it in concealment. On returning to the shore he met the fairest damsel that was ever gazed upon by mortal eyes, lamenting the robbery, by which she had become an exile from her submarine friends, and a tenant of the upper world. Vainly she implored the restitution of her property; the man had drunk deeply of love, and was inexorable; but he offered her protection beneath his roof as his betrothed spouse. The merlady, perceiving that she must become an inhabitant of the earth, found that she could not do better than accept of the offer. This strange attachment subsisted for many years, and the couple had several children. The Shetlander's love for his merwife was unbounded, but his affection was coldly returned. The lady would often steal alone to the desert strand, and, on a signal being given, a large seal would make his appearance, with whom she would hold, in an unknown tongue, an anxious conference. Years had thus glided away, when it happened that one of the children, in the course of his play, found concealed beneath a stack of corn a seal's skin; and, delighted with the prize, he ran with it to his mother. Her eyes glistened with rapture—she gazed upon it as her own—as the means by which she could pass through the ocean that led to her native home. She burst forth into an ecstasy of joy, which was only moderated when she beheld her children, whom she was now about to leave; and, after hastily embracing them, she fled with all speed towards the seaside. The husband immediately returned, learned the discovery that had taken place, ran to overtake his wife, but only arrived in time to see her transformation of shape completed—to see her, in the form of a seal, bound from the ledge of a rock into the sea. The large animal of the same kind with whom she had held a secret converse soon appeared, and evidently congratulated her, in the most tender manner, on her escape. But before she dived to unknown depths, she cast a parting glance at the wretched Shetlander, whose despairing looks excited in her breast a few transient feelings of commiseration.

"Farewell!" said she to him, "and may all good attend you. I loved you very well when I resided upon earth, but I always loved my first husband much better."

## THE FIDDLER AND THE BOGLE OF BOGANDORAN.

"LATE one night, as my grand-uncle, Lachlan Dhu Macpherson, who was well known as the best fiddler of his day, was returning home from a ball, at which he had acted as a musician, he had occasion to pass through the once-haunted Bog of Torrans. Now, it happened at that time that the bog was frequented by a huge bogle or ghost, who was of a most mischievous disposition, and took particular pleasure in abusing every traveller who had occasion to pass through the place betwixt the twilight at night and cock-crowing in the morning. Suspecting much that he would also come in for a share of his abuse, my grand-uncle made up his mind, in the course of his progress, to return the ghost any *civilities* which he might think meet to offer him. On arriving on the spot, he found his suspicions were too well grounded; for whom did he see but the ghost of Bogandoran apparently ready waiting him, and seeming by his ghastly grin not a little overjoyed at the meeting. Marching up to my grand-uncle, the bogle clapped a huge club into his hand, and furnishing himself with one of the same dimensions, he put a spittle in his hand, and deliberately commenced the combat. My grand-uncle returned the salute with equal spirit, and so ably did both parties ply their batons that for a while the issue of the combat was extremely doubtful. At length, however, the fiddler could easily discover that his opponent's vigour was much in the fagging order. Picking up renewed courage in consequence, he plied the ghost with renewed force, and after a stout resistance, in the course of which both parties were seriously handled, the ghost of Bogandoran thought it prudent to give up the night.

"At the same time, filled no doubt with great indignation at this signal defeat, it seems the ghost resolved to re-engage my grand-uncle on some other occasion, under more favourable circumstances. Not long after, as my grand-uncle was returning home quite unattended from another ball in the Braes of the country, he had just entered the hollow of Auldichoish, well known for its 'eerie' properties, when, lo! who presented himself to his view on the adjacent eminence but his old friend of Bogandoran, advancing as large as the gable of a house, and putting himself in the most threatening and fighting attitudes.

"Looking at the very dangerous nature of the ground where they had met, and feeling no anxiety for a second encounter with a combatant of his weight, in a situation so little desirable, the fiddler would have willingly deferred the settlement of their differences till a more convenient season. He, accordingly, assuming the most submissive aspect in the world, endeavoured to pass by his champion in peace, but in vain. Longing, no doubt, to retrieve the disgrace of his late discomfiture, the bogle instantly seized the fiddler, and attempted with all his might to pull the latter down the precipice, with the diabolical intention, it is supposed, of drowning him in the river Avon below. In this pious design the bogle was happily frustrated by the intervention of some trees which grew on the precipice, and to which my unhappy grand-uncle clung with the zeal of a drowning man. The enraged ghost, finding it impossible to extricate him from those friendly trees, and resolving, at all events, to be revenged upon him, fell upon maltreating the fiddler with his hands and feet in the most inhuman manner.

"Such gross indignities my worthy grand-uncle was not accustomed to, and being incensed beyond all measure at the liberties taken by Bogandoran, he resolved again to try his mettle, whether life or death should be the consequence. Having no other weapon wherewith to defend himself but his *biodag*, which, considering the nature of his opponent's constitution, he suspected much would be of little avail to him—I say, in the absence of any other weapon, he sheathed the *biodag* three times in the ghost of Bogandoran's body. And what was the consequence? Why, to the great astonishment of my courageous forefather, the ghost fell down cold dead at his feet, and was never more seen or heard of."

# THOMAS THE RHYMER.

Thomas, of Ercildoun, in Lauderdale, called the Rhymer, on account of his producing a poetical romance on the subject of Tristrem and Yseult, which is curious as the earliest specimen of English verse known to exist, flourished in the reign of Alexander III. of Scotland. Like other men of talent of the period, Thomas was suspected of magic. He was also said to have the gift of prophecy, which was accounted for in the following peculiar manner, referring entirely to the Elfin superstition.

As Thomas lay on Huntly Bank (a place on the descent of the Eildon Hills, which raise their triple crest above the celebrated monastery of Melrose), he saw a lady so extremely beautiful that he imagined she must be the Virgin Mary herself. Her appointments, however, were those rather of an amazon, or goddess of the woods. Her steed was of the highest beauty, and at its mane hung thirty silver bells and nine, which were music to the wind as she paced along. Her saddle was of "royal bone" (ivory), laid over with "orfeverie" (goldsmith's work). Her stirrups, her dress, all corresponded with her extreme beauty and the magnificence of her array. The fair huntress had her bow in hand, and her arrows at her belt. She led three greyhounds in a leash, and three raches, or hounds of scent, followed her closely.

She rejected and disclaimed the homage which Thomas desired to pay her; so that, passing from one extremity to the other, Thomas became as bold as he had at first been humble. The lady warned him he must become her slave if he wished to prosecute his suit. Before their interview terminated, the appearance of the beautiful lady was changed into that of the most hideous hag in existence. A witch from the spital or almshouse would have been a goddess in comparison to the late beautiful huntress. Hideous as she was, Thomas felt that he had placed himself in the power of this hag, and when she bade him take leave of the sun, and of the leaf that grew on the tree, he felt himself under the necessity of obeying her. A cavern received them, in which, following his frightful guide, he for three days travelled in darkness, sometimes hearing the booming of a distant ocean, sometimes walking through rivers of blood, which crossed their subterranean path. At length they emerged into daylight, in a most beautiful orchard. Thomas, almost fainting for want of food, stretched out his hand towards the goodly fruit which hung around him, but was forbidden by his conductress, who informed him that these were the fatal apples which were the cause of the fall of man. He perceived also that his guide had no sooner entered this mysterious ground and breathed its magic air than she was revived in beauty, equipage, and splendour, as fair or fairer than he had first seen her on the mountain. She then proceeded to explain to him the character of the country.

"Yonder right-hand path," she says, "conveys the spirits of the blest to paradise. You downward and well-worn way leads sinful souls to the place of everlasting punishment. The third road, by yonder dark brake, conducts to the milder place of pain, from which prayer and mass may release offenders. But see you yet a fourth road, sweeping along the plain to yonder splendid castle? Yonder is the road to Elfland, to which we are now bound. The lord of the castle is king of the country, and I am his queen; and when we enter yonder castle, you must observe strict silence, and answer no question that is asked you, and I will account for your silence by saying I took your speech when I brought you from middle earth."

Having thus instructed him, they journeyed on to the castle, and, entering by the kitchen, found themselves in the midst of such a festive scene as might become the mansion of a great feudal lord or prince.

Thirty carcasses of deer were lying on the massive kitchen board, under the hands of numerous cooks, who toiled to cut them up and dress them, while the gigantic greyhounds which had taken the spoil lay lapping the blood, and enjoying the sight of the slain game. They came next to the royal hall, where the king received his loving consort; knights and ladies, dancing by threes, occupied the floor of the hall; and Thomas, the fatigue of his journey from the Eildon Hills forgotten, went forward and joined in the revelry. After a period, however, which seemed to him a very short one, the queen spoke with him apart, and bade him prepare to return to his own country.

"Now," said the queen, "how long think you that you have been here?"

"Certes, fair lady," answered Thomas, "not above these seven days."

"You are deceived," answered the queen; "you have been seven years in this castle, and it is full time you were gone. Know, Thomas, that the archfiend will come to this castle to-morrow to demand his tribute, and so handsome a man as you will attract his eye. For all the world would I not suffer you to be betrayed to such a fate; therefore up, and let us be going."

This terrible news reconciled Thomas to his departure from Elfinland; and the queen was not long in placing him upon Huntly Bank, where the birds were singing. She took leave of him, and to ensure his reputation bestowed on him the tongue which *could not lie*. Thomas in vain objected to this inconvenient and involuntary adhesion to veracity, which would make him, as he thought, unfit for church or for market, for king's court or for lady's bower. But all his remonstrances were disregarded by the lady; and Thomas the Rhymer, whenever the discourse turned on the future, gained the credit of a prophet whether he would or not, for he could say nothing but what was sure to come to pass.

Thomas remained several years in his own tower near Ercildoun, and enjoyed the fame of his predictions, several of which are current among the country people to this day. At length, as the prophet was entertaining the Earl of March in his dwelling, a cry of astonishment arose in the village, on the appearance of a hart and hind, which left the forest, and, contrary to their shy nature, came quietly onward, traversing the village towards the dwelling of Thomas. The prophet instantly rose from the board, and acknowledging the prodigy as the summons of his fate, he accompanied the hart and hind into the forest, and though occasionally seen by individuals to whom he has chosen to show himself, he has never again mixed familiarly with mankind.

*Scotch.*

# FAIRY FRIENDS.

It is a good thing to befriend the fairies, as the following stories show :—

There have been from time immemorial at Hawick, during the two or three last weeks of the year, markets once a week, for the disposal of sheep for slaughter, at which the greater number of people, both in the middle and poorer classes of life, have been accustomed to provide themselves with their *marts*. A poor man from Jedburgh who was on his way to Hawick for the purpose of attending one of these markets, as he was passing over that side of Rubislaw which is nearest the Teviot, was suddenly alarmed by a frightful and unaccountable noise. The sound, as he supposed, proceeded from an immense number of female voices, but no objects whence it could come were visible. Amidst howling and wailing were mixed shouts of mirth and jollity, but he could gather nothing articulate except the following words—

"O there's a bairn born, but there's naething to pit on 't."

The occasion of this elfish concert, it seemed, was the birth of a fairy child, at which the fairies, with the exception of two or three who were discomposed at having nothing to cover the little innocent with, were enjoying themselves with that joviality usually characteristic of such an event. The astonished rustic finding himself amongst a host of invisible beings, in a wild moorland place, and far from any human assistance, should assistance be required, full of the greatest consternation, immediately on hearing this expression again and again vociferated, stripped off his plaid, and threw it on the ground. It was instantly snatched up by an invisible hand, and the wailings immediately ceased, but the shouts of mirth were continued with increased vigour. Being of opinion that what he had done had satisfied his invisible friends, he lost no time in making off, and proceeded on his road to Hawick, musing on his singular adventure. He purchased a sheep, which turned out a remarkably good bargain, and returned to Jedburgh. He had no cause to regret his generosity in bestowing his plaid on the fairies, for every day afterwards his wealth multiplied, and he continued till the day of his death a rich and prosperous man.

About the beginning of harvest, there having been a want of meal for *shearers'* bread in the farmhouse of Bedrule, a small quantity of barley (being all that was yet ripe) was cut down, and converted into meal. Mrs. Buckham, the farmer's wife, rose early in the morning to bake the bread, and, while she was engaged in baking, a little woman in green costume came in, and, with much politeness, asked for a loan of a capful of meal. Mrs. Buckham thought it prudent to comply with her request. In a short time afterwards the woman in green returned with an equal quantity of meal, which Mrs. Buckham put into the *meal-ark*. This meal had such a lasting quality, that from it alone the gudewife of Bedrule baked as much bread as served her own family and the reapers throughout the harvest, and when harvest was over it was not exhausted.

# THE SEAL-CATCHER'S ADVENTURE.

THERE was once upon a time a man who lived upon the northern coasts, not far from "Taigh Jan Crot Callow" (John-o'-Groat's House), and he gained his livelihood by catching and killing fish, of all sizes and denominations. He had a particular liking for the killing of those wonderful beasts, half dog half fish, called "Roane," or seals, no doubt because he got a long price for their skins, which are not less curious than they are valuable. The truth is, that the most of these animals are neither dogs nor cods, but downright fairies, as this narration will show; and, indeed, it is easy for any man to convince himself of the fact by a simple examination of his *tobacco-spluichdan*, for the dead skins of those beings are never the same for four-and-twenty hours together. Sometimes the *spluichdan* will erect its bristles almost perpendicularly, while, at other times, it reclines them even down; one time it resembles a bristly sow, at another time a *sleekit cat*; and what dead skin, except itself, could perform such cantrips? Now, it happened one day, as this notable fisher had returned from the prosecution of his calling, that he was called upon by a man who seemed a great stranger, and who said he had been despatched for him by a person who wished to contract for a quantity of seal-skins, and that the fisher must accompany him (the stranger) immediately to see the person who wished to contract for the skins, as it was necessary that he should be served that evening. Happy in the prospect of making a good bargain, and never suspecting any duplicity, he instantly complied. They both mounted a steed belonging to the stranger, and took the road with such velocity that, although the direction of the wind was towards their backs, yet the fleetness of their movement made it appear as if it had been in their faces. On reaching a stupendous precipice which overhung the sea, his guide told him they had now reached their destination.

"Where is the person you spoke of?" inquired the astonished seal-killer.

"You shall see that presently," replied the guide.

With that they immediately alighted, and, without allowing the seal-killer much time to indulge the frightful suspicions that began to pervade his mind, the stranger seized him with irresistible force, and plunged headlong with him into the sea. After sinking down, down, nobody knows how far, they at length reached a door, which, being open, led them into a range of apartments, filled with inhabitants—not people, but seals, who could nevertheless speak and feel like human folk; and how much was the seal-killer surprised to find that he himself had been unconsciously transformed into the like image. If it were not so, he would probably have died from the want of breath. The nature of the poor fisher's thoughts may be more easily conceived than described. Looking at the nature of the quarters into which he had landed, all hopes of escape from them appeared wholly chimerical, whilst the degree of comfort, and length of life which the barren scene promised him were far from being flattering. The "Roane," who all seemed in very low spirits, appeared to feel for him, and endeavoured to soothe the distress which he evinced by the amplest assurances of personal safety. Involved in sad meditation on his evil fate, he was quickly roused from his stupor by his guide's producing a huge gully or joctaleg, the object of which he supposed was to put an end to all his earthly cares. Forlorn as was his situation, however, he did not wish to be killed; and, apprehending instant destruction, he fell down, and earnestly implored for mercy. The poor generous animals did not mean him any harm, however much his former conduct deserved it, and he was accordingly desired to pacify himself, and cease his cries.

"Did you ever see that knife before?" said the stranger to the fisher.

The latter instantly recognised his own knife, which he had that day stuck into a seal, and with which it had escaped, and acknowledged it was formerly his own, for what would be the use of denying it?

"Well," rejoined the guide, "the apparent seal which made away with it is my father, who has lain dangerously ill ever since, and no means can stay his fleeting breath without your aid. I have been obliged to resort to the artifice I have practised to bring you hither, and I trust that my filial duty to my father will readily excuse me."

Having said this, he led into another apartment the trembling seal-killer, who expected every minute to be punished for his own ill-treatment of the father. There he found the identical seal with which he had had the encounter in the morning, suffering most grievously from a tremendous cut in its hind-quarter. The seal-killer was then desired, with his hand, to cicatrise the wound, upon doing which it immediately healed, and the seal arose from its bed in perfect health. Upon this the scene changed from mourning to rejoicing—all was mirth and glee. Very different, however, were the feelings of the unfortunate seal-catcher, who expected no doubt to be metamorphosed into a seal for the remainder of his life. However, his late guide accosting him, said—

"Now, sir, you are at liberty to return to your

wife and family, to whom I am about to conduct you; but it is on this express condition, to which you must bind yourself by a solemn oath, viz. that you will never maim or kill a seal in all your lifetime hereafter."

To this condition, hard as it was, he joyfully acceded; and the oath being administered in all due form, he bade his new acquaintance most heartily and sincerely a long farewell. Taking hold of his guide, they issued from the place and swam up, till they regained the surface of the sea, and, landing at the said stupendous pinnacle, they found their former steed ready for a second canter. The guide breathed upon the fisher, and they became like men. They mounted their horse, and fleet as had been their course towards the precipice, their return from it was doubly swift; and the honest seal-killer was laid down at his own door-cheek, where his guide made him such a present as would have almost reconciled him to another similar expedition, such as rendered his loss of profession, in so far as regarded the seals, a far less intolerable hardship than he had at first considered it.

## THE FAIRIES OF MERLIN'S CRAIG.

EARLY in the seventeenth century, John Smith, a barn-man at a farm, was sent by his master to cast divots (turf) on the green immediately behind Merlin's Craig. After having laboured for a considerable time, there came round from the front of the rock a little woman, about eighteen inches in height, clad in a green gown and red stockings, with long yellow hair hanging down to her waist, who asked the astonished operator how he would feel were she to send her husband to *tir* (uncover) his house, at the same time commanding him to place every *divot* he had cast *in statu quo*. John obeyed with fear and trembling, and, returning to his master, told what had happened. The farmer laughed at his credulity, and, anxious to cure him of such idle superstition, ordered him to take a cart and fetch home the *divots* immediately.

John obeyed, although with much reluctance. Nothing happened to him in consequence till that day twelve months, when he left his master's work at the usual hour in the evening, with a small *stoup* of milk in his hand, but he did not reach home, nor was he ever heard of for years (I have forgotten how many), when, upon the anniversary of that unfortunate day, John walked into his house at the usual hour, with the milk-stoup in his hand.

The account that he gave of his captivity was that, on the evening of that eventful day, returning home from his labour, when passing Merlin's Craig, he felt himself suddenly taken ill, and sat down to rest a little. Soon after he fell asleep, and awoke, as he supposed, about midnight, when there was a troop of male and female fairies dancing round him. They insisted upon his joining in the sport, and gave him the finest girl in the company as a partner. She took him by the hand; they danced three times round in a fairy ring, after which he became so happy that he felt no inclination to leave his new associates. Their amusements were protracted till he heard his master's cock crow, when the whole troop immediately rushed forward to the front of the craig, hurrying him along with them. A door opened to receive them, and he continued a prisoner until the evening on which he returned, when the same woman who had first appeared to him when casting *divots* came and told him that the grass was again green on the roof of her house, which he had *tirred*, and if he would swear an oath, which she dictated, never to discover what he had seen in fairyland, he should be at liberty to return to his family.

John took the oath, and observed it most religiously, although sadly teased and questioned by his helpmate, particularly about the "bonnie lassie" with whom he danced on the night of his departure. He was also observed to walk a mile out of his way rather than pass Merlin's Craig when the sun was below the horizon.

On a subsequent occasion the tiny inhabitants of Merlin's Craig surprised a shepherd when watching his fold at night; he was asleep, and his bonnet had fallen off and rolled to some little distance. He was awakened by the fairies dancing round him in a circle, and was induced to join them; but recollecting the fate of John Smith, he would not allow his female companion to take hold of his hands. In the midst of their gambols they came close to the hillock where the shepherd's bonnet lay,—he affected to stumble, fell upon his bonnet, which he immediately seized, clapping it on his head, when the whole troop instantly vanished. This exorcism was produced by the talismanic power of a Catechism containing the Lord's Prayer and the Apostles' Creed, which the shepherd most fortunately recollected was deposited in the crown of his bonnet.

# RORY MACGILLIVRAY.

ONCE upon a time a tenant in the neighbourhood of Cairngorm, in Strathspey, emigrated with his family and cattle to the forest of Glenavon, which is well known to be inhabited by many fairies as well as ghosts. Two of his sons being out late one night in search of some of their sheep which had strayed, had occasion to pass a fairy turret, or dwelling, of very large dimensions; and what was their astonishment on observing streams of the most refulgent light shining forth through innumerable crevices in the rock—crevices which the sharpest eye in the country had never seen before. Curiosity led them towards the turret, when they were charmed by the most exquisite sounds ever emitted by a fiddle-string, which, joined to the sportive mirth and glee accompanying it, reconciled them in a great measure to the scene, although they knew well enough the inhabitants of the nook were fairies. Nay, overpowered by the enchanting jigs played by the fiddler, one of the brothers had even the hardihood to propose that they should pay the occupants of the turret a short visit. To this motion the otner brother, fond as he was of dancing, and animated as he was by the music, would by no means consent, and he earnestly desired his brother to restrain his curiosity. But every new jig that was played, and every new reel that was danced, inspired the adventurous brother with additional ardour, and at length, completely fascinated by the enchanting revelry, leaving all prudence behind, at one leap he entered the "Shian." The poor forlorn brother was now left in a most uncomfortable situation. His grief for the loss of a brother whom he dearly loved suggested to him more than once the desperate idea of sharing his fate by following his example. But, on the other hand, when he coolly considered the possibility of sharing very different entertainment from that which rang upon his ears, and remembered, too, the comforts and convenience of his father's fireside, the idea immediately appeared to him anything but prudent. After a long and disagreeable altercation between his affection for his brother and his regard for himself, he came to the resolution to take a middle course, that is, to shout in at the window a few remonstrances to his brother, which, if he did not attend to, let the consequences be upon his own head. Accordingly, taking his station at one of the crevices, and calling upon his brother three several times by name, as use is, he uttered the most moving pieces of elocution he could think of, imploring him, as he valued his poor parents' life and blessing, to come forth and go home with him, Donald Macgillivray, his thrice affectionate and unhappy brother. But whether it was the dancer could not hear this eloquent harangue, or, what is more probable, that he did not choose to attend to it, certain it is that it proved totally ineffectual to accomplish its object, and the consequence was that Donald Macgillivray found it equally his duty and his interest to return home to his family with the melancholy tale of poor Rory's fate. All the prescribed ceremonies calculated to rescue him from the fairy dominion were resorted to by his mourning relatives without effect, and Rory was supposed lost for ever, when a "wise man" of the day having learned the circumstance, discovered to his friends a plan by which they might deliver him at the end of twelve months from his entry.

"Return," says the *Duin Glichd* to Donald, "to the place where you lost your brother a year and a day from the time. You will insert in your garment a *Rowan Cross*, which will protect you from the fairies' interposition. Enter the turret boldly and resolutely in the name of the Highest, claim your brother, and, if he does not accompany you voluntarily, seize him and carry him off by force—none dare interfere with you."

The experiment appeared to the cautious contemplative brother as one that was fraught with no ordinary danger, and he would have most willingly declined the prominent character allotted to him in the performance but for the importunate entreaty of his friends, who implored him, as he valued their blessing, not to slight such excellent advice. Their entreaties, together with his confidence in the virtues of the *Rowan Cross*, overcame his scruples, and he at length agreed to put the experiment in practice, whatever the result might be.

Well, then, the important day arrived, when the father of the two sons was destined either to recover his lost son, or to lose the only son he had, and, anxious as the father felt, Donald Macgillivray, the intended adventurer, felt no less so on the occasion. The hour of midnight approached when the drama was to be acted, and Donald Macgillivray, loaded with all the charms and benedictions in his country, took mournful leave of his friends, and proceeded to the scene of his intended enterprise. On approaching the well-known turret, a repetition of that mirth and those ravishing sounds, that had been the source of so much sorrow to himself and family, once more attracted his attention, without at all creating in his mind any extraordinary feelings of satisfaction. On the contrary, he abhorred the sounds most heartily, and felt much greater inclination to recede than to advance. But what was to be done? Courage, character, and everything dear to him were at stake, so that to advance was his only alternative. In short, he reached the "Shian," and, after twenty fruitless attempts, he at length entered the place with trembling footsteps, and amidst the brilliant and jovial scene the not least gratifying spectacle which presented itself to Donald was his brother Rory earnestly engaged at the Highland fling on the floor, at which, as might have been expected, he had greatly improved. Without losing much time in satisfying his curiosity by examining the quality of the company, Donald ran to his brother, repeating, most vehemently, the words prescribed to him by the "wise man," seized him by the collar, and insisted on his immediately accompanying him home to his poor afflicted parents. Rory assented, provided he would allow him to finish his single reel, assuring Donald, very earnestly, that he had not been half an hour in the house. In vain did the latter assure him that, instead of half an hour, he had actually remained twelve months. Nor would he have believed his overjoyed friends when his brother at length got him home, did not the calves, now grown into stots, and the new-born babes, now travelling the house, at length convince him that in his single reel he had danced for a twelvemonth and a day.

# THE HAUNTED SHIPS.

> "Though my mind's not
> Hoodwinked with rustic marvels, I do think
> There are more things in the grove, the air, the flood,
> Yea, and the charnelled earth, than what wise man,
> Who walks so proud as if his form alone
> Filled the wide temple of the universe,
> Will let a frail mind say. I'd write i' the creed
> O' the sagest head alive, that fearful forms,
> Holy or reprobate, do page men's heels;
> That shapes, too horrid for our gaze, stand o'er
> The murderer's dust, and for revenge glare up,
> Even till the stars weep fire for very pity."

ALONG the sea of Solway, romantic on the Scottish side, with its woodland, its bays, its cliffs, and headlands; and interesting on the English side, with its many beautiful towns with their shadows on the water, rich pastures, safe harbours, and numerous ships, there still linger many traditional stories of a maritime nature, most of them connected with superstitions singularly wild and unusual. To the curious these tales afford a rich fund of entertainment, from the many diversities of the same story; some dry and barren, and stripped of all the embellishments of poetry; others dressed out in all the riches of a superstitious belief and haunted imagination. In this they resemble the inland traditions of the peasants; but many of the oral treasures of the Galwegian or the Cumbrian coast have the stamp of the Dane and the Norseman upon them, and claim but a remote or faint affinity with the legitimate legends of Caledonia. Something like a rude prosaic outline of several of the most noted of the northern ballads, the adventures and depredations of the old ocean kings, still lends life to the evening tale; and, among others, the story of the Haunted Ships is still popular among the maritime peasantry.

One fine harvest evening I went on board the shallop of Richard Faulder, of Allanbay, and, committing ourselves to the waters, we allowed a gentle wind from the east to waft us at its pleasure towards the Scottish coast. We passed the sharp promontory of Siddick, and, skirting the land within a stonecast, glided along the shore till we came within sight of the ruined Abbey of Sweetheart. The green mountain of Criffel ascended beside us; and the bleat of the flocks from its summit, together with the winding of the evening horn of the reapers, came softened into something like music over land and sea. We pushed our shallop into a deep and wooded bay, and sat silently looking on the serene beauty of the place. The moon glimmered in her rising through the tall shafts of the pines of Caerlaverock; and the sky, with scarce a cloud, showered down on wood and headland and bay the twinkling beams of a thousand stars, rendering every object visible. The tide, too, was coming with that swift and silent swell observable when the wind is gentle; the woody curves along the land were filling with the flood, till it touched the green branches of the drooping trees; while in the centre current the roll and the plunge of a thousand pellocks told to the experienced fisherman that salmon were abundant.

As we looked, we saw an old man emerging from a path that wound to the shore through a grove of doddered hazel; he carried a halve-net on his back, while behind him came a girl, bearing a small harpoon, with which the fishers are remarkably dexterous in striking their prey. The senior seated himself on a large grey stone, which overlooked the bay, laid aside his bonnet, and submitted his bosom and neck to the refreshing sea breeze, and, taking his harpoon from his attendant, sat with the gravity and composure of a spirit of the flood, with his ministering nymph behind him. We pushed our shallop to the shore, and soon stood at their side.

"This is old Mark Macmoran the mariner, with his granddaughter Barbara," said Richard Faulder, in a whisper that had something of fear in it; "he knows every creek and cavern and quicksand in Solway; has seen the Spectre Hound that haunts the Isle of Man; has heard him bark, and at every bark has seen a ship sink; and he has seen, too, the Haunted Ships in full sail; and, if all tales be true, he has sailed in them himself;—he's an awful person."

Though I perceived in the communication of my friend something of the superstition of the sailor, I could not help thinking that common rumour had made a happy choice in singling out old Mark to maintain her intercourse with the invisible world. His hair, which seemed to have refused all intercourse with the comb, hung matted upon his shoulders; a kind of mantle, or rather blanket, pinned with a wooden skewer round his neck, fell mid-leg down, concealing all his nether garments as far as a pair of hose, darned with yarn of all conceivable colours, and a pair of shoes, patched and repaired till nothing of the original structure remained, and clasped on his feet with two massy silver buckles. If the dress of the old man was rude and sordid, that of his granddaughter was gay, and even rich. She wore a bodice of fine wool, wrought round the bosom with alternate leaf and lily, and a kirtle of the same fabric, which, almost touching her white and delicate ankle, showed her snowy feet, so fairy-light and round that they scarcely seemed to touch the grass where she stood. Her hair, a natural ornament which woman seeks much to improve, was of bright glossy brown, and encumbered rather than adorned with a snood, set thick with marine productions, among which the small clear pearl found in the Solway was conspicuous. Nature had not trusted to a handsome shape and a sylph-like air for young Barbara's influence over the heart of man, but had bestowed a pair of large bright blue eyes, swimming in liquid light, so full of love and gentleness and joy, that all the sailors from Annanwater to far Saint Bees acknowledged their power, and sang songs about the bonnie lass of Mark Macmoran. She stood holding a small gaff-hook of polished steel in her hand, and seemed not dissatisfied with the glances I bestowed on her from time to time, and which I held more than requited by a single glance of those eyes which retained so many capricious hearts in subjection.

The tide, though rapidly augmenting, had not yet filled the bay at our feet. The moon now streamed fairly over the tops of Caerlaverock pines, and showed the expanse of ocean dimpling and swelling, on which sloops and shallops came dancing, and displaying at every turn their extent of white sail against the beam of the moon. I looked on old Mark the mariner, who, seated motionless on his grey stone, kept his eye fixed on the increasing waters with a look of seriousness and sorrow, in which I saw little of the calculating spirit of a mere fisherman. Though he looked on the coming tide, his eyes seemed to dwell particularly on the black and decayed hulls of two vessels, which, half immersed in the quicksand, still addressed to every heart a tale of shipwreck and desolation. The tide wheeled and foamed around them, and, creeping inch by inch up the side, at last fairly threw its waters over the top, and a long and hollow eddy showed the resistance which the liquid element received.

The moment they were fairly buried in the water, the old man clasped his hands together, and said: "Blessed be the tide that will break over and bury ye for ever! Sad to mariners, and sorrowful to maids and mothers, has the time been you have choked up this deep and bonnie bay. For evil were you sent, and for evil have you continued. Every season finds from you its song of sorrow and wail, its funeral processions, and its shrouded corses. Woe to the land where the wood grew that made ye! Cursed be the axe that hewed ye on the mountains, the hands that joined ye together, the bay that ye first swam in, and the wind that wafted ye here! Seven times have ye put my life in peril, three fair sons have ye swept from my side, and two bonnie grand-bairns; and now, even now, your waters foam and flash for my destruction, did I venture my infirm limbs in quest of food in your deadly bay. I see by that ripple and that foam, and hear by the sound and singing of your surge, that ye yearn for another victim; but it shall not be me nor mine."

Even as the old mariner addressed himself to the wrecked ships, a young man appeared at the southern extremity of the bay, holding his halve-net in his hand, and hastening into the current. Mark rose and shouted, and waved him back from a place which, to a person unacquainted with the dangers of the bay, real and superstitious, seemed sufficiently perilous; his granddaughter, too, added her voice to his, and waved her white hands; but the more they strove, the faster advanced the peasant, till he stood to his middle in the water, while the tide increased every moment in depth and strength. "Andrew, Andrew," cried the young woman, in a voice quavering with emotion, "turn, turn, I tell you! O the Ships, the Haunted Ships!" But the appearance of a fine run of fish had more influence with the peasant than the voice of bonnie Barbara, and forward he dashed, net in hand. In a moment he was borne off his feet, and mingled like foam with the water, and hurried towards the fatal eddies which whirled and roared round the sunken ships. But he was a powerful young man, and an expert swimmer; he seized on one of the projecting ribs of the nearest hulk, and clinging to it with the grasp of despair, uttered yell after yell, sustaining himself against the prodigious rush of the current.

From a shealing of turf and straw, within the pitch of a bar from the spot where we stood, came out an old woman bent with age, and leaning on a crutch. "I heard the voice of that lad Andrew Lammie; can the chield be drowning that he skirls sae uncannily?" said the old woman, seating herself on the ground, and looking earnestly at the water. "Ou, ay," she continued, "he's doomed, he's doomed; heart and hand can never save him; boats, ropes, and man's strength and wit, all vain! vain! —he's doomed, he's doomed!"

By this time I had thrown myself into the shallop, followed reluctantly by Richard Faulder, over whose courage and kindness of heart superstition had great power, and with one push from the shore, and some exertion in sculling, we came within a quoitcast of the unfortunate fisherman. He stayed not to profit by our aid; for, when he perceived us near, he uttered a piercing shriek of joy, and bounded towards us through the agitated element the full length of an oar. I saw him for a second on the surface of the water, but the eddying current sucked him down; and all I ever beheld of him again was his hand held above the flood, and clutching in agony at some imaginary aid. I sat gazing in horror on the vacant sea before us; but a breathing-time before, a human being, full of youth and strength and hope, was there; his cries were still ringing in my ears, and echoing in the woods; and now nothing was seen or heard save the turbulent expanse of water, and the sound of its chafing on the shores. We pushed back our shallop, and resumed our station on the cliff beside the old mariner and his descendant.

"Wherefore sought ye to peril your own lives fruitlessly," said Mark, "in attempting to save the doomed? Whoso touches those infernal ships never survives to tell the tale. Woe to the man who is found nigh them at midnight when the tide has subsided, and they arise in their former beauty, with forecastle, and deck, and sail, and pennon, and shroud! Then is seen the streaming of lights along the water from their cabin windows, and then is heard the sound of mirth and the clamour of tongues, and the infernal whoop and halloo and song, ringing far and wide. Woe to the man who comes nigh them!"

To all this my Allanbay companion listened with a breathless attention. I felt something touched with a superstition to which I partly believed I had seen one victim offered up; and I inquired of the old mariner, "How and when came these Haunted Ships there? To me they seem but the melancholy relics of some unhappy voyagers, and much more likely to warn people to shun destruction than entice and delude them to it."

"And so," said the old man with a smile, which had more of sorrow in it than of mirth; "and so, young man, these black and shattered hulks seem to the eye of the multitude. But things are not what they seem: that water, a kind and convenient servant to the wants of man, which seems so smooth and so dimpling and so gentle, has swallowed up a human soul even now; and the place which it covers, so fair and so level, is a faithless quicksand, out of which none escape. Things are otherwise than they seem. Had you lived as long as I have had the sorrow to live; had you seen the storms, and braved the perils, and endured the distresses which have befallen me; had you sat gazing out on the dreary ocean at midnight on a haunted coast; had you seen comrade after comrade, brother after brother, and son after son, swept away by the merciless ocean from your very side; had you seen the shapes of friends, doomed to the wave and the quicksand, appearing to you in the dreams and visions of the night, then would your mind have been prepared for crediting the maritime legends of mariners; and the two haunted Danish ships would have had their terrors for you, as they have for all who sojourn on this coast.

"Of the time and the cause of their destruction," continued the old man, "I know nothing certain; they have stood as you have seen them for uncounted time; and while all other ships wrecked on this unhappy coast have gone to pieces, and rotted and sunk away in a few years, these two haunted hulks have neither sunk in the quicksand, nor has a single spar or board been displaced. Maritime legend says that two ships of Denmark

having had permission, for a time, to work deeds of
darkness and dolor on the deep, were at last
condemned to the whirlpool and the sunken rock,
and were wrecked in this bonnie bay, as a sign to
seamen to be gentle and devout. The night when
they were lost was a harvest evening of uncommon
mildness and beauty: the sun had newly set; the
moon came brighter and brighter out; and the
reapers, laying their sickles at the root of the standing corn, stood on rock and bank, looking at the
increasing magnitude of the waters, for sea and land
were visible from Saint Bees to Barnhourie. The
sails of two vessels were soon seen bent for the
Scottish coast; and, with a speed outrunning the
swiftest ship, they approached the dangerous quicksands and headland of Borranpoint. On the deck
of the foremost ship not a living soul was seen, or
shape, unless something in darkness and form resembling a human shadow could be called a shape,
which flitted from extremity to extremity of the
ship, with the appearance of trimming the sails, and
directing the vessel's course. But the decks of its
companion were crowded with human shapes; the
captain and mate, and sailor and cabin-boy, all
seemed there; and from them the sound of mirth and
minstrelsy echoed over land and water. The coast
which they skirted along was one of extreme danger,
and the reapers shouted to warn them to beware of
sandbank and rock; but of this friendly counsel no

notice was taken, except that a large and famished dog, which sat on the prow, answered every shout with a long, loud, and melancholy howl. The deep sandbank of Carsethorn was expected to arrest the career of these desperate navigators; but they passed, with the celerity of water-fowl, over an obstruction which had wrecked many pretty ships.

"Old men shook their heads and departed, saying, 'We have seen the fiend sailing in a bottomless ship; let us go home and pray;' but one young and wilful man said, 'Fiend! I'll warrant it's nae fiend, but douce Janet Withershins the witch, holding a carouse with some of her Cumberland cummers, and mickle red wine will be spilt atween them. Dod I would gladly have a toothfu'! I'll warrant it's nane o' your cauld sour slae-water like a bottle of Bailie Skrinkie's port, but right drap-o'-my-heart's-blood stuff, that would waken a body out of their last linen. I wonder where the cummers will anchor their craft?' 'And I'll vow,' said another rustic, 'the wine they quaff is none of your visionary drink, such as a drouthie body has dished out to his lips in a dream; nor is it shadowy and unsubstantial, like the vessels they sail in, which are made out of a cockel-shell or a cast-off slipper, or the paring of a seaman's right thumb-nail. I once got a hansel out of a witch's quaigh myself—auld Marion Mathers, of Dustiefoot, whom they tried to bury in the old kirkyard of

Dunscore; but the cummer raise as fast as they laid her down, and naewhere else would she lie but in the bonnie green kirkyard of Kier, among douce and sponsible fowk. So I'll vow that the wine of a witch's cup is as fell liquor as ever did a kindly turn to a poor man's heart; and be they fiends, or be they witches, if they have red wine asteer, I'll risk a drouket sark for ae glorious tout on't."

"'Silence, ye sinners,' said the minister's son of a neighbouring parish, who united in his own person his father's lack of devotion with his mother's love of liquor. 'Whist!—speak as if ye had the fear of something holy before ye. Let the vessels run their own way to destruction: who can stay the eastern wind, and the current of the Solway sea? I can find ye Scripture warrant for that; so let them try their strength on Blawhooly rocks, and their might on the broad quicksand. There's a surf running there would knock the ribs together of a galley built by the imps of the pit, and commanded by the Prince of Darkness. Bonnily and bravely they sail away there, but before the blast blows by they'll be wrecked; and red wine and strong brandy will be as rife as dyke-water, and we'll drink the health of bonnie Bell Blackness out of her left-foot slipper.'

"The speech of the young profligate was applauded by several of his companions, and away they flew to the bay of Blawhooly, from whence they never returned. The two vessels were observed all at once to stop in the bosom of the bay, on the spot where their hulls now appear; the mirth and the minstrelsy waxed louder than ever, and the forms of maidens, with instruments of music and wine-cups in their hands, thronged the decks. A boat was lowered; and the same shadowy pilot who conducted the ships made it start towards the shore with the rapidity of lightning, and its head knocked against the bank where the four young men stood who longed for the unblest drink. They leaped in with a laugh, and with a laugh were they welcomed on deck; wine-cups were given to each, and as they raised them to their lips the vessels melted away beneath their feet, and one loud shriek, mingled with laughter still louder, was heard over land and water for many miles. Nothing more was heard or seen till the morning, when the crowd who came to the beach saw with fear and wonder the two Haunted Ships, such as they now seem, masts and tackle gone; nor mark, nor sign, by which their name, country, or destination could be known, was left remaining. Such is the tradition of the mariners; and its truth has been attested by many families whose sons and whose fathers have been drowned in the haunted bay of Blawhooly."

"And trow ye," said the old woman, who, atracted from her hut by the drowning cries of the young fisherman, had remained an auditor of the mariner's legend,—" And trow ye, Mark Macmoran, that the tale of the Haunted Ships is done? I can say no to that. Mickle have mine ears heard; but more mine eyes have witnessed since I came to dwell in this humble home by the side of the deep sea. I mind the night weel; it was on Hallowmas Eve; the nuts were cracked, and the apples were eaten, and spell and charm were tried at my fireside; till, wearied with diving into the dark waves of futurity, the lads and lasses fairly took to the more visible blessings of kind words, tender clasps, and gentle courtship. Soft words in a maiden's ear, and a kindly kiss o' her lip were old-world matters to me, Mark Macmoran; though I mean not to say that I have been free of the folly of daunering and daffin with a youth in my day, and keeping tryst with him in dark and lonely places. However, as I say, these times of enjoyment were passed and gone with me—the mair's the pity that pleasure should fly sae fast away—and as I couldna make sport I thought I should not mar any; so out I sauntered into the fresh cold air, and sat down behind that old oak, and looked abroad on the wide sea. I had my ain sad thoughts, ye may think, at the time: it was in that very bay my blythe goodman perished, with seven more in his company; and on that very bank where ye see the waves leaping and foaming, I saw seven stately corses streeked, but the dearest was the eighth. It was a woful

sight to me, a widow, with four bonnie boys, with
nought to support them but these twa hands, and
God's blessing, and a cow's grass. I have never
liked to live out of sight of this bay since that
time; and mony's the moonlight night I sit looking
on these watery mountains and these waste shores;
it does my heart good, whatever it may do to my
head. So ye see it was Hallowmas Night, and
looking on sea and land sat I; and my heart wandering to other thoughts soon made me forget my
youthful company at hame. It might be near the
howe hour of the night. The tide was making, and
its singing brought strange old-world stories with
it, and I thought on the dangers that sailors endure,
the fates they meet with, and the fearful forms they
see. My own blythe goodman had seen sights
that made him grave enough at times, though he
aye tried to laugh them away.

"Aweel, atween that very rock aneath us and
the coming tide, I saw, or thought I saw—for the
tale is so dreamlike that the whole might pass for
a vision of the night,—I saw the form of a man;
his plaid was grey, his face was grey; and his hair,
which hung low down till it nearly came to the
middle of his back, was as white as the white sea-
foam. He began to howk and dig under the bank;
an' God be near me, thought I, this maun be the
unblessed spirit of auld Adam Gowdgowpin the
miser, who is doomed to dig for shipwrecked treasure,

and count how many millions are hidden for ever from man's enjoyment. The form found something which in shape and hue seemed a left-foot slipper of brass; so down to the tide he marched, and, placing it on the water, whirled it thrice round, and the infernal slipper dilated at every turn, till it became a bonnie barge with its sails bent, and on board leaped the form, and scudded swiftly away. He came to one of the Haunted Ships, and striking it with his oar, a fair ship, with mast and canvas and mariners, started up; he touched the other Haunted Ship, and produced the like transformation; and away the three spectre ships bounded, leaving a track of fire behind them on the billows which was long unextinguished. Now wasna that a bonnie and fearful sight to see beneath the light of the Hallowmas moon? But the tale is far frae finished, for mariners say that once a year, on a certain night, if ye stand on the Borran Point, ye will see the infernal shallops coming snoring through the Solway; ye will hear the same laugh and song and mirth and minstrelsy which our ancestors heard; see them bound over the sandbanks and sunken rocks like sea-gulls, cast their anchor in Blawhooly Bay, while the shadowy figure lowers down the boat, and augments their numbers with the four unhappy mortals to whose memory a stone stands in the kirkyard, with a sinking ship and a shoreless sea cut upon it. Then the spectre ships vanish, and the drowning shriek of mortals and the rejoicing laugh of fiends are heard, and the old hulls are left as a memorial that the old spiritual kingdom has not departed from the earth. But I maun away, and trim my little cottage fire, and make it burn and blaze up bonnie, to warm the crickets and my cold and crazy bones that maun soon be laid aneath the green sod in the eerie kirkyard." And away the old dame tottered to her cottage, secured the door on the inside, and soon the hearth-flame was seen to glimmer and gleam through the keyhole and window.

"I'll tell ye what," said the old mariner, in a subdued tone, and with a shrewd and suspicious glance of his eye after the old sibyl, "it's a word that may not very well be uttered, but there are many mistakes made in evening stories if old Moll Moray there, where she lives, knows not mickle more than she is willing to tell of the Haunted Ships and their unhallowed mariners. She lives cannily and quietly; no one knows how she is fed or supported; but her dress is aye whole, her cottage ever smokes, and her table lacks neither of wine, white and red, nor of fowl and fish, and white bread and brown. It was a dear scoff to Jock Matheson, when he called old Moll the uncanny carline of Blawhooly: his boat ran round and round in the centre of the Solway—everybody said it was enchanted—and down it went head foremost; and hadna Jock been a swimmer equal to a sheldrake, he would have fed the fish. But I'll warrant it sobered the lad's speech; and he never reckoned himself safe till he made old Moll the present of a new kirtle and a stone of cheese."

"O father!" said his granddaughter Barbara, "ye surely wrong poor old Mary Moray; what use could it be to an old woman like her, who has no wrongs to redress, no malice to work out against mankind, and nothing to seek of enjoyment save a canny hour and a quiet grave—what use could the fellowship of fiends and the communion of evil spirits be to her? I know Jenny Primrose puts rowan-tree above the door-head when she sees old Mary coming; I know the goodwife of Kittlenaket wears rowan-berry leaves in the headband of her blue kirtle, and all for the sake of averting the unsonsie glance of Mary's right ee; and I know that the auld Laird of Burntroutwater drives his seven cows to their pasture with a wand of witch-tree, to keep Mary from milking them. But what has all that to do with haunted shallops, visionary mariners, and bottomless boats? I have heard myself as pleasant a tale about the Haunted Ships and their unworldly crews as any one would wish to hear in a winter evening. It was told me by young Benjie Macharg, one summer night, sitting on Arbigland-bank: the lad intended a sort of love meeting; but all that he could talk of was about smearing sheep and shearing sheep, and of the wife which the Norway elves of the Haunted Ships made for his uncle Sandie Macharg. And I shall tell ye the tale as the honest lad told it to me.

"Alexander Macharg, besides being the laird of three acres of peatmoss, two kale gardens, and the owner of seven good milch cows, a pair of horses, and six pet sheep, was the husband of one of the handsomest women in seven parishes. Many a lad sighed the day he was brided; and a Nithsdale laird and two Annandale moorland farmers drank themselves to their last linen, as well as their last shilling, through sorrow for her loss. But married was the dame; and home she was carried, to bear rule over her home and her husband, as an honest woman should. Now ye maun ken that though the flesh-and-blood lovers of Alexander's bonnie wife all ceased to love and to sue her after she became another's, there were certain admirers who did not consider their claim at all abated, or their hopes lessened by the kirk's famous obstacle of matrimony. Ye have heard how the devout minister of Tinwald had a fair son carried away, and wedded against his liking to an unchristened bride, whom the elves and the fairies provided; ye have heard how the bonnie bride of the drunken Laird of Soukitup was stolen by the fairies out at the back-window of the bridal chamber, the time the bridegroom was groping his way to the chamber door; and ye have heard—but why need I multiply cases? Such things in the ancient days were as common as candle-light. So ye 'll no hinder certain water elves and sea fairies, who sometimes keep festival and summer mirth in these old haunted hulks, from falling in love with the weel-faured wife of Laird Macharg; and to their plots and contrivances they went how they might accomplish to sunder man and wife; and sundering such a man and such a wife was like sundering the green leaf from the summer, or the fragrance from the flower.

"So it fell on a time that Laird Macharg took his halve-net on his back, and his steel spear in his hand, and down to Blawhooly Bay gaed he, and into the water he went right between the two haunted hulks, and placing his net awaited the coming of the tide. The night, ye maun ken, was mirk, and the wind lowne, and the singing of the increasing waters among the shells and the peebles was heard for sundry miles. All at once light began to glance and twinkle on board the two Haunted Ships from every hole and seam, and presently the sound as of a hatchet employed in squaring timber echoed far and wide. But if the toil of these unearthly workmen amazed the laird, how much more was his amazement increased when a sharp shrill voice called out, 'Ho, brother! what are you doing now?' A voice still shriller responded from the other haunted ship, 'I 'm making a wife to Sandie Macharg!' And a loud quavering laugh running from ship to ship, and from bank to bank, told the joy they expected from their labour.

"Now the laird, besides being a devout and a God-fearing man, was shrewd and bold; and in plot and contrivance, and skill in conducting his designs, was fairly an overmatch for any dozen land elves; but the water elves are far more subtle; besides their haunts and their dwellings being in the great deep, pursuit and detection is hopeless if they succeed in carrying their prey to the waves. But ye shall hear. Home flew the laird, collected his family around the hearth, spoke of the signs and the sins of the times, and talked of mortification and prayer for averting calamity; and, finally, taking his father's Bible, brass clasps, black print, and covered with calf-skin, from the shelf, he proceeded without let or stint to perform domestic worship. I should have told ye that he bolted and locked the door, shut up all inlet to the house, threw salt into the fire, and proceeded in every way like a man skilful in guarding against the plots of fairies and fiends. His wife looked on all this with wonder; but she saw something in her husband's looks that hindered her from intruding either question or advice, and a wise woman was she.

"Near the mid-hour of the night the rush of a horse's feet was heard, and the sound of a rider leaping from its back, and a heavy knock came to the door, accompanied by a voice, saying, 'The cummer drink's hot, and the knave bairn is expected at Laird Laurie's to-night; sae mount, goodwife, and come.'

"'Preserve me!' said the wife of Sandie Macharg, 'that's news indeed; who could have thought it? The laird has been heirless for seventeen years! Now, Sandie, my man, fetch me my skirt and hood.'

"But he laid his arm round his wife's neck, and said, 'If all the lairds in Galloway go heirless, over this door threshold shall you not stir to-night; and I have said, and I have sworn it; seek not to know why or wherefore—but, Lord, send us thy blessed mornlight.' The wife looked for a moment in her husband's eyes, and desisted from further entreaty.

"'But let us send a civil message to the gossips, Sandy; and hadna ye better say I am sair laid with a sudden sickness? though it's sinful-like to send the poor messenger a mile agate with a lie in his mouth without a glass of brandy.'

"'To such a messenger, and to those who sent him, no apology is needed,' said the austere laird; 'so let him depart.' And the clatter of a horse's hoofs was heard, and the muttered imprecations of its rider on the churlish treatment he had experienced.

"'Now, Sandie, my lad,' said his wife, laying an arm particularly white and round about his neck as she spoke, 'are you not a queer man and a stern?

I have been your wedded wife now these three years; and, beside my dower, have brought you three as bonnie bairns as ever smiled aneath a summer sun. O man, you a douce man, and fitter to be an elder than even Willie Greer himself, I have the minister's ain word for 't, to put on these hard-hearted looks, and gang waving your arms that way, as if ye said, "I winna take the counsel of sic a hempie as you;" I'm your ain leal wife, and will and maun have an explanation.'

"To all this Sandie Macharg replied, 'It is written, "Wives, obey your husbands"; but we have been stayed in our devotion, so let us pray;' and down he knelt: his wife knelt also, for she was as devout as bonnie; and beside them knelt their household, and all lights were extinguished.

"'Now this beats a',' muttered his wife to herself; 'however, I shall be obedient for a time; but if I dinna ken what all this is for before the morn by sunket-time, my tongue is nae langer a tongue, nor my hands worth wearing.'

"The voice of her husband in prayer interrupted this mental soliloquy; and ardently did he beseech to be preserved from the wiles of the fiends and the snares of Satan; from witches, ghosts, goblins, elves, fairies, spunkies, and water-kelpies; from the spectre shallop of Solway; from spirits visible and invisible; from the Haunted Ships and their unearthly tenants; from maritime spirits that plotted against godly men, and fell in love with their wives——'

"'Nay, but His presence be near us!' said his wife, in a low tone of dismay. 'God guide my gudeman's wits: I never heard such a prayer from human lips before. But, Sandie, my man, Lord's sake, rise. What fearful light is this? Barn and byre and stable maun be in a blaze; and Hawkie, and Hurley, Doddie, and Cherrie, and Damsonplum will be smoored with reek, and scorched with flame.'

"And a flood of light, but not so gross as a common fire, which ascended to heaven and filled all the court before the house, amply justified the goodwife's suspicions. But to the terrors of fire Sandie was as immovable as he was to the imaginary groans of the barren wife of Laird Laurie; and he held his wife, and threatened the weight of his right hand—and it was a heavy one—to all who ventured abroad, or even unbolted the door. The neighing and prancing of horses, and the bellowing of cows, augmented the horrors of the night; and to any one who only heard the din, it seemed that the whole onstead was in a blaze, and horses and cattle perishing in the flame. All wiles, common or extraordinary, were put in practice to entice or force the honest farmer and his wife to open the door; and when the like success attended every new stratagem, silence for a little while ensued, and a long, loud, and shrilling laugh wound up the dramatic efforts of the night. In the morning, when Laird Macharg went to the door, he found standing against one of the pilasters a piece of black ship oak, rudely fashioned into something like human form, and which skilful people declared would have been clothed with seeming flesh and blood, and palmed upon him by elfin adroitness for his wife, had he admitted his visitants. A synod of wise men and women sat upon the woman of timber, and she was finally ordered to be devoured by fire, and that in the open air. A fire was soon made, and into it the elfin sculpture was tossed from the prongs of two pairs of pitchforks. The blaze that arose was awful to behold; and hissings and burstings and loud cracklings and strange noises were heard in the midst of the flame; and when the whole sank into ashes, a drinking-cup of some precious metal was found; and this cup, fashioned no doubt by elfin skill, but rendered harmless by the purification with fire, the sons and daughters of Sandie Macharg and his wife drink out of to this very day. Bless all bold men, say I, and obedient wives!"

# THE BROWNIE.

The Scottish Brownie formed a class of being distinct in habit and disposition from the freakish and mischievous elves. He was meagre, shaggy, and wild in his appearance. Thus Cleland, in his satire against the Highlanders, compares them to

> "Faunes, or Brownies, if ye will,
> Or Satyres come from Atlas Hill."

In the day-time he lurked in remote recesses of the old houses which he delighted to haunt, and in the night sedulously employed himself in discharging any laborious task which he thought might be acceptable to the family to whose service he had devoted himself. But the Brownie does not drudge from the hope of recompense. On the contrary, so delicate is his attachment that the offer of reward, but particularly of food, infallibly occasions his disappearance for ever. It is told of a Brownie, who haunted a border family now extinct, that the lady having fallen unexpectedly ill, and the servant, who was ordered to ride to Jedburgh for the *sage-femme*, showing no great alertness in setting out, the familiar spirit slipped on the greatcoat of the lingering domestic, rode to the town on the laird's best horse, and returned with the midwife *en croupe*. During the short space of his absence, the Tweed, which they must necessarily ford, rose to a dangerous height. Brownie, who transported his charge with all the rapidity of the ghostly lover of Lenore, was not to be stopped by the obstacle. He plunged in with the terrified old lady, and landed her in safety where her services were wanted. Having put the horse into the stable (where it was afterwards found in a woful plight), he proceeded to the room of the servant, whose duty he had discharged, and finding him just in the act of drawing on his boots, he administered to him a most merciless drubbing with his own horsewhip. Such an important service excited the gratitude of the laird, who, understanding that Brownie had been heard to express a wish to have a green coat, ordered a vestment of the colour to be made, and left in his haunts. Brownie took away the green coat, but was never seen more. We may suppose that, tired of his domestic drudgery, he went in his new livery to join the fairies.

The last Brownie known in Ettrick Forest resided in Bodsbeck, a wild and solitary spot, near the head of Moffat Water, where he exercised his functions undisturbed, till the scrupulous devotion of an old lady induced her to "hire him away," as it was termed, by placing in his haunt a porringer of milk and a piece of money. After receiving this hint to depart, he was heard the whole night to howl and cry, "Farewell to bonnie Bodsbeck!" which he was compelled to abandon for ever.

## MAUNS' STANE.

In the latter end of the autumn of 18—, I set out by myself on an excursion over the northern part of Scotland, and during that time my chief amusement was to observe the little changes of manners, language, etc., in the different districts. After having viewed on my return the principal curiosities in Buchan, I made a little ale-house, or "public," my head-quarters for the night. Having discussed my supper in solitude, I called up mine host to enable me to discuss my bottle, and to give me a statistical account of the country around me. Seated in the "blue" end, and well supplied with the homely but satisfying luxuries which the place afforded, I was in an excellent mood for enjoying the communicativeness of my landlord; and, after speaking about the cave of Slaines, the state of the crops, and the neighbouring franklins, edged him, by degrees, to speak about the Abbey of Deer, an interesting ruin which I had examined in the course of the day, formerly the stronghold of the once powerful family of Cummin.

"It's dootless a bonnie place about the abbey," said he, "but naething like what it was when the great Sir James the Rose came to hide i' the Buchan woods wi' a' the Grahames rampagin' at his tail, whilk you that's a beuk-learned man 'ill hae read o', an' may be ye'll hae heard o' the saughen bush where he forgathered wi' his jo; or aiblins ye may have seen 't, for it's standing yet just at the corner o' gaukit Jamie Jamieson's peat-stack. Ay, ay, the abbey was a brave place once; but a' thing, ye ken, comes till an end." So saying, he nodded to me, and brought his glass to an end.

"This place, then, must have been famed in days of yore, my friend?"

"Ye may tak my word for that," said he, "'Od, it *was* a place! Sic a sight o' fechtin' as they had about it! But gin ye'll gan up the trap-stair to the laft, an' open Jenny's kist, ye'll see sic a story about it, printed by ane o' your learned Aberdeen's fouk, Maister Keith, I think; she coft it in Aberdeen for twal' pennies, lang ago, an' battered it to the lid o' her kist. But gang up the stair canny, for fear that you should wauken her, puir thing; or, bide, I'll just wauken Jamie Fleep, an' gar him help me down wi't, for our stair's no just that canny for them 't's no acquaint wi't, let alane a frail man wi' your infirmity."

I assured him that I would neither disturb the young lady's slumber nor Jamie Fleep's, and begged him to give me as much information as he could about this castle.

"Weel, wishin' your guid health again.—Our minister ance said that Solomon's Temple was a' in ruins, wi' whin bushes, an' broom and thistles growin' ower the bonnie carved wark an' the cedar wa's, just like our ain abbey. Noo, I judge that the Abbey o' Deer was just the marrow o 't, or the minister wadna hae said that. But when it was biggit, Lord kens, for I dinna. It was just as you see it, lang afore your honour was born, an' aiblins, as the by-word says, may be sae after ye 're hanged. But that's neither here nor there. The Cummins o' Buchan were a dour and surly race; and, for a fearfu' time, nane near han' nor far awa could ding them, an' yet mony a ane tried it. The fouk on their ain lan' likit them weel enough; but the Crawfords, an' the Grahames, an' the Mars, an' the Lovats, were aye trying to comb them against the hair, an' mony a weary kempin' had they wi' them. But some way or ither they could never ding them; an' fouk said that they gaed and learned the black art frae the Pope o' Room, wha, I myself heard the minister say, had aye a colleague wi' the Auld Chiel. I dinna ken fou it was, in the tail o' the day, the hale country raise up against them, an' besieged them in the Abbey o' Deer. Ye 'll see, my frien'" (by this time mine host considered me as one of his cronies), " tho' we ca' it the abbey, it had naething to do wi' papistry; na, na, no sae bad as a' that either, but just a noble's castle, where they keepit sodgers gaun about in airn an' scarlet, wi' their swords an' guns, an' begnets, an' sentry-boxes, like the local militia in the barracks o' Aberdeen.

"Weel, ye see, they surrounded the castle, an' lang did they besiege it; but there was a vast o' meat in the castle, an' the Buchan fouk fought like the vera deil. They took their horse through a miscellaneous passage, half a mile long, aneath the hill o' Saplinbrae, an' watered them in the burn o' Pulmer. But a' wadna do; they took the castle at last, and a terrible slaughter they made amo' them; but they were sair disappointed in ae partic'ler, for Cummin's fouk sank a' their goud an' siller in a draw-wall, an' syne filled it up wi' stanes. They got naething in the way of spulzie to speak o'; sae out o' spite they dang doon the castle, an'. it's never been biggit to this day. But the Cummins were no sae bad as the Lairds o' Federat, after a'."

"And who were these Federats?" I inquired.

"The Lairds o' Federat?" said he, moistening his mouth again as a preamble to his oration. "Troth, frae their deeds ane would maist think that they had a drap o' the deil's blude, like the pyets. Gin a' tales be true, they hae the warmest place at his bink this vera minute. I dinna ken vera muckle about them though, but the auldest fouk said they were just byous wi' cruelty. Mony a good man did they hing up i' their ha', just for their ain sport; ye'll see the ring to the fore yet in the roof o't. Did ye never hear o' Mauns' Stane, neebour?"

"Mauns' what?" said I.

"Ou, Mauns' Stane. But it's no likely. Ye see it was just a queer clump o' a roun'-about heathen, waghlin' may be twa tons or thereby. It wasna like ony o' the stanes in our countra, an' it was as roun' as a fit-ba'; I'm sure it wad ding Professor Couplan himsel' to tell what way it cam' there. Noo, fouk aye thought there was something uncanny about it, an' some gaed the length o' saying that the deil used to bake ginshbread upon't; and, as sure as ye're sitting there, frien', there was knuckle-marks upon't, for my ain father has seen them as aften as I have taes an' fingers. Aweel, ye see, Mauns Crawford, the last o' the Lairds o' Federat, an' the deil had coost out (may be because the laird was just as wicked an' as clever as he was himsel'), an' ye perceive the evil ane wantit to play him a trick. Noo, Mauns Crawford was ae day lookin' ower his castle wa', and he saw a stalwart carle, in black claes, ridin' up the loanin'. He stopped at this chuckie o' a stane, an' loutin' himsel', he took it up in his arms, and lifted it three times to his saddle-bow, an' syne he rade awa out o' sight, never comin' near the castle, as Mauns thought he would hae done. 'Noo,' says the baron till himsel', says he, 'I didna think that there was ony ane in a' the land that could hae played sic a ploy; but deil fetch me if I dinna lift it as weel as he did!' Sae aff he gaed, for there wasna sic a man for birr in a' the countra, an' he kent it as weel, for he never met wi' his match. Weel, he tried, and tugged, and better than tugged at the stane, but he coudna mudge it ava; an' when he looked about, he saw a man at his ilbuck, a' smeared wi' smiddy-coom, snightern an' laughin' at him. The laird d——d him, an' bade him lift it, whilk he did as gin 't had been a little pinnin. The laird was like to burst wi' rage at being fickled by sic a hag-ma-hush carle, and he took to the stane in a fury, and lifted it till his knee; but the weight o' t amaist ground his banes to smash. He held the stane till his een-strings crackit, when he was as blin' as a moudiwort. He was blin' till the day o' his death,—that 's to say, if ever he died, for there were queer sayings about it—vera queer! vera queer! The stane was ca'd Mauns' Stane ever after; an' it was no thought that canny to be near it after gloaming; for what says the Psalm—hem!—I mean the sang—

   'Tween Ennetbutts an' Mauns' Stane
   Ilka night there walks ane!

"There never was a chief of the family after; the men were scattered, an' the castle demolished. The doo and the hoodie-craw nestle i' their towers, and the hare mak's her form on their grassy hearth-stane."

"Is this stone still to be seen?"

"Ou, na. Ye see, it was just upon Johnie Forbes's craft, an' fouk cam' far an' near to leuk at it, an' trampit down a' the puir cottar-body's corn; sae he houkit a hole just aside it, and tumbled it intil 't; by that means naebody sees 't noo, but its weel kent that it's there, for they're livin' yet wha 've seen it."

"But the well at the Abbey—did no one feel a desire to enrich himself with the gold and silver buried there?"

"Hoot, ay; mony a ane tried to find out whaur it was, and, for that matter, I've may be done as foolish a thing myself; but nane ever made it out. There was a scholar, like yoursel', that gaed ae night down to the Abbey, an', ye see, he summoned up the deil."

"The deuce he did!" said I.

"Weel, weel, the deuce, gin ye like it better," said he. "An' he was gaun to question him where the treasure was, but he had eneuch to do to get him laid without deaving him wi' questions, for a' the deils cam' about him, like bees biggin' out o' a byke. He never coured the fright he gat, but cried out, 'Help! help!' till his very enemy wad hae been wae to see him; and sae he cried till he died, which was no that lang after. Fouk sudna meddle wi' sic ploys!"

"Most wonderful! And do you believe that Beelzebub actually appeared to him?"

"Believe it! What for no?" said he, consequentially tapping the lid of his snuff-horn. "Didna my ain father see the evil ane i' the schule o' Auld Deer?"

"Indeed!"

"Weel, I wot he did that. A wheen idle callants, when the dominie was out at his twal'-hours, read the Lord's Prayer backlans, an' raised him, but couldna lay him again, for he threepit ower them that he wadna gang awa unless he gat ane o' them wi' him. Ye may be sure this put them in an awfu' swither. They were a' squallin' an' crawlin' and sprawlin' amo' the couples to get out o' his grips. Ane o' them gat out an' tauld the maister about it, an' when he cam' down, the melted lead was runnin' aff the roof o' the house wi' the heat, sae, flingin' to the black thief a young bit kittlen o' the schulemistress's, he sank through the floor wi' an awsome roar. I mysel' have heard the mistress misca'in her man about offering up the puir thing, baith saul and body, to Baal. But troth, I'm no clear to speak o' the like o' this at sic a time o' night; sae if your honour bena for another jug, I'll e'en wus you a gude-night, for it's wearin' late, an I maun awa' to Skippyfair i' the mornin'."

I assented to this, and quickly lost in sleep the remembrance of all these tales of the olden times.

## "HORSE AND HATTOCK."

The power of the fairies was not confined to unchristened children alone; it was supposed frequently to be extended to full-grown people, especially such as in an unlucky hour were devoted to the devil by the execrations of parents and of masters; or those who were found asleep under a rock, or on a green hill, belonging to the fairies, after sunset, or, finally, to those who unwarily joined their orgies. A tradition existed, during the seventeenth century, concerning an ancestor of the noble family of Duffers, who, " walking abroad in the fields near to his own house, was suddenly carried away, and found the next day at Paris, in the French king's cellar, with a silver cup in his hand. Being brought into the king's presence, and questioned by him who he was, and how he came thither, he told his name, his country, and the place of his residence, and that on such a day of the month, which proved to be the day immediately preceding, being in the fields, he heard a noise of a whirlwind, and of voices crying ' Horse and hattock!' (this is the word which the fairies are said to use when they remove from any place), whereupon he cried 'Horse and hattock!' also, and was immediately caught up and transported through the air by the fairies to that place, where, after he had drunk heartily, he fell asleep, and before he woke the rest of the company were gone, and had left him in the posture wherein he was found. It is said the king gave him a cup which was found in his hand, and dismissed him." The narrator affirms " that the cup was still preserved, and known by the name of the fairy cup." He adds that Mr. Steward, tutor to the then Lord Duffers, had informed him that, " when a boy at the school of Forres, he and his school-fellows were once upon a time whipping their tops in the churchyard, before the door of the church, when, though the day was calm, they heard a noise of a wind, and at some distance saw the small dust begin to rise and turn round, which motion continued advancing till it came to the place where they were, whereupon they began to bless themselves; but one of their number being, it seems, a little more bold and confident than his companion, said, 'Horse and hattock with my top!' and immediately they all saw the top lifted up from the ground, but could not see which way it was carried, by reason of a cloud of dust which was raised at the same time. They sought for the top all about the place where it was taken up, but in vain; and it was found afterwards in the churchyard, on the other side of the church." This legend is contained in a letter from a learned gentleman in Scotland to Mr. Aubrey, dated 15th March 1695, published in *Aubrey's Miscellani*.

# SECRET COMMONWEALTH.

*By* Mr. Robert Kirk, *Minister of Aberfoyle*, 1691.

THE Siths, or Fairies, they call *Sluagh Maith*, or the Goodpeople, it would seem, to prevent the dint of their ill attempts (for the Irish used to bless all they fear harm of), and are said to be of a middle nature betwixt man and angel, as were demons thought to be of old, of intelligent studious spirits, and light changeable bodies (like those called astral), somewhat of the nature of a condensed cloud, and best seen in twilight. These bodies be so pliable through the subtlety of the spirits that agitate them, that they can make them appear or disappear at pleasure. Some have bodies or vehicles so spongeous, thin, and defecat [pure] that they are fed by only sucking into some fine spirituous liquors, that pierce like pure air and oil; others feed more gross on the foyson [abundance] or substance of corn and liquors, or corn itself that grows on the surface of the earth, which these fairies steal away, partly invisible, partly preying on the grain, as do crows and mice; wherefore in this same age they are sometimes heard to break bread, strike hammers, and to do such like services within the little hillocks they most do haunt; some whereof of old, before the Gospel dispelled Paganism, and in some barbarous places as yet, enter houses after all are at rest, and set the kitchens in order, cleansing all the vessels. Such drags go under the name of Brownies. When we have plenty, they have scarcity at their homes; and, on the contrary (for they are not empowered to catch as much prey everywhere as they please), their robberies, notwithstanding, ofttimes occasion great ricks of corn not to bleed so well (as they call it), or prove so copious by very far as was expected by the owner.

Their bodies of congealed air are sometimes carried aloft, other whiles grovel in different shapes, and enter into any cranny or clift of the earth where air enters, to their ordinary dwellings; the earth being full of cavities and cells, and there being no place, no creature, but is supposed to have other animals (greater or lesser) living in or upon it as inhabitants; and no such thing as a pure wilderness in the whole universe.

We then (the more terrestrial kind have now so numerously planted all countries) do labour for that abstruse people, as well as for ourselves. Albeit, when several countries were uninhabited by us, these had their easy tillage above ground, as we now. The print of those furrows do yet remain to be seen on the shoulders of very high hills, which was done when the campaign ground was wood and forest.

They remove to other lodgings at the beginning of each quarter of the year, so traversing till doomsday, being impotent of staying in one place, and finding some ease by so purning [journeying] and changing habitations. Their chameleon-like bodies swim in the air near the earth with bag and baggage; and at such revolution of time, seers, or men of the second sight (females being seldom so qualified) have very terrifying encounters with them, even on highways; who, therefore, awfully shun to travel abroad at these four seasons of the year, and thereby have made it a custom to this day among the Scottish-Irish to keep church duly every first Sunday of the quarter to *seun* or hallow themselves, their corn and cattle, from the shots and stealth of these wandering tribes; and many of these superstitious people will not be seen in church again till the next quarter begins, as if no duty were to be learnt or done by them, but all the use of worship and sermons were to save them from these arrows that fly in the dark.

They are distributed in tribes and orders, and have children, nurses, marriages, deaths, and burials in appearance, even as we (unless they so do for a mock-show, or to prognosticate some such things among us).

They are clearly seen by these men of the second sight to eat at funerals [and] banquets. Hence many of the Scottish-Irish will not taste meat at these meetings, lest they have communion with, or be poisoned by, them. So are they seen to carry the bier or coffin with the corpse among the middle-earth men to the grave. Some men of that exalted sight (whether by art or nature) have told me they have seen at these meetings a double man, or the shape of some man in two places; that is a super-terranean and a subterranean inhabitant, perfectly resembling one another in all points, whom he, notwithstanding, could easily distinguish one from another by some secret tokens and operations, and so go and speak to the man, his neighbour and familiar, passing by the apparition or resemblance of him. They avouch that every element and different state of being has animals resembling those of another element; as there be fishes sometimes at sea resembling monks of late order in all their hoods and dresses; so as the Roman invention of good and bad demons, and guardian angels particularly assigned is called by them an ignorant mistake, sprung only from this original. They call this reflex man a co-walker, every way like the man, as a twin brother and companion, haunting him as his shadow, as is oft seen and known among men (resembling the original), both before and after the original is dead; and was often seen of old to enter a house, by which the people knew that the person of that likeness was to visit them within a few days. This copy, echo, or living picture, goes at last to his own herd. It accompanied that person so long and frequently for ends best known to itself, whether to guard him from the secret assaults of some of its own folk, or only as a sportful ape to counterfeit all his actions. However, the stories of old witches prove beyond contradiction that all sorts of people, spirits which assume light airy bodies, or crazed bodies coacted by foreign spirits, seem to have some pleasure (at least to assuage some pain or melancholy) by frisking and capering like satyrs, or whistling and screeching (like unlucky birds) in their unhallowed synagogues and Sabbaths. If invited and earnestly required, these companions make themselves known and familiar to men; otherwise, being in a different state and element, they neither can nor will easily converse with them. They avouch that a *heluo* or great eater has a voracious elve to be his attender, called a joint-eater or just-halver, feeding on the pith and quintessence of what the man eats; and that, therefore, he continues lean like a hawk or heron, notwithstanding his devouring appetite; yet it would seem they convey that substance elsewhere, for these subterraneans eat but little in their dwellings, their food being exactly clean, and served up by pleasant children, like enchanted puppets.

Their houses are called large and fair, and (unless

at some odd occasions) unperceivable by vulgar eyes, like Rachland and other enchanted islands, having fir lights, continual lamps, and fires, often seen without fuel to sustain them. Women are yet alive who tell they were taken away when in childbed to nurse fairy children, a lingering voracious image of them being left in their place (like their reflection in a mirror), which (as if it were some insatiable spirit in an assumed body) made first semblance to devour the meats that it cunningly carried by, and then left the carcass as if it expired and departed thence by a natural and common death. The child and fire, with food and all other necessaries, are set before the nurse how soon she enters, but she neither perceives any passage out, nor sees what those people do in other rooms of the lodging. When the child is weaned, the nurse dies, or is conveyed back, or gets it to her choice to stay there. But if any superterraneans be so subtle as to practise sleights for procuring the privacy to any of their mysteries (such as making use of their ointments, which, as Gyges' ring, make them invisible or nimble, or cast them in a trance, or alter their shape, or make things appear at a vast distance, etc.), they smite them without pain, as with a puff of wind, and bereave them of both the natural and acquired sights in the twinkling of an eye (both these sights, when once they come, being in the same organ and inseparable), or they strike them dumb. The tramontanes to this day place bread, the Bible, or a piece of iron, to save their women at such times from being thus stolen, and they commonly report that all uncouth, unknown wights are terrified by nothing earthly so much as cold iron. They deliver the reason to be that hell lying betwixt the chill tempests and the firebrands of scalding metals, and iron of the north (hence the loadstone causes a tendency to that point), by an antipathy thereto, these odious, far-scenting creatures shrug and fright at all that comes thence relating to so abhorred a place, whence their torment is either begun, or feared to come hereafter.

Their apparel and speech is like that of the people and country under which they live; so are they seen to wear plaids and variegated garments in the Highlands of Scotland, and suanachs [plaids] therefore in Ireland. They speak but little, and that by way of whistling, clear, not rough. The very devils conjured in any country do answer in the language of the place; yet sometimes the subterraneans speak more distinctly than at other times. Their women are said to spin very fine, to dye, to tossue, and embroider; but whether it be as manual operation of substantial refined stuffs, with apt and solid instruments, or only curious cobwebs, unpalpable rainbows, and a phantastic imitation of the actions of more terrestrial mortals, since it transcended all the senses of the seer to discern whether, i leave to conjecture as I found it.

Their men travel much abroad, either presaging or aping the dismal and tragical actions of some amongst us; and have also many disastrous doings of their own, as convocations, fighting, gashes, wounds, and burials, both in the earth and air. They live much longer than we; yet die at last, or [at] least vanish from that state. 'Tis one of their tenets that nothing perisheth, but (as the sun and year) everything goes in a circle, lesser or greater, and is renewed and refreshed in its revolutions; as 'tis another, that every body in the creation moves (which is a sort of life); and that nothing moves but has another animal moving on it; and so on, to the utmost minutest corpuscle that's capable of being a receptacle of life.

They are said to have aristocratical rulers and laws, but no discernible religion, love, or devotion towards God, the blessed Maker of all: they disappear whenever they hear His name invoked, or the name of Jesus (at which all do bow willingly, or by constraint, that dwell above or beneath, within the earth), (Philip. ii. 10); nor can they act ought at that time after hearing of that sacred name. The Taiblsdear or seer, that corresponds with this kind of familiars, can bring them with a spell to appear to himself or others when he pleases, as readily as Endor Witch did those of her own kind. He tells they are ever readiest to go on hurtful errands, but seldom will be the messengers of great good to men. He is not terrified with their sight when he calls them, but seeing them in a surprise (as often as he does) frights him extremely, and glad would he be quit of such, for the hideous spectacles seen among them; as the torturing of some wight, earnest, ghostly, staring looks, skirmishes, and the like. They do not all the harm which appearingly they have power to do; nor are they perceived to be in great pain, save that they are usually silent and sullen. They are said to have many pleasant toyish books; but the operation of these pieces only appears in some paroxysms of antic, corybantic jollity, as if ravished and prompted by a new spirit entering into them at that instant, lighter and merrier than their own. Other books they have of involved, abstruse sense, much like the Rosurcian [Rosicrucian] style. They have nothing of the Bible, save collected parcels for charms and counter-charms; not to defend themselves withal, but to operate on other animals, for they are a people invulnerable by our weapons, and albeit werewolves' and witches' true bodies are (by the union of the spirit of nature that runs through all echoing and doubling the blow towards another) wounded at home, when the astral assumed bodies are stricken elsewhere—as the strings of a second harp, tuned to a unison, sound, though only one be struck,—yet these people have not a second, or so gross a body at all, to be so pierced; but as air which when divided unites again; or if they feel pain by a blow, they are better physicians than we, and quickly cure. They are not subject to sore sicknesses, but dwindle and decay at a certain period, all about an age. Some say their continual sadness is because of their pendulous state (like those men, Luke xiii. 2-6), as uncertain what at the last revolution will become of them, when they are locked up into an unchangeable condition; and if they have any frolic fits of mirth, 'tis as the constrained grinning of a mort-head [death's-head], or rather as acted on a stage, and moved by another, ther [than?] cordially coming of themselves. But other men of the second sight, being illiterate, and unwary in their observations, learn from [differ from] those; one averring those subterranean people to be departed souls, attending a while in this inferior state, and clothed with bodies procured through their alms-deeds in this life; fluid, active, ethereal vehicles to hold them that they may not scatter nor wander, and be lost in the totum, or their first nothing; but if any were so impious as to have given no alms, they say, when the souls of such do depart, they sleep in an inactive state till they resume the terrestrial bodies again; others, that what the low-country Scotch call a wraith, and the Irish *taibhse*, or death's messenger (appearing sometimes as a little rough dog, and if crossed and conjured in time, will be pacified by the death of any other creature instead of the sick man), is only exuvious fumes of the man approaching death, exhaled and congealed into a various likeness (as ships and armies are sometimes shaped in the air), and called astral bodies, agitated as wild-fire with wind, and are neither souls nor counterfeiting spirits; yet not a few avouch (as is said) that surely these are a numerous people by themselves, having their own politics, which diversities of judgment may occasion several inconsonancies in this rehearsal, after the narrowest scrutiny made about it.

Their weapons are most-what solid earthly bodies, nothing of iron, but much of stone, like to yellow soft flint spa, shaped like a barbed arrow-head, but flung like a dart, with great force. These arms (cut by art and tools, it seems, beyond human) have somewhat of the nature of thunderbolt subtlety, and mortally wounding the vital parts without breaking the skin; of which wounds I have observed in beasts, and felt them with my hands. They are not as infallible Benjamites, hitting at a hair's-breadth; nor are they wholly unvanquishable, at least in appearance.

The men of the second sight do not discover strange things when asked, but at fits and raptures, as if inspired with some genius at that instant, which before did work in or about them. Thus I have frequently spoken to one of them, who in his transport told me he cut the body of one of those people in two with his iron weapon, and so escaped this onset, yet he saw nothing left behind of that appearing divided; at other times he outwrested [wrestled?] some of them. His neighbours often perceived this man to disappear at a certain place, and about an hour after to become visible, and discover himself near a bow-shot from the first place. It was in that place where he became invisible, said he, that the subterraneans did encounter and combat with him. Those who are *unseund*, or unsanctified (called fey), are said to be pierced or wounded with those people's weapons, which makes them do somewhat very unlike their former practice, causing a sudden alteration, yet the cause thereof unperceivable at present; nor have they power (either they cannot make use of their natural powers, or asked not the heavenly aid) to escape the blow impendent. A man of the second sight perceived a person standing by him (sound to other's view) wholly gored in blood. and he (amazed like) bid him instantly flee. The whole man laughed at his *airt* [notice] and warning, since there was no appearance of danger. He had scarce contracted his lips from laughter when unexpectedly his enemies leaped in at his side and stabbed him with their weapons. They also pierce cows or other animals, usually said to be Elf-shot, whose purest substance (if they die) these subterraneans take to live on, viz. the aërial and ethereal parts, the most spirituous matter for prolonging of life, such as aquavitæ (moderately taken) is amongst liquors, leaving the terrestrial behind. The cure of such hurts is only for a man to find out the hole with his finger, as if the spirits flowing from a man's warm hand were antidote sufficient against their poisoned darts.

As birds, as beasts, whose bodies are much used to the change of the free and open air, foresee storms, so those invisible people are more sagacious to understand by the books of nature things to come, than we, who are pestered with the grossest dregs of all elementary mixtures, and have our purer spirits choked by them. The deer scents out a man and powder (though a late invention) at a great distance; a hungry hunter, bread; and the raven, a carrion; their brains, being long clarified by the high and subtle air, will observe a very small change in a trice. Thus a man of the second sight, perceiving the operations of these forecasting invisible people among us (indulged through a stupendous providence to give warnings of some remarkable events, either in the air, earth, or waters), told he saw a winding shroud creeping on a walking healthful person's leg till it came to the knee, and afterwards it came up to the middle, then to the shoulders, and at last over the head, which was visible to no other person. And by observing the spaces of time betwixt the several stages, he easily guessed how long the man was to live who wore the shroud; for when it approached the head, he told that such a person was ripe for the grave.

There be many places called fairy-hills, which the mountain people think impious and dangerous to peel or discover, by taking earth or wood from them, superstitiously believing the souls of their predecessors to dwell there. And for that end (say they) a mole or mound was dedicate beside every churchyard to receive the souls till their adjacent bodies arise, and so became as a fairy-hill; they using bodies of air when called abroad. They also affirm those creatures that move invisibly in a house, and cast huge great stones, but do no much hurt, because counter-wrought by some more courteous and charitable spirits that are everywhere ready to defend men (Dan. x. 13), to be souls that have not attained their rest, through a vehement desire of revealing a murder or notable injury done or received, or a treasure that was forgot in their lifetime on earth, which, when disclosed to a conjuror alone, the ghost quite removes.

In the next country to that of my former residence, about the year 1676, when there was some scarcity of grain, a marvellous illapse and vision strongly struck the imagination of two women in one night, living at a good distance from one another, about a treasure hid in a hill called *Sith-bruthach*, or fairy-hill. The appearance of a treasure was first represented to the fancy, and then an audible voice named the place where it was to their awaking senses. Whereupon both rose, and meeting accidentally at the place, discovered their design; and jointly digging, found a vessel as large as a Scottish peck full of small pieces of good money, of ancient coin; and halving betwixt them, they sold in dishfuls for dishfuls of meal to the country people. Very many of undoubted credit saw and had of the coin to this day. But whether it was a good or bad angel, one of the subterranean people, or the restless soul of him who hid it, that discovered it, and to what end it was done, I leave to the examination of others.

These subterraneans have controversies, doubts, disputes, feuds, and siding of parties; there being some ignorance in all creatures, and the vastest created intelligences not compassing all things. As to vice and sin, whatever their own laws be, sure according to ours, and equity, natural, civil, and revealed, they transgress and commit acts of injustice and sin by what is above said, as to their stealing of nurses to their children, and that other sort of plaginism in catching our children away (may seem to heir some estate in those invisible dominions) which never return. For swearing and intemperance, they are not observed so subject to those irregularities, as to envy, spite, hypocrisy, lying, and dissimulation.

As our religion obliges us not to make a peremptory and curious search into these abstrusenesses, so the histories of all ages give as many plain examples of extraordinary occurrences as make a modest inquiry not contemptible. How much is written of pigmies, fairies, nymphs, syrens, apparitions, which though not the tenth part true, yet could not spring of nothing; even English authors relate [of] Barry Island, in Glamorganshire, that laying your ear into a cleft of the rocks, blowing of bellows, striking of hammers, clashing of armour, filing of iron, will be heard distinctly ever since Merlin enchanted those subterranean wights to a solid manual forging of arms to Aurelius Ambrosius and his Britons, till he returned; which Merlin being killed in a battle, and not coming to loose the knot, these active vulcans are there tied to a perpetual labour.

## THE FAIRY BOY OF LEITH.

'About fifteen years since, having business that letained me for some time at Leith, which is near Edinburgh, in the kingdom of Scotland, I often met some of my acquaintance at a certain house there, where we used to drink a glass of wine for our refection. The woman which kept the house was of honest reputation among the neighbours, which made me give the more attention to what she told me one day about a fairy boy (as they called him) who lived about that town. She had given me so strange an account of him, that I desired her I might see him the first opportunity, which she promised; and not long after, passing that way, she told me there was the fairy boy, but a little before I came by; and, casting her eye into the street, said, 'Look you, sir, yonder he is, at play with those other boys'; and pointing him out to me, I went, and by smooth words, and a piece of money, got him to come into the house with me; where, in the presence of divers people, I demanded of him several astrological questions, which he answered with great subtlety; and, through all his discourse, carried it with a cunning much above his years, which seemed not to exceed ten or eleven.

"He seemed to make a motion like drumming upon the table with his fingers, upon which I asked him whether he could beat a drum? To which he replied, 'Yes, sir, as well as any man in Scotland; for every Thursday night I beat all points to a sort of people that used to meet under yonder hill' (pointing to the great hill between Edinburgh and Leith). 'How, boy?' quoth I, 'what company have you there?' 'There are, sir,' said he, 'a great company both of men and women, and they are entertained with many sorts of music besides my drum; they have, besides, plenty of variety of meats and wine, and many times we are carried into France or Holland in the night, and return again, and whilst we are there, we enjoy all the pleasures the country doth afford.' I demanded of him how they got under that hill? To which he replied that there was a great pair of gates that opened to them, though they were invisible to others, and that within there were brave large rooms, as well accommodated as most in Scotland. I then asked him how I should know what he said to be true? Upon which he told me he would read my fortune, saying, I should have two wives, and that he saw the forms of them over my shoulders; and both would be very handsome women.

The woman of the house told me that all the people in Scotland could not keep him from the rendezvous on Thursday night; upon which, by promising him some more money, I got a promise of him to meet me at the same place in the afternoon, the Thursday following, and so dismissed him at that time. The boy came again at the place and time appointed, and I had prevailed with some friends to continue with me (if possible) to prevent his moving that night. He was placed between us, and answered many questions, until, about eleven of the clock, he was got away unperceived by the company; but I, suddenly missing him, hastened to the door, and took hold of him, and so returned him into the same room. We all watched him, and, of a sudden, he was again got out of doors; I followed him close, and he made a noise in the street, as if he had been set upon, and from that time I could never see him."

# THE DRACÆ.

THESE are a sort of water-spirits who inveigle women and children into the recesses which they inhabit, beneath lakes and rivers, by floating past them, on the surface of the water, in the shape of gold rings or cups. The women thus seized are employed as nurses, and after seven years are permitted to revisit earth. Gervase mentions one woman in particular who had been allured by observing a wooden dish, or cup, float by her, while she was washing clothes in the river. Being seized as soon as she reached the depths, she was conducted into one of the subterranean recesses, which she described as very magnificent, and employed as nurse to one of the brood of the hag who had allured her. During her residence in this capacity, having accidentally touched one of her eyes with an ointment of serpent's grease, she perceived, at her return to the world, that she had acquired the faculty of seeing the *Dracæ*, when they intermingle themselves with men. Of this power she was, however, deprived by the touch of her ghostly mistress, whom she had one day incautiously addressed. It is a curious fact that this story, in almost all its parts, is current in both the Highlands and Lowlands of Scotland, with no other variation than the substitution of Fairies for Dracæ, and the cavern of a hill for that of a river. Indeed many of the vulgar account it extremely dangerous to touch anything which they may happen to find without saining (blessing) it, the snares of the enemy being notorious and well-attested. A poor woman of Teviotdale having been fortunate enough, as she thought herself, to find a wooden beetle, at the very time when she needed such an implement, seized it without pronouncing a proper blessing, and, carrying it home, laid it above her bed to be ready for employment in the morning. At midnight the window of her cottage opened, and a loud voice was heard calling up some one within by a strange and uncouth name. The terrified cottager ejaculated a prayer, which, we may suppose, ensured her personal safety; while the enchanted implement of housewifery, tumbling from the bedstead, departed by the window with no small noise and precipitation. In a humorous fugitive tract, Dr. Johnson has been introduced as disputing the authenticity of an apparition, merely because the spirit assumed the shape of a teapot and a shoulder of mutton. No doubt, a case so much in point as that we have now quoted would have removed his incredulity.

# A SUCCINCT ACCOUNT

OF

## MY LORD TARBAT'S RELATIONS,

IN A LETTER TO THE HONORABLE ROBERT BOYLE, ESQUIRE, OF THE PREDICTIONS MADE BY SEERS, WHEREOF HIMSELF WAS EAR- AND EYE-WITNESS.

SIR,—I heard very much, but believed very little of the second sight; yet its being assumed by several of great veracity, I was induced to make inquiry after it in the year 1652, being then confined in the north of Scotland by the English usurpers. The more general accounts of it were that many Highlanders, yet far more Islanders, were qualified with this second sight; and men, women, and children, indistinctly, were subject to it, and children where parents were not. Sometimes people came to age who had it not when young, nor could any tell by what means produced. It is a trouble to most of them who are subject to it, and they would be rid of it at any rate if they could. The sight is of no long duration, only continuing so long as they can keep their eyes steady without twinkling. The hardy, therefore, fix their look that they may see the longer; but the timorous see only glances—their eyes always twinkle at the first sight of the object. That which generally is seen by them are the species of living creatures, and of inanimate things, which be in motion, such as ships, and habits upon persons. They never see the species of any person who is already dead. What they foresee fails not to exist in the mode, and in that place where it appears to them. They cannot well know what space of time shall intervene between the apparition and the real existence. But some of the hardiest and longest experience have some rules for conjectures; as, if they see a man with a shrouding sheet in the apparition, they will conjecture at the nearness or remoteness of his death by the more or less of his body that is covered by it. They will ordinarily see their absent friends, though at a great distance, sometimes no less than from America to Scotland, sitting, standing, or walking in some certain place; and then they conclude with an assurance that they will see them so, and there. If a man be in love with a woman, they will ordinarily see the species of that man standing by her, and so likewise if a woman be in love. If they see the species of any person who is sick to die, they see them covered over with the shrouding sheet.

These generals I had verified to me by such of them as did see, and were esteemed honest and sober by all the neighbourhood; for I inquired after such for my information. And because there were more of these seers in the isles of Lewis, Harris, and Uist than in any other place, I did entreat Sir James M'Donald (who is now dead), Sir Normand M'Loud, and Mr. Daniel Morison, a very honest person (who are still alive), to make inquiry in this uncouth sight, and to acquaint me therewith; which they did, and all found an agreement in these generals, and informed me of many instances confirming what they said. But though men of discretion and honour, being but at second-hand, I will choose rather to put myself than my friends on the hazard of being laughed at for incredible relations.

I was once travelling in the Highlands, and a good number of servants with me, as is usual there; and one of them, going a little before me, entering into a house where I was to stay all night, and going hastily to the door, he suddenly slipped back with a screech, and did fall by a stone, which hit his foot. I asked what the matter was, for he seemed to be very much frighted. He told me very seriously that I should not lodge in that house, because shortly a dead coffin would be carried out of it, for many were carrying of it when he was heard cry. I, neglecting his words, and staying there, he said to other of his servants he was sorry for it, and that surely what he saw would shortly come to pass. Though no sick person was then there, yet the landlord, a healthy Highlander, died of an apoplectic fit before I left the house.

In the year 1653 Alexander Monro (afterwards Lieutenant-Colonel to the Earl of Dumbarton's regiment) and I were walking in a place called Ullapool, in Loch Broom, on a little plain at the foot of a rugged hill. There was a servant walking with a spade in the walk before us; his back was to us, and his face to the hill. Before we came to him he let the spade fall, and looked toward the hill. He took notice of us as we passed near by him, which made me look at him, and perceiving him to stare a little strangely I conjectured him to be a seer. I called at him, at which he started and smiled. "What are you doing?" said I. He answered, "I have seen a very strange thing: an army of Englishmen, leading of horses, coming down that hill; and a number of them are coming down to the plain, and eating the barley which is growing in the field near to the hill." This was on the 4th May (for I noted the day), and it was four or five days before the barley was sown in the field he spoke of. Alexander Monro asked him how he knew they were Englishmen. He said because they were leading of horses, and had on hats and boots, which he knew no Scotchman would have there. We took little notice of the whole story as other than a foolish vision, but wished that an English party were there, we being then at war with them, and the place almost inaccessible for horsemen. But in the beginning of August thereafter, the Earl of Middleton (then Lieutenant for the King in the Highlands), having occasion to march a party of his towards the South Highlands, he sent his Foot through a place called Inverlawell; and the fore-party, which was first down the hill, did fall off eating the barley which was on the little plain under it. And Monro calling to mind what the seer told us in May preceding, he wrote of it, and sent an express to me to Lochslin, in Ross (where I then was), with it.

I had occasion once to be in company where a young lady was (excuse my not naming of persons), and I was told there was a notable seer in the company. I called him to speak with me, as I did ordinarily when I found any of them; and after he had answered me several questions, I asked if he knew any person to be in love with that lady. He said he did, but he knew not the person; for, during the two days he had been in her company, he perceived one standing near her, and his head leaning on her shoulder, which he said did foretell that the man should marry her, and die before her, according to his observation. This was in the year 1655. I desired him to describe the person, which he did, so that I could conjecture, by the description, of such a one, who was of that lady's acquaintance, though there were no thoughts of their marriage till two years thereafter. And having occasion in the year 1657 to find this seer, who was an islander, in company with the other person whom I conjectured to have been described by him, I called him aside, and asked if that was the person he saw beside the lady near two years then past. He said it was he indeed, for he had seen that lady just then standing by him hand in hand. This was some few months before their marriage, and that man is now dead, and the lady alive.

I shall trouble you but with one more, which I thought most remarkable of any that occurred to me.

In January 1652, the above-mentioned Lieutenant, Colonel Alex. Monro, and I, happened to be in the house of one William M'Clend, of Ferrinlea, in the county of Ross. He, the landlord, and I, were sitting in three chairs near the fire, and in the corner of the great chimney there were two islanders, who were that very night come to the house, and were related to the landlord. While the one of them was talking with Monro, I perceived the other to look oddly toward me. From this look, and his being an islander, I conjectured him a seer, and asked him at what he stared. He answered by desiring me to rise from that chair, for it was an unlucky one. I asked him why? He answered, because there was a dead man in the chair next to me. "Well," said I, "if it be in the next chair, I may keep my own. But what is the likeness of the man?" He said he was a tall man, with a long grey coat, booted, and one of his legs hanging over the arm of the chair, and his head hanging dead to the other side, and his arm backward, as if it was broken. There were some English troops then quartered near that place, and there being at that time a great frost after a thaw, the country was covered all over with ice. Four or five of the English riding by this house some two hours after the vision, while we were sitting by the fire, we heard a great noise, which proved to be those troopers, with the help of other servants, carrying in one of their number, who had got a very mischievous fall, and had his arm broke; and falling frequently in swooning fits, they brought him into the hall, and set him in the very chair, and in the very posture that the seer had prophesied. But the man did not die, though he recovered with great difficulty.

Among the accounts given me by Sir Normand M'Loud, there was one worthy of special notice, which was thus:—There was a gentleman in the Isle of Harris, who was always seen by the seers with an arrow in his thigh. Such in the Isle who thought those prognostications infallible, did not doubt but he would be shot in the thigh before he died. Sir Normand told me that he heard it the subject of their discourse for many years. At last he died without any such accident. Sir Normand was at his burial at St. Clement's Church in the Harris. At the same time the corpse of another gentleman was brought to be buried in the same very church. The friends on either side came to debate who should first enter the church, and, in a trice, from words they came to blows. One of the number (who was armed with bow and arrows) let one fly among them. (Now every family in that Isle have their burial-place in the Church in stone chests, and the bodies are carried in open biers to the burial-place.) Sir Normand having appeased the tumult, one of the arrows was found shot in the dead man's thigh. To this Sir Normand was a witness.

In the account which Mr. Daniel Morison, parson in the Lewis, gave me, there was one, though it be heterogeneous from the subject, yet it may be worth your notice. It was of a young woman in this parish, who was mightily frightened by seeing her own image still before her, always when she came to the open air; the back of the image being always to her, so that it was not a reflection as in a mirror, but the species of such a body as her own, and in a very like habit which appeared to herself continually before her. The parson kept her a long while with him, but had no remedy of her evil, which troubled her exceedingly. I was told afterwards that when she was four or five years older she saw it not

These are matters of fact, which I assure you they are truly related. But these and all others that occurred to me, by information or otherwise, could never lead me into a remote conjecture of the cause of so extraordinary a phenomenon. Whether it be a quality in the eyes of some people in these parts, concurring with a quality in the air also; whether such species be everywhere, though not seen by the want of eyes so qualified, or from whatever other cause, I must leave to the inquiry of clearer judgments than mine. But a hint may be taken from this image which appeared still to this woman above mentioned, and from another mentioned by Aristotle, in the fourth of his Metaphysics (if I remember right, for it is long since I read it), as also from the common opinion that young infants (unsullied with many objects) do see apparitions which were not seen by those of elder years; as likewise from this, that several did see the second sight when in the Highlands or Isles, yet when transported to live in other countries, especially in America, they quite lose this quality, as was told me by a gentleman who knew some of them in Barbadoes, who did see no vision there, although he knew them to be seers when they lived in the Isles of Scotland.

*Thus far my Lord Tarbat.*

# THE BOGLE.

This is a freakish spirit who delights rather to perplex and frighten mankind than either to serve or seriously hurt them. The *Esprit Follet* of the French, Shakespeare's Puck, or Robin Goodfellow, and Shellycoat, a spirit who resides in the waters, and has given his name to many a rock and stone on the Scottish coast, belong to the class of bogles. One of Shellycoat's pranks is thus narrated:—Two men in a very dark night, approaching the banks of the Ettrick, heard a doleful voice from its waves repeatedly exclaim, "Lost! lost!" They followed the sound, which seemed to be the voice of a drowning person, and, to their astonishment, found that it ascended the river; still they continued to follow the cry of the malicious sprite, and, arriving before dawn at the very sources of the river, the voice was now heard descending the opposite side of the mountain in which they arise. The fatigued and deluded travellers now relinquished the pursuit, and had no sooner done so, than they heard Shellycoat applauding, in loud bursts of laughter, his successful roguery

# DAOINE SHIE, OR THE MEN OF PEACE.

They are, though not absolutely malevolent, believed to be a peevish, repining, and envious race, who enjoy, in the subterranean recesses, a kind of shadowy splendour. The Highlanders are at all times unwilling to speak of them, but especially on Friday, when their influence is supposed to be particularly extensive. As they are supposed to be invisibly present, they are at all times to be spoken of with respect. The fairies of Scotland are represented as a diminutive race of beings, of a mixed or rather dubious nature, capricious in their dispositions, and mischievous in their resentment. They inhabit the interior of green hills, chiefly those of a conical form, in Gaelic termed *Sighan*, on which they lead their dances by moonlight, impressing upon the surface the marks of circles, which sometimes appear yellow and blasted, sometimes of a deep green hue, and within which it is dangerous to sleep, or to be found after sunset. The removal of those large portions of turf, which thunderbolts sometimes scoop out of the ground with singular regularity, is also ascribed to their agency. Cattle which are suddenly seized with the cramp, or some similar disorder, are said to be elf-shot, and the approved cure is to chafe the parts affected with a blue bonnet, which, it may be readily believed, often restores the circulation. The triangular flints frequently found in Scotland, with which the ancient inhabitants probably barbed their shafts, are supposed to be the weapons of fairy resentment, and are termed elf arrowheads. The rude brazen battle-axes of the ancients, commonly called " celts," are also ascribed to their manufacture. But, like the Gothic duergar, their skill is not confined to the fabrication of arms; for they are heard sedulously hammering in linns, precipices, and rocky or cavernous situations, where, like the dwarfs of the mines mentioned by George Agricola, they busy themselves in imitating the actions and the various employments of men. The Brook of Beaumont, for example, which passes in its course by numerous linns and caverns, is notorious for being haunted by the fairies; and the perforated and rounded stones which are formed by trituration in its channels are termed by the vulgar fairy cups and dishes. A beautiful reason is assigned by Fletcher for the fays frequenting streams and fountains. He tells us of

> "A virtuous well, about whose flowery banks
> The nimble-footed fairies dance their rounds
> By the pale moonshine, dipping oftentimes
> Their stolen children, so to make them free
> From dying flesh and dull mortality."

It is sometimes accounted unlucky to pass such places without performing some ceremony to avert the displeasure of the elves. There is upon the top of Minchmuir, a mountain in Peeblesshire, a spring called the Cheese Well, because, anciently, those who passed that way were wont to throw into it a piece of cheese as an offering to the fairies, to whom it was consecrated.

Like the *feld elfen* of the Saxons, the usual dress of the fairies is green; though, on the moors, they have been sometimes observed in heath-brown, or in weeds dyed with the stone-raw or lichen. They often ride in invisible procession, when their presence is discovered by the shrill ringing of their bridles. On these occasions they sometimes borrow mortal steeds, and when such are found at morning, panting and fatigued in their stalls, with their manes and tails dishevelled and entangled, the grooms, I presume, often find this a convenient excuse for their situation, as the common belief of the elves quaffing the choicest liquors in the cellars of the rich might occasionally cloak the delinquencies of an unfaithful butler.

The fairies, besides their equestrian processions, are addicted, it would seem, to the pleasures of the chase. A young sailor, travelling by night from Douglas, in the Isle of Man, to visit his sister residing in Kirk Merlugh, heard a noise of horses, the holloa of a huntsman, and the sound of a horn.

Immediately afterwards, thirteen horsemen, dressed in green, and gallantly mounted, swept past him. Jack was so much delighted with the sport that he followed them, and enjoyed the sound of the horn for some miles, and it was not till he arrived at his sister's house that he learned the danger which he had incurred. I must not omit to mention that these little personages are expert jockeys, and scorn to ride the little Manx ponies, though apparently well suited to their size. The exercise, therefore, falls heavily upon the English and Irish horses brought into the Isle of Man. Mr. Waldron was assured by a gentleman of Ballafletcher that he had lost three or four capital hunters by these nocturnal excursions. From the same author we learn that the fairies sometimes take more legitimate modes of procuring horses. A person of the utmost integrity informed him that, having occasion to sell a horse, he was accosted among the mountains by a little gentleman plainly dressed, who priced his horse, cheapened him, and, after some chaffering, finally purchased him. No sooner had the buyer mounted and paid the price than he sank through the earth, horse and man, to the astonishment and terror of the seller, who, experienced, however, no inconvenience from dealing with so extraordinary a purchaser.

# THE DEATH "BREE."

THERE was once a woman, who lived in the Campdel-more of Strathavon, whose cattle were seized with a murrain, or some such fell disease, which ravaged the neighbourhood at the time, carrying off great numbers of them daily. All the forlorn fires and hallowed waters failed of their customary effects; and she was at length told by the wise people, whom she consulted on the occasion, that it was evidently the effect of some infernal agency, the power of which could not be destroyed by any other means than the never-failing specific—the juice of a dead head from the churchyard,—a nostrum certainly very difficult to be procured, considering that the head must needs be abstracted from the grave at the hour of midnight. Being, however, a woman of a stout heart and strong faith, native feelings of delicacy towards the sanctuary of the dead had more weight than had fear in restraining her for some time from resorting to this desperate remedy. At length, seeing that her stock would soon be annihilated by the destructive career of the disease, the wife of Camp-del-more resolved to put the experiment in practice, whatever the result might be. Accordingly, having with considerable difficulty engaged a neighbouring woman as her companion in this hazardous expedition, they set out a little before midnight for the parish churchyard, distant about a mile and a half from her residence, to execute her determination. On arriving at the churchyard her companion, whose courage was not so notable, appalled by the gloomy prospect before her, refused to enter among the habitations of the dead. She, however, agreed to remain at the gate till her friend's business was accomplished. This circumstance, however, did not stagger the wife's resolution. She, with the greatest coolness and intrepidity, proceeded towards what she supposed an old grave, took down her spade, and commenced her operations. After a good deal of toil she arrived at the object of her labour. Raising the first head, or rather skull, that came in her way, she was about to make it her own property, when a hollow, wild, sepulchral voice exclaimed, "That is my head; let it alone!" Not wishing to dispute the claimant's title to this head, and supposing she could be otherwise provided, she very good-naturedly returned it and took up another. "That is my father's head," bellowed the same voice. Wishing, if possible, to avoid disputes, the wife of Camp-del-more took up another head, when the

www.ingramcontent.com/pod-product-compliance
Lightning Source LLC
Chambersburg PA
CBHW032009220426
43664CB00006B/192